THE
JAIN PATH

ANCIENT WISDOM FOR THE WEST

Aidan Rankin

Winchester, UK
Washington, USA)

First published by O Books, 2006
O Books is an imprint of John Hunt Publishing Ltd.,
The Bothy, Deershot Lodge, Park Lane, Ropley, Hants, SO24 0BE, UK
office1@o-books.net
www.o-books.net

Distribution in:

UK and Europe
Orca Book Services
orders@orcabookservices.co.uk
Tel: 01202 665432 Fax: 01202 666219 Int. code (44)

USA and Canada
NBN
custserv@nbnbooks.com
Tel: 1 800 462 6420 Fax: 1 800 338 4550

Australia
Brumby Books
sales@brumbybooks.com
Tel: 61 3 9761 5535 Fax: 61 3 9761 7095

New Zealand
Peaceful Living
books@peaceful-living.co.nz
Tel: 64 7 57 18105 Fax: 64 7 57 18513

Singapore
STP
davidbuckland@tlp.com.sg
Tel: 65 6276 Fax: 65 6276 7119

South Africa
Alternative Books
altbook@peterhyde.co.za
Tel: 021 447 5300 Fax: 021 447 1430

Text copyright Aidan Rankin 2006

Design: Stuart Davies

ISBN-13: 978 1 905047 21 5
ISBN-10: 1 905047 21 5

A CIP catalogue record for this book is available from the British Library.

Printed in the US by Maple Vail

THE
JAIN PATH

ANCIENT WISDOM FOR THE WEST

Aidan Rankin

BOOKS

Winchester, UK
Washington, USA

CONTENTS

FOR MY MOTHER AND FATHER,

ANNE AND DAVID RANKIN

I ask pardon of all living creatures; may all of them pardon me. May I have a friendly relationship with all beings and unfriendly with none.

JAIN PRAYER, RECITED AT SAMVATSARI
(ANNUAL CEREMONY OF PUBLIC CONFESSION).

PREFACE

I can still clearly remember an occasion when I was young, perhaps four years old, and trod on a small snail when playing in the garden. I do not recall whether this was an act of child-like callousness or a careless accident. Whatever it was, my mother who was nearby was horrified. 'You have killed a living creature,' she told me, and she proceeded to remind me of the need to be careful at all times not to do avoidable harm.

Her words would be very familiar to a Jain. Indeed I thought of them when years later I heard of Jainism, and learned of its deep reverence for life in all its rich variety. For the first premise of this ancient philosophy is that all life has intrinsic value and each life form is unique, special and has the possibility of achieving enlightenment. Thousands of years ago, the Jains of India recognised that all living things depended on each other, and that the concept of life extended beyond humans to animals and plants, to water and rock, to deserts, forests and mountain ranges. All natural formations contained life, indeed many lives, all of which were crucial in their own ways to the health of the planet. As human beings, our relatively advanced state of consciousness gives us the ability to conserve and protect life, but also arms us with immense powers to destroy, whether through active malevolence or simple carelessness.

The Jain path is one of continuous caution. It urges us to exercise constant care in the way we use our intelligence and in all decisions we make, great and small, because what can so easily seem trivial to us can have global, or indeed universal importance. Jainism makes explicit the links between damage to the environment and damage to ourselves, the way we treat other species and the way we behave to each other. Jains have always realised that if we treat nature as a resource, to be consumed without conscience or foresight, then human relationships will be built on aggression and domination. They sensed that all violence, even to the tiniest forms of life, can inflict a much larger psychic harm.

In this in-built caution or cosmic conservatism, we can find radical implications for the way we conduct our lives and our order of priorities. Far from being repressive, the emphasis on restraint sets us free from our obsessions with unsatisfying material gain and superficial competitive 'success'. It shows us that these obsessions are not only destructive but rooted in delusion. In Jainism, the idea of social justice begins in our daily lives. We are enjoined to live simply, so that others may simply live and so that the balance of nature may be preserved. But at the same time, we are asked to avoid violent thoughts, fixed ideas, impatience and inflexibility. We improve our own lives, and those of our fellows, through equanimity instead of zealous passion. The Jain principle of restraint sets us free from the irrational attachments that have corrupted and embittered humanity. By cultivating inner calm, we do not become coldly and narrowly rationalist. Instead, we are liberated from the unwanted attachments that make us unhappy and are able to focus on aspects of our lives that really matter, such as friendship and love, and beyond that compassion for all beings and affinity with the whole of nature.

Jains have arrived at these insights by meditation, philosophical exploration and the intuitive faculty that is too often undervalued by supposedly 'rational' human beings. Their faith can trace its origins to the earliest settled communities of the Indian subcontinent.[1] Yet what better spiritual tonic could there be than this ancient wisdom for a Western society that for all its apparent wealth and technological prowess is undergoing a deepening crisis of the soul? What better inspiration could there be for those of us who see true growth as spiritual rather than merely economic? Hundreds of years before the time of Christ, the Jains understood that the protection of the environment was the most critical question facing human society. This gives them an impressive prescience, and also makes their teachings resonate with modern concerns, especially in the affluent (but still divided and unequal) Western world.

Our diverse and growing knowledge of ecology, climate science and human psychology all now give credence to the Jain view of life. Individually, and as a human family, we are discovering – albeit reluctantly at times - that the pursuit of happiness is usually the pursuit of less rather than the pursuit of more. We are becoming aware of the connection between emotional and environmental health, and that in order to survive at all, we have to accept limitations and cannot go on expanding and consuming eternally. Many social forces, and human impulses, still militate against these conclusions and threaten to pull us towards physical and spiritual catastrophe. Therefore, all wisdom traditions that point us towards restraint and balance are of increasing relevance value to us. Jainism expresses with a particular clarity the sacredness of all life, but it does so gently and subtly, with affection rather than simple exhortation. This surely makes it resonate especially with our present cultural and social problems, as well as our innermost spiritual needs.

The Jain path also impressed me as a political scientist and a qualified stress counsellor. At the political level, Jainism supported and gave shape to my increasing awareness that the left/right polarity was sterile and unsatisfactory. The study of Jain principles confirmed my belief that modern political theory merely scratched the surface of the human predicament. Our current difficulties, be they political or economic, connected with terrorism or conventional war, are symptoms of a spiritual malaise. In the West, this is reflected in the increasing fragmentation of society into mutually hostile interest groups, the increasing isolation of individuals from each other and a state of disconnection from the natural world.

NB even in small towns

Jainism's concept of 'many-sidedness' offers an alternative based on integration and true tolerance. It invites all who have open minds and compassionate hearts to embark on a search for the truth. More than that, it enables us as a society to reach beyond arbitrary divisions, such as left and right, but to think for ourselves and evaluate issues on their merit. Central to Jainism is the individual conscience and respect for the intelligence and potential of each man and woman, indeed every being. This provides a healthy inoculation against all forms of fanaticism or fundamentalism, religious or secular, and the adversarial 'either you're with us or against us' mentality that blights us in peacetime and leads us to war.

DC?

As a stress counsellor, I am also aware that our civilisation's chronic anxiety arises out of attachment. The belief that we can and should always have more is at the root of our culture of insane over-work, the mindless cult of celebrity, the breakdown of relationships (social and intimate), and the despair that comes when materialistic dreams dissolve. Recovery from stress is about casting aside attachments and finding hidden creative energies, letting go of ambition and fulfilling our true goals as human beings. Jainism can help us make sense of all this, and give the reduction of stress an ethical purpose.

There are many people who have contributed, directly or indirectly, to the thoughts and impressions I have brought together in this book. In particular, I would like to thank my mother for teaching me respect for life, my publisher, John Hunt, for his enthusiasm for this project and his gentle encouragement, 'Anant Shah, the dynamic former Chair of *Jain Spirit*, and Dr Harshad N. Sanghrajka, of the Institute of Jainology, whose erudition and wisdom I have greatly valued. However I wish to give special thanks to Atul K. Shah,', founder of *Jain Spirit* magazine and former colleague from the London School of Economics. Atul's friendship and generosity have contributed greatly to my understanding of Jainism, and the experience of guest editing *Jain Spirit* led directly to the writing of this book.

INTRODUCTION

By Dr David Frawley

Introducing a religious and spiritual tradition is not an easy task, particularly one that is based on a very different vision of humanity and the universe. It requires both an understanding of the background of that tradition and an ability to communicate it to the modern reader. Aidan Rankin has brought such a deep examination to his new book on Jainism, one of humanity's deepest, most ancient and yet least understood religious traditions. His approach is not merely academic but shows the living aspect of Jain thought from one who has understood it in a western context. Therefore his book is bound to remain one of the most important introductions to Jainism available and brings the light of this ancient teaching out for everyone to see clearly. For those who want to learn about Jainism, *The Jain Path* is a great place to start. It makes the Jain tradition relevant both in its social and its personal significance in the context of the great challenges of life today.

India is a land that has produced a great variety of spiritual teachings, so much so that the western mind finds it difficult to fathom or even recognize all of these, much like the proverbial blind man looking at an elephant. The Hindu tradition itself, with its many schools of Yoga and Vedanta, is highly diverse. Buddhism, though it is more homogenous in nature, has different aspects as well and many local variations.

Jainism is another tradition from India that is worthy of respect and greatly in need of a closer examination. Jain Dharma stands between the Hindu and Buddhist ways and has much in common with both, as well as a highly distinctive character of its own. It shares a similar dharmic view of the world based on natural law, a recognition of the process of karma and rebirth, and a seeking of liberation through various yogic and meditative practices.

More ancient even than Buddhism, Jain Dharma has all the richness of a major world religion, including many marvellous temples and a great literature extending to philosophy, art, science and mathematics. Indeed much that the modern mind associates with Buddhism, with its theory of karma, its monasticism and emphasis on non-violence, already existed in Jain culture and practice well before the time of the Buddha.

Jainism is best known for holding to non-violence as the supreme principle in life, and this facet of its teaching had a substantial impact on the thought and action of Mahatma Gandhi. Yet the non-violence of Jainism is not just a principle of political activism; it is first and foremost a principle of right living, leading to spiritual practice. There is no living being that has ever existed which wants to be harmed. We ourselves do not want to be harmed. So, accepting this universal order, which in India is called 'dharma', we should not wish for the harm of others or seek it in any way.

Non-violence in Jainism, as in Indic thought in general, is not a passive principle either. It is a proactive principle that asks us to act and live in such a way so as to reduce the amount of harm that takes place in the world. While some harm is unavoidable in a life in which the interests of various creatures compete, there is much we can do to lessen this and make life happier for all. Non-violence is a call to action to encourage us to make the world more peaceful.

Jainism has another important philosophical principle for the modern world, which is as important as its approach to non-violence, which is its honouring of pluralism (syadvada). This Aidan Rankin eloquently defines as 'the non-violence of the mind'. Jainism holds that on any given topic there will always be any number of points of view. Each mind is different and is therefore inclined to see things differently, according to its own perspective. So one should tolerate and even honour a diversity of points of view on any subject. There is no need to promote any belief, ideology or philosophy as the only truth, the final truth or the last word for all humanity.

Such 'intellectual pluralism' is the foundation of non-violent action, whereas intellectual absolutism generally leads to violence. This violence occurs when absolutism is imposed in the political sphere, for example through cultural or nationalistic chauvinism. It also takes place, notoriously, in the name of religion, or rather through the exclusivism and intolerance that is a distortion of faith. The need for 'the non-violence of the mind' has probably never been greater than today, and so Rankin's book comes at an opportune time to provide us with this insight.

Indeed much of the violence in the world arises from hegemonic and monolithic approaches to economics, politics and religion. We cannot live and let live if we believe that only our way is valid and the other ways are not only wrong but dangerous or even heretical. Rather than condemning one another to religious or political incorrectness, it is better to try to find a common ground. Rankin has done this in his own reflections on ecology and politics, where he looks beyond the boundaries of existed warring camps and vested interested to the greater common good of all creatures. In his words and thoughts one finds a natural affinity with this aspect of Jainism.

Jain non-violence and pluralism are therefore critically important teachings for the world today. The Jain view is to express these principles in action rather than in mere theorising. It is easy to talk about world peace while we are promoting our own particular personal or social agenda, but it is very hard to live in a peaceful manner, not only with our fellow human beings but with the entire world of nature – and with ourselves.

Aidan Rankin is a notable European thinker on social, cultural and spiritual issues. He has been at the forefront of a deeper approach to ecological thinking in the West. He looks to the deeper truth behind an issue and is never merely a propagandist for one group, party, faction or point of view. He brings this approach which is both objective and sensitive to his examination of Jainism, which makes this ancient spiritual teaching accessible today with its great insights and noble practices.

Rankin resonates with Jain dharma and shows its relevance in the world today in a way that the modern reader can understand and appreciate. As we move into an ecological and global age, Jainism provides many of the insights that can direct us forward and help us along the way.

David Frawley is Director of the American Institute of Vedic Studies, Santa Fe, New Mexico (www.vedanet.com). His books include *Yoga and the Sacred Fire*, *Yoga and Ayurveda* and *Gods, Sages and Kings*.

परस्परोपग्रहो जीवानाम्

The Pratika, a symbol of Jainism adopted in 1975, the 2,500th anniversary of Mahavira's enlightenment. The hand is an expression of the ideal of peace, with the word Ahimsa (non-injury) inscribed in the palm. Above it is the svastika, a symbol of life whose arms represent the Fourfold Order consisting of male ascetics, female ascetics, lay men and lay women, and equally the four destinies of human, animal or plant, heavenly and hellish being. The three dots represent the Triratna (Three Jewels) of Right Faith, Right Knowledge and Right Action, the crescent marks out the place of enlightened souls, and the dot above it signifies the liberated jiva, the unit of pure consciousness that has thrown off the bonds of karma. Beneath the Pratika is the inscription Parasparopagraho Jivanam: all life is interdependent.

CHAPTER ONE

WHY JAINISM?

I do not know if there is rebirth or not, or life after
death. But if it is true, then I would like to be born in
India as a Jain.

ALBERT EINSTEIN

ay the word 'Jain' to most well informed Westerners and a
haunting image of an ascetic will arise in their minds. They
will think of a man or woman clad in white, with mouth
covered, holding a brush to sweep gently aside all animal life that
might be injured by the human tread. Some, especially those who
know India, will think of the animal sanctuaries of Ahmedabad, a
Jain stronghold. There, ill or wounded birds and beasts are cared
for as they cling to life, because life is so sacred that it cannot
under any circumstances be taken by humans, whose advanced
moral conscience enables them to make choices. Those who know
still more will be aware that some Jain ascetics let themselves die
so that they can transcend the body and the material aspect of the
universe, revealing (in Western terms) the shadow side of Jainism,
an ambivalence towards earthly existence.

For some, another paradox will spring to mind, that of wealthy
lay Jains, successful in business and the professions and enjoying
the full benefits of that success. Others might know the atmosphere
of stillness and calm that is associated with Jain temples and sacred

sites, or the statues, rounded and elegant rather than ornate, which are not worshipped as images of the divine, but revered as exemplars for humanity. Within the Western frame of reference, Jainism is quietly mysterious. Its respect for all life is admirable and reassuring, its apparent austerities forbidding and sinister, its philosophy an enigma.

Jainism, therefore, is to the Western mind a series of fragments without an underlying theme. It is somewhat like an incomplete mosaic or jigsaw puzzle, whose few remaining pieces are striking enough to tease and tantalise. Moreover, Jainism is not a missionary religion, like Christianity or many forms of Buddhism. It is a living tradition passed down within families and communities and characterised by modesty and privacy, concerned with seeking the light within rather than shining a light on the rest of the world. This is why many in the West, including those who consider themselves spiritual seekers, are still wholly unaware of Jainism, or treat it as a subset of Hinduism; the latter impression is affirmed by some Jains, through their silence, and asserted by some Hindus, who emphasise the Indian roots that both traditions share. Often, Jainism comes across as complex and impenetrable, too disciplined and 'difficult' for the modern secular mind, too extreme in its demands and too inaccessible, because it does not consciously seek 'converts' and does not always reveal itself enthusiastically to inquirers.

In spite of many superficial similarities, the Jain path is not immediately compatible with the New Age consciousness of the West. The New Age is eclectic and sometimes overtly consumerist in its approach, although it arises out of a sense that the materialistic, mechanistic model of 'progress' is not enough, and that without spiritual leavening is imposing an intolerable stress on the individual, the human community and the planet. To access the Jain *dharma*, the natural law or underlying truth, and make it relevant to our lives, we need to go beyond the simple political and spiritual slogans that have become the moral absolutes of the counter-culture. At the same time, we need to reach beneath the more extreme outward manifestations of Jain austerity, to look beyond the paradoxes, which only seem contradictory according to the limited and adversarial mindset that has restricted our society's capacity to adapt to its present social and ecological challenges.

But why should we bother? The 'spiritual tourist' has enough possible journeys available. A by-product of this age of instant communication and the global economy is that once exclusive cultural traditions are now available to all. Spiritual disciplines and practices that, until recently, were associated with specific human groups or regions of the world have become universal, whether their adherents wish it or not. In an era dominated by the ideals of the free market and private ownership, culture, thought and faith have become common property. At one level, this creates an atmosphere of intense competition, in which faiths, traditions and individual gurus vie with each other for the attention of spiritual inquirers whose attention needs to be held and for whom the various paths to enlightenment need to be made attractive. At another, it leads to the dilution and absorption of ancient beliefs or ways of life, so that they are readily accessible to the urban sophisticate.

Upholders of indigenous spiritual paths have come to resent this bowdlerisation of their cultures, and to be less open to sharing their knowledge with outsiders. Native Americans, for example, are increasingly resentful of the appropriation of their cultural norms by affluent 'white' Westerners. Academics and writers such as Vine Deloria, Jr, have likened this process to spiritual colonisation.[1] In Australia, some Aboriginal elders have objected to white women visitors playing the didgeridoo, considered to be a male preserve in many Native Australian cultures. That seems a minor matter, but symbols are important for peoples who are struggling for their survival and their spiritual inheritance, and this is a potent symbol, because it illustrates the clash between traditional spiritual paths and the nostrums of Western liberalism, and therefore a clash between two visions of justice, one universalist, the other culturally specific, to which there is no 'correct' solution. When such clashes occur, they can be every bit as extreme as the conflict with openly reactionary or blatantly exploitative forces.

The rise of Hindutva in India, loosely translated in the West as Hindu nationalism, has been interpreted in the context of fundamentalism and so is often likened to right-wing Evangelical Christianity and radical Islam. However, we understand it better if we view it as part of the reclamation of indigenous knowledge, an assertion of the Indian-ness of Hindu culture, accompanied by a growing ecological consciousness. Therefore, it is akin to the revival of interest in Native American spirituality, or Daoism in China and Shinto in Japan, or indeed Neo-Paganism the resurgence of Celtic or Germanic faith traditions amongst those of European descent world-wide. Jains, in turn, are starting increasingly to assert their distinctiveness, including their distinction from Hindus. They too represent the continuity of an ancient, indigenous faith tradition, but one that includes universal themes, many of which are profoundly pertinent to today's global concerns.

Jainism is the continuation in modern form of an ancient consciousness, a strand of thought that that stretches back for millennia. For this reason, it is held by its adherents to be the most authentic expression of Indian culture, although Jains do not make this claim in a supremacist or chauvinistic manner, because this would be diametrically opposed to the philosophy that underpins their lives. Within Jainism, therefore, there are all the characteristics of an indigenous faith. There is an archaic cosmology, in which an eternal universe surrounds and encloses a finite material or 'known' universe. For each individual human being, the ultimate goal is immortality and with it omniscience. The known universe, for Jains, is teeming with life. Like the most primeval of human cultures, they find souls in trees and shrubs as well as animals, and discern conscious life in mountains, rivers, waterfalls and rocks. All these forms of life have equal value, in the sense that they are connected to each other by the possession of souls. In recognising this connection, Jains – again like native peoples today – display an advanced ecological consciousness, the sense of a world of interdependent parts, which reflect an underlying unity, rather than independent parts that largely sustain themselves.

'Only Connect', the author E.M. Forster's watchword for literary criticism, could also be a Jain motto, for connectedness is the beginning, middle and ending of the Jain path, and awareness of it is the base on which the more advanced layers of doctrine are superimposed. But the sense of connectedness also assumes a more literal form. Jains share with other Indian traditions the idea of the karmic journey, in which progress towards enlightenment usually takes place over many lifetimes as the soul, the unit of true life, is continuously reborn. They take the concept of *karma* more literally than most Buddhists and Hindus, however, because they believe that souls can transmigrate from humans to animals (or plants) and that every life form in the material universe has to be handled with care because it contains souls that have the potential to become enlightened. Indeed failure to handle them with care is one of the principle causes of regression to a less advanced life form, such as rebirth as an animal. Even karma itself is not a mere abstract concept, but a physical process, a formation of subtle matter that encases the soul, clouding its judgement and enclosing it in a bodily trap.

In Jainism, there is the atmosphere of enchantment associated with 'primitive' folk religion, along with a very deep consciousness of nature and the sacredness of all life. Yet Jainism is also a sophisticated philosophy, the product of literate urban minds that engage in abstract, speculative thought rather than mere interaction with natural forces. There is in the Jain path a continuous interplay between the use of abstract reason in the search for objective knowledge, or higher truth, and a wordless, intuitive awareness of that truth. There is, in one dimension, a celebration of life in all its intricacy and richness, and in another there is a powerful awareness of life's limitations and the need to transcend the world. Jains have a mystical appreciation of the life force embedded in the most primitive or microscopic beings, in the air and in the landscape, to the extent that they plan every conscious action to minimise damage to that life. Yet they also regard lived experience as a vale of tears, a state of physical and intellectual limitation, beyond which the spiritually awakened must aim to move.

Similarly, enlightenment, the moment of liberation or *moksha*, is identified with escape from the limits of the known world, including emotions of the highest order, such as the capacity for love and friendship. For even these are subjective and insignificant when measured against the state of pure reason, the perfect objectivity which is the ultimate goal of all Jains. Jainism eschews the competitive struggle. The men and women who live nearest to its ideals are ascetics who have abjured all the trappings of earthly success, and have abjured any human relationships that most others would regard as essential and normal. But the *Jina*, the one who achieves enlightenment, is one who has at once conquered himself and overcome the vicissitudes of earthly life. Jainism means 'the faith of the conquerors', those who have worked through all levels of existence and won out. Jains inhabit a known universe in which the souls of all life forms can be discerned and supernatural beings, the 'shining ones' or *devas*, exist in magical realms. Yet their universe is also eternal and constantly regenerating itself. Life and the universe were not 'created' by a divine being, because Jains discerned thousands of years, it seems, before Westerners, that energy can neither be created nor destroyed.

Consciousness is identified by Jains with energy, and the *jiva*, loosely translated as the soul, is a unit of pure consciousness, fully alive, rather than partially alive and semi-consciousness as we are on Earth. Thus Jainism is a primal, or pre-modern religion, but also a literate, modern – arguably 'post-modern' - philosophy. It reveres nature and works within its rhythms, and yet it also ultimately rejects nature in favour of an intellectual ideal of perfection. It is at once deeply intuitive, appealing to powerful emotions, such as compassion for all living beings and strict commitment to non-violence, and at the same time objective and rational to the point of apparent coldness. Jainism appears hard to decipher, but is also founded upon the simplest idea, that of interconnectedness, an idea grasped by humans aeons before written scripts or organised religions were devised. For the Western spiritual inquirer, of which there are many in a period of increasing dislocation, even crisis, Jainism seems to blow hot and cold. It is a mystery because it is built on paradox, because its twin views of the universe seem to cancel each other out.

This interpretation of Jainism is rooted in a worldview based on opposition, on either/or logic, on 'straight' choices. It is an approach by which strength, intellectual and moral, is identified with doctrinaire certainty and progress is conceived of as a narrow movement forward, in which the superstitions of the past are shed as new knowledge supplants old ways. This worldview is very dynamic and has been a motive force for individual creativity, discovery, experimentation in the arts and sciences, and social reform. However it has also laid the foundations for the disconnection of humanity from nature and as a result an ecological crisis, which is simultaneously a crisis of the spirit. Increasingly, we are aware of the consequences of human impact on the environment and the climate, which stem from the idea that we can dominate and triumph over the natural world, and so rise above and beyond it.

The separation of humanity from nature – the rest of nature – has strong roots in Western thought, and these roots are religious and spiritual as well as rational and scientific. It has found its logical conclusion in a society that values material possessions over spiritual insights, youth and glamour over experience and reflection, noise over contemplation, which favours mass-produced consumer goods over craftsmanship and in which the ultimate goal seems to be to win the Lottery. There is far, far more to Western society than this, and there is much to give us hope, but the overwhelming atmosphere of materialism and the separation from nature have created a mood of anxiety, a gnawing sense that something is deeply wrong. That 'something' is the basis of the social and environmental problems, which despite all the knowledge for which we pride ourselves, we have singularly failed to resolve.

It is increasingly clear that the reason for this failure lies in the very ideology of progress that has produced so much dynamism and creativity, which has made our Western civilisation value freedom, the centrality of the individual and, at its best moments, social justice and the equality of rights. The ideology of progress is reflected in the dominant religious and spiritual traditions of the West. These emphasise salvation and, even in these ecumenical times, assume superiority or precedence over other belief systems. This spirit is equally – or perhaps even more – present in the secular ideas of the European Enlightenment that have prevailed over the past two centuries, which have done so much to shape our concepts of human rights and freedom of expression, as well as our understanding of other cultures. However these dynamic and creative aspects of Western civilisation also have their darker side. This finds expression principally in the adversarial mentality, the belief that an idea can only prove its validity by defeating and driving out another, the sense that progress is a narrow line instead of a winding path, and that enlightenment means staring straight ahead rather than looking around, still less behind.

Such narrowness of focus, and the accompanying emphasis on 'struggle' and 'victory' can produce advances in thought and understanding. However these are invariably cancelled out by a climate of intellectual intolerance and cultural prejudice. At worst, the adversarial mindset gives rise to such phenomena as racism and imperialism, which seem to run contrary to the Enlightenment ideal, but are justified in terms of 'superior' technology and thought. At the other end of the political spectrum, 'progressive' movements adopt adversarial positions, which pervert their original aims and make them appear tyrannical and unjust. Too often, for instance, feminism in the modern West has seemed to mutate into an anti-male ideology or struggle between the genders, rather than a movement for equal rights and a just balance between the sexes. Likewise, 'anti-racism' can easily mutate into 'racism in reverse', because its premise is adversarial rather than holistic. Indeed the Achilles heel of the Western left has been its emphasis on punishment and retribution of 'oppressor' groups rather than the emancipation of all of humanity. This has made it a mirror image of the right, rather than a coherent alternative or a path beyond fear and bigotry.

Above all, the Western adversarial mode of thought has led us to view the environment as a resource to be infinitely plundered for our use, to be subdued and 'conquered' like an adversary, so that it will respond to our needs, rather than our living and working within its limits. The ecological consequences of this approach are catching up with us, and forcing us to look again at our relation-ship with nature, with our fellow human beings, and at our entire way of looking at the world. Increasingly, we are seeing that despite our very definite advances, there is something profoundly missing, a gap in our consciousness that we increasingly long to fill.

In this context, the apparent paradoxes of Jainism become an advantage, an inner strength from which we have much to learn. Jains are not asked to 'choose' between faith and reason, between abstract and concrete, the mystical and the scientific, emotion and objectivity. Nor is Jainism about exclusivity, about being the 'only' path to enlightenment, for it explicitly rejects such doctrines. Jains do not see the 'reasoning' and 'feeling' sides of their faith as polarities, or diametrically opposed worldviews, but as complementary principles that form essential parts of a whole. The rational and intuitive aspects of Jainism can be likened loosely to the hemispheres of the brain, the left being mainly concerned with reason and data, the right with more primal forces of creativity and the unconscious. The hemispheres need each other and are not 'separate' but physically joined and constantly overlapping in their functions, instead of adopting contradictory roles. Western thought needs that roundedness, for in its pursuit of knowledge it neglects and devalues the intuitive, in its quest for certainty, it confuses doubt with weakness. But Western civilisation, in its present phase, can seem almost irretrievably 'left brained', suppressing the sense of wonder and equating reason with the absence of doubt.

Jainism explicitly recognises the value of doubt and sees it as an intellectual strength. Only the Jina can be certain of anything after all, and against the ideal of moksha, all human knowledge is relative. The pursuit of truth is the duty of all conscious human beings, who are enjoined to cast around, consider other possibilities, think and above all else avoid arbitrary certainties. To be certain does not clarify anything in reality, but limits the exercise of compassion and the capacity to evaluate. It is also an illusion. In the West, the revival of an interest in the spiritual dimension arises out of a quest for wholeness, a desire to reconnect our increasingly fragmentary – although materially advanced – society, and a realisation that our political and even spiritual doctrines no longer have the ability to do so on their own.

Therefore, it is probably most useful for us in the West to look on the extreme practices of the Jain ascetics as if they were a decoy or disguise. Seeing them in this way does not diminish their importance to Jain belief and the lives of lay Jains. However it also enables us to view asceticism, in its more profound manifestations, as a deterrent to the superficial inquirer and an invitation to those who seek more. At the same time, it would be quite wrong to see Jain asceticism as archaic or reactionary – a conclusion to which the 'progressive' and hedonistic are inclined to leap. For in an age of environmental crisis, they dramatise some of the most pressing human preoccupations and take them to their logical conclusion. Environmental campaigners, policy-makers and scientific experts now speak fairly routinely of 'ecological footprints' and our need, individually and collectively, to minimise their impact. The Jain monk or nun sees every footprint as an individual act that has a direct bearing on other lives. Surely, this is an example to all of us whose thinking is influenced by 'green' concerns. It is, and will always be, impossible for us to copy their actions, but they provide an ideal standard against which we can measure our efforts.

Because Jains do not look for converts to their faith, there is no pressure on the inquirer into Jainism to 'become a Jain' or renounce his or her own beliefs and way of life. Indeed precisely because Jainism is not a missionary faith, it is more genuinely inclusive. Anyone who accepts the principle that life is sacred – all life, that is, not merely human – and does their best to live accordingly is regarded as following the Jain path. So is anyone who minimises his or her consumption or uses honestly acquired wealth for positive social ends. For Jains, the word 'social' encompasses the animal world and the environment as well as the way in which human communities are organised. Through exploring the main tenets of Jainism, Western men and women can adopt a more three-dimensional view of their own culture, applying it to the new situations we face, or rescuing from antiquity beliefs and practices that have been suppressed or overlooked by the prevailing adversarial view of 'progress'. Reverence for nature, for example, is part of the Western cultural inheritance, and is wholly compatible with reason. With the planet in danger from industrial pollution and over-consumption, it is indeed the only rational stance.

The Jain path therefore allows us to rediscover our instinctive affinity for the natural world. This is reflected in the sense of wonder and enchantment that is found in the heritage of pre-Christian Europe, as much as in today's aboriginal cultures. It is found as well in early Christianity, in the teachings of St Francis of Assisi or the 'heretical' sects of the Middle Ages that in the name of centralised progress were driven underground. These alternative Western viewpoints, pagan and Christian, thought of time as a series of cycles rather than a simple linear progression. Some accepted ideas of reincarnation and karmic destiny, either as an advanced philosophical system, as in the case of 'heretics' like the Cathars or, as with the Celtic and Germanic religions, at the intuitive level and so largely beneath the surface of consciousness. An understanding of Jainism puts us back in touch with these neglected areas of our culture, without our having to adopt 'Eastern' names, dress as Native Americans or Druids, or dance around sacred groves – unless of course we wish to do any of these things. On the Jain path, we can be better Christians or Jews, better secular humanists, better pagans, better radicals or conservatives. We are not required to renounce but we are invited constantly to question.

Jainism can therefore help us access the primitive, the instinctual, the unconscious, and put them to positive use in the modern world. However it is also, as we have noted, a rational faith or philosophy (the word 'dharma' covers both aspects) that can be applied in startlingly clear ways to questions bearing upon the modern human predicament. Science, for example, is moving increasingly away from the mechanistic view of the universe and finding common ground with the spiritual impulse within humanity. It is concerned, as never before, with the role and critical importance of sub-atomic particles, the existence and significance of which Jains have always implicitly understood. The ancient Jain seers were right to conceive of the universe as full of life forms, each one significant. The Jain tradition also anticipates, and reinforces, the concepts of rights that Western societies express through legal frameworks, even if, at home and abroad, they often fall short. The idea that each individual has value, is a conscious being, and is endowed with inalienable rights is central to the Jain dharma, the rights in question balanced by responsibilities, principally to human and animal welfare. The sense of the individual, and his or her freedoms and obligations, is arguably stronger in Jainism than in other Indian-derived traditions. The aim is not to annihilate the self, or to merge the self with a larger cosmic consciousness, but to do all that one can in one's lifetime to realise the true self. This is achieved through leading a measured, careful life, reducing or eliminating feelings of anger or hatred and being mindful of the rights of all living beings.

Equality is also one of this ancient yet modern tradition's most revered precepts. In the context of Jainism, I use the phrase 'his or her' less for 'politically correct' and more for reasons of strict accuracy. The Jain path was not, and never has been, restricted either to men or women, who are regarded as spiritual equals and, for the most part, just as likely to attain enlightenment. Jainism does not define or restrict people by gender, but values their individual qualities and contributions. At the same time, it does not identify the idea of equality with identical feelings and characteristics, any more than it assumes that any two individuals are 'the same'. The duty of Jains – or those who identify with Jain values – is to try to achieve as much spiritual insight as they can within one lifetime, whether they are female or male, and regardless of racial background, level of education, intellectual ability, sexual orientation or any of the other factors that be used to divide and classify human beings. The enlightened being, or the inner self, is neither male nor female and transcends these categories along with all conventional human labels.

Jainism's stance on equality was revolutionary in its day, and remains so in vast areas of the world, including (contrary to our complacent assumptions) the 'developed' West. Furthermore, Jainism is distinguished from other religions by explicitly extending the idea of rights to all species, placing a moral obligation on humans to respect those rights and be aware of them in even the most mundane decisions. Other traditions acknowledge the connections between species, within the cycle of life. Most of the world's mythologies involve an interaction and an overlap between humans and animals, but Jainism is distinctive in its insistence on the intrinsic worth of all life forms. Animal liberation, and the 'animal rights' movement in its varied manifestations, is gradually transforming social and cultural attitudes in the West, especially in such areas of life as laboratory experimentation, factory farming and 'blood' sports. It is recognised more and more that such practices, as well as inflicting needless harm, are scientifically misleading, detrimental to human health and psychologically damaging to those who carry them out. They represent the worst form of cruelty, rationalised cruelty, and so are destructive of the human spirit and, in Jain terms, generators of negative karma. Those who reflect on such issues, or who seek to alleviate suffering, are following the Jain path whether they are conscious of it or not.

The purpose of this book is to offer an overview of the principal and defining tenets of Jainism. I have concentrated on those which, although distinctively Jain, have a transcendent or universal significance. They are ideas that enable us to 'get at' Jainism, to explore its essential truths and be spiritually enriched by them. The book is not an academic study, but a personal exploration of a philosophy and spiritual path that has influenced my attitude towards politics, economics and culture, as well as spirituality. The Jain path is one that deserves more attention than it has hitherto received outside India and Indian communities around the world, despite its many indirect and subtle influences. I use the term 'path' to describe Jainism, because learning to follow Jain principles is a journey, not only in terms of spiritual development, but also of practical changes in the conduct of our lives.

More than anything else, the Jain dharma is a path that directs us to a different way of thinking, one that is more rounded, more holistic, less based on polarised arguments that are never resolved. The book is aimed principally at non-Jains, and at those who are influenced by the prevailing Western assumptions about progress, whether they live in North America and Europe, or other areas of the world, including burgeoning economic giants such as India. The term 'West' might be problematic for some, but it is shorthand for a system of values as much as a geographical area. It is a system of values that is superficially confident, but in a process of self-criticism and change, some would say spiritual crisis. One aspect of this crisis is reflected in the movement loosely categorised as the 'New Age', which is at base an attempt to fill the empty space in our lives created by materialism and the manic emphasis on progress. Yet this quest for 'something more' can often become the continuation of shopping by other means, a consumerism of the spirit.

At a more sinister level, the suppression of spirituality in Western culture – the triumph of the 'left brain' – contributes to the prevalent atmosphere of aggression. Sometimes, this is directed against the self, through the epidemics of substance abuse and self-harm. It is also directed against society, through increasingly random violence and cruelty, family breakdown and a culture in which rudeness is rewarded, harshness and indifference elevated into virtues. Such symptoms of spiritual breakdown are also expressed in acts of aggression towards other countries and the growing climate of hostility towards non-Western cultures, a rejection of other ways of knowing and acting. These developments are signs of weakness rather than strength. In spiritual terms, they are a cry for help, the expression of a need for healing. Jainism contains healing energy. In a world that is at once more closely connected and more ideologically fragmented, we would do well to draw upon the Jain concepts of non-violence, living lightly upon the Earth and respecting difference. There is no single 'Jain solution' to the problems facing Western humanity. Far better than that, the ancient dharma provides a series of principles, which we can use as a guide and which give us a welcome and long overdue humility. Jainism gently challenges the assumption that Western civilisation is always right and that its technological power is unassailable.

This is perhaps why Einstein so admired the religion of the conquerors that he wished to be reborn as a Jain. The scientist who for many personifies the Western rational tradition saw in this philosophy of the East a way to reconcile the absolute and the relative, the pursuit of knowledge with the leap of faith.

CHAPTER TWO

THE FAITH OF THE PATHFINDERS

I am not Rama. I have no desire for material things.
Like a Jina, I want to establish peace within myself.

SRI RAMA, IN THE HINDU *YOGA VASISHTHA*

J ainism, being a non-theistic faith, does not offer its followers recourse to a divine creator with redemptive powers. Instead, it asks individuals to discover the power within themselves, a power at once spiritual and intellectual, by which we redeem ourselves from the karmic cycle. That cycle consists, in essence, of material preoccupations and passions – good as well as bad, creative as well as destructive – that obscure our understanding of the truth. The path of Jainism is about the search for truth, which can never be fully achieved because of the human condition's natural limits, but which we should none the less work towards through our actions, our thoughts and our social relationships. In this way Jainism, despite the rigorous demands it can make of its followers, acknowledges our imperfections in a compassionate and humane way.

Truth is a spiritual and social goal, which we are obliged to pursue although it is impossible fully to attain. This might seem illogical, until we remember that equality and justice are goals that remain central to the Western political project, even though they can never be achieved in perfect form: utopia after all, means 'no place'. Jainism's search for truth resembles the Western scientific quest, in that it values the pursuit of knowledge for its own sake. Unlike the cult of 'pure', mechanistic reasoning, it values the power of intuition. At the same time it eschews the blind faith that leads to fundamentalism. Knowledge is only worthwhile, only real, when it is tempered by reasoned judgement. And the responsibility for that reasoning lies with all of us, as rational men and women as well as spiritual inquirers.

To the modern sensibility, the Jain view of the individual's quest for knowledge can appear stark. In a society where self-expression and 'emoting' are encouraged by opinion formers in the media and academia, and equated with personal liberation, Jainism seems to offer little to the spiritual consumer. This is why it is less immediately appealing to the New Age movement of the West than some other Eastern cultural traditions. It is not accessible to 'converts', after the fashion of Buddhism. Nor does it appeal directly to our sentiments, like the *bhakti* or devotional movements within Hinduism, where fervour is the starting point and understanding comes later. Jainism draws no distinction between the intellectual and spiritual search. It appeals at once to our minds and our hearts, our instinctive 'feelings' and our rational assumptions.

Unlike secular humanism, the Jain dharma does not confine the pursuit of knowledge to one lifetime, after which consciousness is snuffed out for eternity. Instead, knowledge is built up over many material existences, as the soul acquires knowledge and experience by being continuously reborn, by moving forward - or regressing – towards escape from karma. This, for Jains, is the karmic journey, but it corresponds to the evolutionary cycle, which encompasses regression as well as advancement. Similarly, human communities can make great strides forward, technologically and socially, and then lapse into the darkest forms of barbarity. The technological prowess that has enabled us to overcome disease and break down cultural barriers has also made possible concentration camps, nuclear weapons and sophisticated methods of repression and torture. Such backward steps are, for Jains, part of the experience of karma. We cannot count on society to create the conditions for a balanced and rational way of living, and there is no all-powerful creator to intervene and rescue us. Therefore, it is up to the individual to work out how best to live according to the principles of non-violence and restraint, how to play a benevolent role in society – or in spiritual terms generate 'positive' karma – and eventually move beyond worldly concerns altogether.

At one level, Jainism strongly emphasises the individual's autonomy and consequent responsibility for his or her actions and attitudes. Human responsibilities, like human rights, derive from our ability to make conscious decisions as well as act from instinct or learned behaviour, the overlapping forces of nature and nurture. The Jain path also reminds us, equally strongly, that we are intimately connected to each other through a karmic chain of being. The 'we' in question are all beings that have life, not only humans. Whilst all lives are equally valid, there is still in a sense a spiritual hierarchy, for human beings alone, in normal circumstances, are held to have the rational power to reach the highest levels of knowledge – although for exactly the same reasons they can also plumb the depths of degradation and ignorance. Humans themselves are spiritually inferior to fully enlightened beings, which are held to have evolved to new levels of consciousness that have broken the fetters of materialism. In the Jain tradition, we do not find a total explanation for the universe, any more than in Western physics we find a total 'explanation' for energy. The universe we inhabit was neither created nor can be destroyed by an external power, but it can expand, contract and regenerate itself in continuous cycles. Nor do we find an underlying cosmic 'purpose', except for our individual purpose of acquiring as much knowledge and understanding as possible, and living a harmonious relationship with other beings. This can be interpreted in terms of practising compassion towards fellow human beings and creatures, as well as reducing our impact on the planet, but it cannot be made to fit into the neat pigeonholes of (increasingly inadequate) secular political ideologies. Neither the 'left' nor the 'right', for example, have exclusive claims on Jain allegiance. The dharma is holistic, in that it gives the individual a context, a spiritual goal and a sense of connection with much larger forces. But that is very different from providing a total and universal explanation. This is because the doctrine known as Jainism is seen as the expression of the most advanced human consciousness. Human knowledge is held to be inherently limited and so from the start the dharma accepts its own limitations and works within them.

Without a creator, without an overall explanation akin to that provided (for instance) by Christianity or Marxism, and offering only spiritual and intellectual challenge, the Jain path can seem a rocky one. It offers little incentive to Westerners whose culture, despite its dynamism and capacity for experimentation, is still made up largely of closed ideological systems, secular and religious. These tend to demand absolute allegiance and with varying degrees of subtlety call upon us to be either 'for' or 'against' them. Jainism, by contrast, does not seek to superimpose itself upon or drive out other ideas and does not demand exclusive loyalty. It is these aspects of the Jain path that should make it attractive to those of us in the West who are schooled in rational thought but wish for something more than 'pure' reason. For we appreciate the value of our enlightened and – in the broadest sense - humanist tradition, but are also aware of its limitations, which have been and remain dangerous limitations, inflicting much misery and perhaps threatening the very survival of our planet.

Yet negotiating the Jain path without the light provided by a creator God, without the certainties conferred by most faiths, is a difficult process. This is why the Jains make sense of their lives, and help themselves on their journey, by their reverence for the *Tirthankaras*. These twenty-four outstanding human beings have all progressed to enlightenment and freed themselves from karma, that is to say they have evolved beyond human status. They connect Jains living today with prehistory, a preliterate culture with a highly educated and largely urban population in India and across the globe. The word Tirthankara literally means 'ford-maker', the one who makes a clearing for us through the river that represents karmic influences and material distractions. Tirthankara also implies the concept of 'pathfinder' and this is the essential role of these Jain heroes. They point us towards the path that leads to liberation form karma, the cycle of birth, death and rebirth. They also show us how to make the best of our karma, and how to live according to the *Triratna* or 'Three Jewels' of Jainism: Right Faith, Right Knowledge and Right Action. These pathfinders are part icons and part role models. They are meditated upon, either as images or ideas, they are looked to for inspiration, and they are also revered as a link with antiquity. However they are not gods, and nor are they *avataras*, like Krishna and Rama in the Hindu tradition: divine beings incarnated in human form to redeem humanity. Instead, the Tirthankaras have unequivocally human origins and are evidence of what human beings have the potential to become.

In the origins of Jainism, as with most faith traditions, myth and history overlap. When exploring China's Daoist history, for example, we are unable to prove the existence of Lao Tse in terms acceptable to modernity. Many of the details we have are shrouded in mystery, such as the 'journey to the West', in which he dictated the *Dao de Jing* to a border guard and subsequently vanished. Christian theologians and lay people argue over details of the life of the historical Jesus. Are the miracles, for instance, to be interpreted as literal truths, or are they symbolic representations of spiritual power? Within the Hindu dharma, there is no single 'founding' event. It is seen as an eternal, timeless wisdom that evolves and adapts. The same is true of Jainism. As a distinctive religious and philosophical movement, it began to take shape in ninth century BCE (Before Common Era) under the influence of Parshva, who is also known by the honorific title Parshva-natha.

Parshva is the twenty-third Tirthankara. This means that the Jain tradition is regarded as having existed for many centuries, indeed thousands of years. Its distinctive characteristics, including vegetarianism and the cultivation of non-violence as the highest ethical goal, are seen as having deep roots in Indian civilisation. They precede even the development of the caste system and the establishment of a written script. Modern Jains describe their tradition as 'millions of years old'. This is because they measure time in terms of twin cycles of 600 million years, one ascending, the other declining. Tirthankaras appear, and reappear, in each half-cycle. The term 'million' need not be interpreted literally, but represents instead a very long period of time, time that cannot easily be measured in human terms. For Jains, their path represents the earliest human insights and impulses, onto which new layers of knowledge are continuously grafted. It this genuinely inclusive approach, and with it the concept of knowledge and intuition as a continuum, that enables Jains to reconcile their spiritual insights with modern science, their lived experience of modernity with their ancient wisdom – and to do so without a crisis of conscience.

The word 'Jina' – and with it the idea of 'Jain', the religion of the Jinas – is relatively new, if we accept that the faith has profoundly ancient roots. Linguistically, it was first associated with *Ardha-Magadhi*, a dialect of the *Prakrit* language that was spoken and written in large swathes of India, a rival to Sanskrit with a somewhat more popular touch. Prakrit – its Ardha Magadhi dialect in particular – is the language of much of early Jain scripture and story-telling. Jina means 'spiritual victor' or 'one who has conquered himself' in both Prakrit and Sanskrit: in the latter the word 'ji' means to conquer or overcome.

The first Tirthankara, Rishabha (also known as Rikhava) is described in Prakrit texts as a Jina who lived 'many thousands of years' ago. The semi-mythical Rishabha is seen as more than the founder of a religious tradition. He is an ancient lawgiver, after the fashion of Lycurgus for the ancient Spartans. Unlike Sparta, however, the society described in Jain texts is distinctly anti-militarist. It is a settled community, based on the cultivation of grain, with cities, currency and trade, a legal system, marriage and family structures.

Rishabha is the lawgiver who yoked a nomadic, tribal population into an ordered, settled society with a tranquil ethos. However, he also recognised in the wandering, uncluttered old way of life a special sense of purity and freedom, the latter spiritual as well as personal. He identified possessions and worldly concerns with karmic bondage, and preached liberation from this bondage by embarking on a life of wandering austerity. It is through this conclusion, rather than his former achievements as a lawgiver, that he became a Jina and is recognised as the first Tirthankara. Whether or not he existed in a literal form, Rishabha established the Jain path, which recognises the value of civilisation over barbarism, but seeks to move beyond the civilised world. Rishabha's settled community corresponds in character to the Indus Valley civilisation of Northern India and Pakistan, about which little is known save for its peace and stability, and its cultivation of grain in around 7000 BCE. Archaeological evidence reveals advanced urban communities, such as Harappa and Mohanjo-daro, and the likelihood that yogic practices existed: surviving sculptures and pottery depict figures in what we recognise today as lotus postures.

The story of Rishabha is the founding myth of Jainism, but it also dramatises one of the most important aspects of the human predicament: the tension between freedom and constraint, individual conscience and social obligation, codified laws and unwritten ancient customs. It is the story of Lao Tse, who saw that the pure reason and order represented by Confucius could become arid and cold. He, like Rishabha, left civilisation to set out on a journey to the West, the world of the barbarians beyond the border. Diogenes, the Cynic philosopher, astounded the ancient Athenians by rejecting material possessions, living in a large earthen pitcher and famously carrying a lantern through the marketplace in search of an honest man. The Roman historian Tacitus contrasted the decadent urbanites of the imperial city unfavourably with the village-dwelling Germanic tribal peoples, in whose society he found integrity as well as the republican virtues of equality and justice. In the Europe of the Enlightenment, at the birth of the modern era, there was continuous tension between freedom and reason, faith and deduction. The *Social Contract* of Jean-Jacques Rousseau begins with the famous phrase 'man is born free and is everywhere in chains' and seeks to reconcile these two ways of being, so that order is achieved whilst ancient virtues are retained.

Through his life's journey, Rishabha straddles this divide between liberty and order, the worldly and the transcendent. This is why he remains the model for Jains through the ages. The regulated way of life of the householder has enduring value, but ultimately it is still a generator of karma and the true path to enlightenment is through renouncing all material concerns, that is to say all that 'matters' to a householder. This is why the ideal goal of the lay Jain is to become an ascetic, or failing that to engage in charitable or voluntary work, when the tasks of the householder are complete. Rishabha's life also symbolises the path of karmic progress, which can take the individual, the *jiva*, through many lifetimes and stages of moral and spiritual evolution, to the point of transcendence. Thirdly, Rishabha's life represents the Jain path itself and its journey through the levels of consciousness, from primal insight, through reasoned knowledge to an enlightenment that is a fusion of the two, and yet beyond both.

Rishabha's journey is also reflected in the ideal life of the Brahmin, the Hindu man of the highest caste, that of priests and scholars. The Brahmin's aim is to fulfil his duties as a householder and then renounce family life for a wandering asceticism and search for a higher truth. Yet Jainism in the sense that we now understand it arose partly in opposition to the new caste-dominated order known as Brahmanism. As such, it was the reassertion of an earlier spiritual path, and with it a social system that was less divided by caste and ethnic divisions and so possessed more of an underlying unity. The hierarchical society was based on Brahmanic interpretations of the Vedas, the corpus of religious and social doctrines that form the basis of what we call Hinduism today, and around which the society of North India came to revolve between approximately 1500 and 900 BCE. In the four principal Vedas, the *Rig Veda*, the *Yajur Veda, Sama Veda and Atharva Veda*, scant mention is made of transmigration, the doctrine or birth, death and rebirth, or karma, the process of cause and effect.

There was, according to Brahmanism's critics, more emphasis on ritual and outward show than on the inner life, more emphasis – by extension – on expanding politically and economically than on the inward journey. Respect for life itself had been undermined, as Brahmanic ritual sometimes included animal sacrifice, whilst war and conquest were increasingly exalted. This attitude of militarism and domination is reflected in the widespread reference to darker-skinned Indic peoples as 'dasyus', a derogatory term implying the 'blackness' and inferior social status of conquered races. The term 'dasyu' did not always refer to race and colour, but could also be used to mean anti-social, hostile or un-spiritual individuals and groups within Vedic culture. Nor were animal sacrifice and caste unique to Brahmanic society. Both were common throughout the ancient world, East and West. Yet in the period when Jainism in its present form began to take shape, there seems to have been a widespread belief that the original Indian ideals of peace and co-operation were being compromised, giving way to the centralisation of power, both spiritual and temporal.

These aspects of Brahmanic society led to a revival of *sramanic* beliefs and practices, as part of a search for authenticity, for a true 'Veda' that would point the spiritual seeker on a path out of material enthralment. 'Sramanic' means committed to ascetic disciplines, and some argue for a linguistic link to the word 'shaman', derived originally from the Tungus language of Siberia and meaning 'one who knows', or one who gains knowledge or insight by travelling to higher and lower worlds. The words shaman and shamanism are well known to us today, with the renewal of interest in tribal societies, past and present, and the sense that their insights can guide us in a society that over-emphasises technology and has lost touch with the natural world. The shaman, like the ascetic, reaches higher levels of consciousness and gains advanced spiritual knowledge through a process of initiation that involves renouncing earthly pleasures and stimuli. Shamanic practices include fasting, sexual abstinence and periods of isolation away from settled communities, chiefly in mountains, deserts and forests. These experiences are central to Jain ascetic practice, ancient and modern, but unlike shamans Jain ascetics are not the locus of political power, but are outside conventional structures, even the conventional Jain structures such as self-governing temples, on which they often depend.

The *sramanas,* or followers of ascetic disciplines, have in common with shamans a sense of the interconnectedness of all life forms, a community of beings that includes humanity but reaches well beyond it. Jains, like members of shamanic cultures, revere mountains and see the spiritual element in everything around them – indeed they go further than shamans in arguing that even the most humble plants – and not just sacred trees – have souls within them. Unlike shamanic cultures, sramanic teachings such as Jainism seek ultimately to move beyond the material realm, rather than merely to help us live better within it. Their reverence for nature is a means to an end, instead of an end in itself. The Vedas identify Rishabha with one of the manifestations of Shiva, and the *Rig Veda*, specifically, speaks of *vrata dharmi* or *yogins*, ascetics who live by vows (*vratas*) and outside established social norms.

Parshva, the twenty-third Tirthankara, is said to have lived between 872 and 772 BCE and there is some evidence for his historical existence. He kept alive an ancient flame of ascetic practice and renunciation at a time when society was changing, when ritual and formality were taking precedence and the highly stratified caste-based society was beginning to take shape. Amongst the Jains, Parshva is seen, one might say, as a John the Baptist equivalent, who 'prepares the way' for the one who gave form and content to modern Jainism, the twenty-fourth Tirthankara: Mahavira.

Bhagvan (Lord) Mahavira (599 – 527 BCE) was not a contemporary of Parshva, but Gautama Buddha (563-483 BCE), the other founder of a major sramanic faith. His original name was

Vardhamana Jnanputra, and he was born near modern Patna, in Bihar, north India, to a princely family of the Kshatriya, or warrior caste, who were just beneath the Brahmins in the Vedic hierarchy but wielded much of the political and all the military power. Aged thirty, he gave up family, property and worldly responsibility to lead the life of a wandering ascetic. During these wanderings, he took five vows: never to stay at places where his presence would cause inconvenience to others; precedence to the soul over all material considerations; only to speak in answer to the questions of disciples or seekers; to accept only alms that he could hold in the palm of his hand, and not to render services to householders merely to fulfil his material needs. Mahavira reaffirmed the essence of Jain teachings, reverence for all life and personal responsibility to abstain from harm:

All breathing, existing, living, sentient creatures should not be slain, nor treated with violence, nor abused, nor tormented, nor driven away. This is the pure, unchangeable, eternal law which the clever ones, who understand the world, have proclaimed.

This simple, independent and non-violent life remains the model for Jain ascetics, building upon the traditions associated with Rishabha. Mahavira's chosen way of life also matches the Five Vows of Jainism, which Mahavira initiated: *ahimsa* (non-injury), *satya* (Truth), *asteya* (non-theft), *brahmacharya* (chastity) and *aparigraha* (non-possessiveness). These vratas are lived out by ascetic men and women in a very literal way. Lay Jains conform to a modified version, which they interpret according to their circumstances and conditions, relying on their intellect and conscience because they have no priesthood to compel obedience or impose an official 'line'. *Asteya*, or abstinence from theft, can also apply to taking anything to which one is not entitled, such as unjustified profits. *Bramacharya* might mean celibacy for ascetics. For lay Jains, it means the avoidance of promiscuity. Unjust profits and promiscuity are both exploitative and cause *himsa* (injury) to the self and others, as does the pursuit of material possessions as ends in themselves. *Ahimsa* is the Alpha and Omega of the Five Vows and the life they prescribe, but each vow is dependent on the others. The life of the Jains is, above all, about balance.

It is also interesting to note that the leaders of the *sramanic* revival, including Mahavira and the Buddha, came from the *Kshatriya* or warrior caste. In one sense, this is ironic, given the sramanic emphasis on non-violence. However, the sramanic path is about spiritual discipline, the conquest of narrowly selfish desire in order to realise the true self. The warrior spirit is therefore directed within. Rather than creating a rift with the Brahmins, with accompanying religious strife, the sramanic revival influenced the future development of Brahmanism. The *Upanishads* (800-500 BCE) are texts that emphasise individual devotion rather than ritual, the practice of *tapas* (austerities), the value of non-possessiveness and the overcoming of materialistic passions. Central to the *Upanishads* are the doctrines of karma and transmigration: the cycle of rebirth until enlightenment. Yet unlike Jainism, the individual soul (*atman*) merges at the point of enlightenment with a universal, all-encompassing soul, or *Brahman*. The Jains balance their belief in interdependence with a sense of the crucial importance of the individual. Therefore the individual soul, which is the true self, survives as a unit of pure, undefiled consciousness, achieving full independence as well as becoming 'at one' with the eternal universe.

Buddhism has grown over the centuries into a distinctive and easily recognisable faith tradition, declining (until very recently) in its native India but expanding over the Asian land mass, to offshore Japan and subsequently the West. The faith of the pathfinders, by contrast, was cultivated quietly and remained distinctively Indian in character. It did not set itself up as a rival to Brahmanic practice, or separate itself militantly from the mainstream Vedic system that evolved into modern Hinduism. As a result, many external observers, including Hindus, have seen Jainism as a sect within the Hindu dharma, or as an 'offshoot' of Hinduism. A Jain, if wishing to make a gentle point, would turn this suggestion on its head and claim that Hinduism is an offshoot of the Jain tradition. The path of non-violence and light living on the Earth is, they justifiably maintain, the basis of Indian spirituality, which they have continued to follow unobtrusively in a pure form. Whilst Jains see themselves as the keepers of an ancient flame, they do not seek to suppress, or even triumph politically over other faiths. They respect boundaries, but accept a common essence out of which arise all faiths, all spiritual aspirations. The absence of supremacist dogma in any form distinguishes the Jain path and also provides Jains with ideal equipment for life in a multi-faith society – and participation in a global community where, for good or ill, faiths continuously interact. They are, indeed, pioneers of what we would now call 'inter-faith' activity, although they would call 'inter-faith' the doctrine of many-sidedness, or intellectual non-violence.

Jainism's essence is not paraded before outsiders. Nor is there a centralised Jain 'authority' to which the inquirer might refer, in order to be clear on precise points of doctrine. For Jains, to an extent like the Quakers within the Christian tradition, or the Sufi orders within Islam, trust in the inner light. This *is* the essence, rather than any corpus of belief. Moksha, or liberation, is the point when the soul emerges, illuminated, and the karmic cycle is broken. Shrimad Rajchandra, confidant and mentor to the young Mahatma Gandhi, described the process in these terms:

> On the cessation of the identification of the soul with the body, you are neither the performer of the action nor the experiencer of its result. This is the secret of true religion. By this religion, there is liberation; you are liberation itself. You are infinite insight and knowledge; you are un-disturbable bliss itself.

The Jain path of good works, followed by withdrawal as a means towards individual salvation is one with which the culture of the West is profoundly familiar. The Christian message is also one of individual salvation and Christ, like Mahavira, asked his followers to put their faith before materialistic concerns, indeed to renounce possessions and earthly ties. Both Christ and Mahavira claimed that their 'kingdoms' were 'not of this world', the material realm being mired in suffering for one tradition and weighed down by the bonds of karma for the other. The parallel goes further, because neither Mahavira nor Christ aimed to found a new religion. They – and Gautama Buddha – sought instead to revive the original spirit of the religious tradition in which they worked.

Jainism is distinctive, in its own time and today, in that it regards all life as having the potential for liberation, or at least the potential for spiritual growth. All living things, therefore, are assumed to have the 'right' to live, and that is not merely a political right, but a spiritual entitlement, because all living things have souls. It is assumed that they have the right to live and make spiritual progress, but it is also taken as inevitable that the process of living causes harm as well as good, that life is destroyed unwittingly as we breathe and consume. What is essential is to give as much and take as little as possible, to minimise our destructive impact on the Earth and seek to reduce our consumption of energy. In the era of climate change, where the limits of technological society are apparent as the advantages, there is no message that could be more topical or more 'relevant'.

Humans are not inherently more virtuous than other creatures because of their 'superior' intellectual aptitude and capacity for spiritual awareness. Indeed, they often reduce themselves to lower levels, when those very capacities are distorted into cruelty, bigotry or fanaticism. And, when it comes to it, how do we know that animals or even plants lack highly developed spiritual sensitivities? Jains do not rule out that possibility at all, and nor increasingly, does modern science. Yet humans also have the capacity to rise to the highest levels of consciousness, which they are obliged to use to avoid less auspicious rebirths. Human birth is one of the stages along the road to spiritual liberation, from which many wrong turnings, some disastrous, might be taken, but where personal salvation and freedom from karma are both within reach. Jains are unique in equating karma directly with the material world. For them, it is composed of living particles, albeit particles of subtle matter that exist at a parallel level of consciousness. This subtle matter, however, imprisons the soul in the world of gross matter, the mundane existence that at once impedes our spiritual progress but also offers us great opportunities for spiritual development. Our actions increase or reduce our levels of karmic accretion. There is negative karma, which binds us uncompromisingly, and positive karma, which is lighter and which points us towards personal salvation. Rooted in ancient cosmology, this view of karma connects moral purpose with physical laws, and so symbolically breaches the divide between the world of direct experience – the so-called 'real world' – and the spiritual domain.

The Jain message to humans is egalitarian and, in Western parlance, democratic. The idea of 'community' extends to all life forms, but there is also a specifically human community or *sangha* (a term shared with the Buddhists), to which Jains voluntarily belong. The sangha is open equally to men and women, young and old, rich and poor, recognising no divisions of caste or class, race, gender or sexual orientation, and regarding disability as no impediment. It was conceived of by Mahavira and his successors as a Fourfold Order, often represented by the *svastika*, that Indo-European symbol of life whose purpose was so badly perverted in mid-twentieth century Europe, when it was used falsely as an agent of death. In the Fourfold Order, each arm of the svastika corresponds to an aspect of the sangha: male ascetics, female ascetics, lay men and lay women. Thus equality and interdependence are acknowledged, but differences venerated at the same time. The svastika also represents the four principal 'destinies' (*gati*) or categories of rebirth, each arm signifying the the human, animal or plant, heavenly and hellish states. These destinies are interchangeable and intertwined.

Jainism is the path of 'both/and' rather than 'either/or' and in this sense, above all, it holds lessons for the polarised West. The

Jain world view, one of equality and diversity, non-violence and personal liberation, is expressed by the public symbol of Jainism, the *pratika*. It depicts a human hand imprinted with the word 'Ahimsa'. Above it, the fourfold order is represented by a svastika, and orbs that represent each of the Three Jewels – Right Faith, Right Knowledge and Right Action. Above them stands the liberated jiva in a state of grace. The framework in which these representations are encased reflects the ancient Jain picture of the universe, which resembles that of Shamanic societies, with a lower, middle and upper world, reflecting different levels of consciousness, along with (unlike Shamanic cosmologies) the *siddha loka*, where the liberated souls reside. These levels of the universe are not discrete but connected entities.

After the death (or rather enlightenment) of Mahavira, divisions occurred within Jainism. The most important of these was the divide, which continues to this day, between the *Svetambaras* and *Digambaras*, the latter a minority tradition, albeit an influential one. The names of these two categories of Jain derive from the garb (or lack thereof) of their ascetics. The *svetambar* (white clad) monks and nuns wear simple white robes, whereas the male ascetics of the Digambara (sky-clad) order go naked. Svetambaras and Digambaras are at variance over aspects of the life of Mahavira and over the position of women within the sangha. To the Digambaras, the naked way of life expresses aparigraha (non-possessiveness) in its purest form, but women ascetics cannot achieve this state for reasons of practicality and decency. They go on to maintain that to achieve moksha, rebirth as a man is essential, because only a male can live out the full ascetic ideal. Svetambaras admit women to all levels of ascetic life and do not regard nakedness as essential to 'pure' renunciation. They believe that the nineteenth Tirthankara, Malli, was a woman and that Mahavira was married with a daughter before he renounced his worldly goods (the Digambaras accept neither of these interpretations as true). It is worth noting here that the Digambara 'side' does not base its argument on the alleged spiritual inequality of women, but on supposedly pragmatic arguments. Jains of all types were unique in the sramanic era in treating women as spiritual equals, a characteristic they share with many 'primal' and shamanic religious traditions, as well as the 'progressive' theology of Western societies today. Digambaras and Svetambaras have not faced each other in conflict, like Sunni and Shia Muslims, for instance, or the Catholic and Protestant wings of Christianity. Instead, they often share facilities, including (occasionally) temples, and for the most part they respect, listen to and influence each other. They can be seen, therefore, less as two principal 'wings' of Jainism and more as two complementary aspects of the sangha.

Whilst we should not underplay the significance of these differences among Jains, or their interest to academics and scholars, there is no reason why they should be of much concern to the Western seeker of spiritual insight. Such seekers are not attempting to 'become' or even imitate Jains, but to find in Jain ideas inspiration, guidance and renewal. Walking the Jain path, for them, is a way to make better sense of their lives, strengthen or re-evaluate their beliefs and engage positively with their own culture rather than reject it. This is because the Jain path is a thread connecting the preliterate society's sense of enchantment and reverence for nature with Mahatma Gandhi's philosophy of non-violence and the ecological movement's aim to rebalance human need with the interests of the natural world, to re-embed humanity in nature.

Jains are encouraged to think independently and apply the whole mind to spiritual as to all other concerns. Theirs is not a path of submission to external authorities or rigid interpretations of rules and texts. Because faith and reason ultimately as one, there is no virtue or spiritual advantage in closing sections of the mind down in order to accept ideas and practices without question. A true understanding of Jainism therefore involves applying the principles of the Five Vows with imagination and sensitivity to the pleasures, problems and many dilemmas that the process of living brings. This is especially true for lay men and women. Ascetics are expected to follow a stricter, and so more literal, interpretation of the Vows. Even they, however, cannot allow either their philosophy or its practice to become ends in themselves, that is to say they must not allow themselves to become attached to ideas or actions, because such attachment strips the ideas and actions of their value. In this context, Jain texts are not objects of worship or blueprints for blind obedience, but guides along the spiritual path that protect against materialism and falsehood. They are also repositories of Jain history.

Among the best-known Jain scriptures are the *Acaranga Sutra* and the *Tattvartha Sutra*. These testimonies to the distinctiveness and power of Jain ideas are presented in the crisp style of the Indian *sutra* tradition, verses of philosophical import. The *Acaranga* is one of eleven 'Angas', or limbs, of post-Mahavira Jain doctrine and practice. These 'limbs', so-called because they are said to form the 'body' of Jain ideas, were not composed by

Mahavira himself, but in the proceeding centuries by *sthaviras* (elders), unknown men of learning who sought to express the Jain dharma in terms of scholarship and ritual, in order to ensure its permanence. Hermann Jacobi, an Indologist of the late nineteenth and early twentieth century who did much to make Jainism accessible to the West, became aware that the Angas were not transmitted or transcribed at the same time, but at irregular intervals over centuries, with frequent variations of Prakrit spelling and grammar. The *Acaranga* is the limb that refers to conduct (*acara*) and guides ascetics towards the best forms of outward behaviour and, more importantly, the frame of mind that accords best with their vocation and status. As Professor Padmanabh H. Jaini has written, the *Acaranga* 'is accorded great reverence, ... because it contains what is certainly the most authoritative account of the life of Mahavira, ... and it may well have preserved Mahavira's own words on the cardinal doctrine of ahimsa'.[1]

The *Acaranga* is widely acknowledged to be the oldest written portion of the Jain canon. The *Tattvartha Sutra* was composed by Umasvati in the second century CE and so represents a mature and well-established body of post-Mahavira Jain doctrines. It is written in Sanskrit, the traditional language of the Brahmanic texts. This is testimony to the spread of Jain influence and, as Professor Jaini suggests, a sign that Jains wished to engage in debate and dialogue with other schools of thought. As such, the *Tattvartha* (That Which Is) carves out a distinctive philosophical niche for both Svetambara and Digambara Jains, with the unique approach to karma and the liberation of the soul distilled in three hundred and fifty verses with succinct commentaries. These Jain scriptures, and the scholarly tradition that surrounds them, do not represent the heart of Jainism, but act as facilitators to good understanding and good conduct.[2]

In Jainism, the ancient spiritual goal of transcending worldly concerns converges with the new political goal of light living on Earth. Just as the warrior instinct of the Kshatriyas was once turned inwards and converted into a struggle for self-mastery, so our impulse towards economic growth should be converted into an impulse to grow spiritually, so that we might survive and so that our lives have lasting value. The faith of the pathfinders can help us recover our social compass and rebalance our personal lives. Its starting point is the individual man or woman, whose steps along that path are a journey towards self-conquest.

CHAPTER THREE

THE GENTLE CONQUERORS

Jai Jinendra.

This popular Jain greeting is used as much in casual conversation as on occasions of spiritual significance. It can be used as a mark of respect by non-Jains, and non-Indians, and yet it expresses profound underlying truths about a faith that lays strong and just claims to be India's most ancient.

'Jai Jinendra' means 'Hail to the Conqueror'. At first glance, this phrase sounds militaristic. In the Western mind, which is divided to the point of schizophrenia on questions of war and the use of force, such imagery arouses feelings of confusion, anger and disquiet. Frequently, these feelings find expression in the rhetoric of violence and rejection. In itself a paradox, but one that Jains would readily understand. Jainism is a philosophy that acknowledges, indeed delights in, paradox. For it is based, after all, on an awareness of the complexity of the universe and each unique life form within it, and on the interconnectedness of all aspects of that universe. Thus Jains take a long view of existence and, perhaps more importantly than that, a rounded view, in which all manner of perspectives can be considered and the truth may be reached by an infinite variety of paths that climb or wind towards it.

It is important to realise here that Jainism is pluralist in its outlook, without abandoning the idea of objective truth, as the post-modern movement in Western culture seeks to do. However the Jain world view transcends the limitations placed on Western thought by the tendency to seek after certainty, to reduce complicated experience to simplified dogmas. This finds its lowest expression in political slogans – pro-this and anti-that – and in religious fundamentalism, but is contained in all ideologies and creeds that proclaim a monopoly of truth. As the philosophy of both/and rather than either/or, Jainism regards as unnecessary and artificial the 'choices' conventionally imposed by Western thought. These can be between, for example, freedom and equality, or faith and reason, emotion and intellect, change and continuity, individual and society, humanity and 'the rest' of nature. In Jainism, the successful and provident householder is valued along with the wandering, propertyless ascetic. They are not opposites, but complements, representing two crucial stages of spiritual development. The discipline of the warrior combines effectively with the ideals of peaceful conduct and renunciation of the world. A Jain is one who is on the way towards spiritual victory, a human being who can understand the complexities, paradoxes and limitations of earthly life and risen above the constraints of humanity.

Jainism's notion of conquest is the reverse of militarism and domination in the ways in which these have come to be widely understood. The warrior ethic is driven inwards, intellectually and spiritually, in a quest not to dominate other human beings or creatures, but to purify and thus realise the essential self. For the Jain, conquest is an internal process of discipline and overcoming the negative aspects of the self, those which attach that self to the world of gross matter, weighing it down, quite literally, with karmic bonds and blocking its spiritual evolution. The Jain path is a process of spiritual growth, in which the individual soul, the jiva, evolves usually over many lifetimes into an enlightened being, referred to as either *kevalin* or Jina, one who has conquered – and so realised – his or her self. The jiva is identified with the true self, clear minded, fully conscious and uncluttered by worldly considerations.   To the enlightened being, the concerns of the material world have become meaningless. Jain conquest involves the removal of layers of illusion: fictitious 'needs' and 'wants'; competition; the accumulation of possessions for their own sake; political power, and all the trappings of attachment to temporary 'things' rather than the pursuit of eternal truths.

Thus the Jain hero, like the existentialist of Western philosophy but at a more profound level, can see 'beyond good and evil'. He – or she – can also see beyond the will to power, which is the most destructive form of attachment. The wish to exercise power, to suppress and dominate other human beings or living creatures – to say nothing of the planet and the wider universe – is the ultimate expression of spiritual indiscipline and lack of inner conquest. Jainism therefore points towards withdrawal from earthly power, and this includes an active commitment to non-violence, or ahimsa, the principle at the core of Jain philosophy that influences all other aspects of Jain life and thought. The Jain must therefore aim to avoid damage to other life forms and ecosystems. For the ascetic or *muni*, the monk or nun who has withdrawn from the materialistic domain and lives by subsistence, ahimsa means pursuing a rigorously eco-centric lifestyle in which consumption is kept to a bare minimum and a special effort is taken to avoid harm to any other forms of life. The lay Jain must also learn to respect and live within the limits imposed by nature and keep his or her 'ecological footprint' as light as possible. This is not only a moral and social good, but also essential to personal salvation, the conquest of the superficial self by the true self. As Mahavira, whose name means 'Great Hero', reminded his followers:

> Non-violence and kindness to living beings is kindness to oneself. For thereby one's own self is saved from various kinds of sins and resultant sufferings and is able to secure one's own welfare.

The Jain tradition identifies the pursuit of a 'sustainable' way of life, as we would now call it, with the quest for self-knowledge, self-mastery and the transcendence of ordinary reality in pursuit of moksha as liberating enlightenment. This goal strikes strong chords with those pursuing a modern, secular 'green' agenda, which is why Jainism can have an enriching effect on green political thought and help the ecological movement to overcome some of its present limitations. That said, the overtly spiritual path towards moksha is distinct from, if sometimes parallel to, the emerging green consciousness, which is political in nature and so rooted or at least deeply involved in worldly concerns. Yet the Jain concern with the individual learning to live in a sustainable way and modify his behaviour dovetails nicely with the element of rational self-interest in green philosophy. One of the aims of green education is to persuade people that reducing consumption is in their long-term interests as well as those of the planet. Many greens would include amongst those long-term interests a spiritual dimension, for green thought at its best challenges the division between social and spiritual realms. Jainism is quite often described as a 'green religion' by Westerners who are seeking to understand it better. From a Jain standpoint, however, it would be better to see green consciousness as part of an individual's spiritual development, an important part, but by no means the whole. At best, green consciousness is an important stage on the path towards moksha, but like all forms of political consciousness, green thought can lead to self-righteous inflexibility, when the campaigning stance overrides compassion, humility and self-awareness.

Jainism's emphasis on the value of the individual matches another broad area of ecological thinking. The non-partisan environmentalism of a growing generation of thoughtful men and women bears a resemblance to certain forms of 'small-c' conservative thought, although few environmentalists admit this. It stresses the role of the individual, and the power of each individual to make a practical difference, however small-scale their action and however large the problem. This principle of individual consciousness contrasts with the top-down approach that has come to be associated with state socialism, in which government is held to be the agent of change and so the individual counts for very little. It also contrasts with the right, which puts 'tradition', 'national sovereignty' and narrow interpretations of sexual morality above the public or individual good. Most of all, the Jain approach to the individual challenges the modern cult of free-market economics, which favours large, impersonal corporations over human communities and places a superstitious faith in 'market forces'. Materialistic ideologies, whether market-based or rooted in the state and the collective, point in the opposite direction from the Jain idea of conquest. They represent the conquest of human beings by systems of values that are superficial and self-limiting, that promote a two-dimensional view of humanity and nature, ignoring the spiritual element that lends a sense of perspective to all human activities. Such ideologies overlook the Christian insight, very much shared by Jains, that 'Man cannot live on bread alone', that material satisfaction is merely a means to various ends, instead of an end in itself. It is this lack of perspective that leads to fanaticism, oppression, the pursuit of unrealisable utopias, along with an over-preoccupation with the material and the mundane, in ways that turn out to be quite literally soul-destroying.

Jainism values highly a sense of proportion and a measured response to all areas of human experience. It goes beyond many spiritual traditions in urging restraint and balance on its followers and discouraging zeal, excess or the fanaticism that corrupts genuine faith, because it is itself a form of attachment. Conquest involves overcoming egocentric emotions and desires, whether these take the form of base materialism or misguided forms of spiritual expression, notably those which are really concerned with authoritarian control. This is why the sense of proportion and the emphasis on restraint at the heart of Jainism can connect well with the growing ecological consciousness of a generation of Westerners who are starting to see through the illusions of the consumer society. Equally, these principles resonate with those in the so-called Third World who believe that the forms of 'development' being foisted upon them are inappropriate and destructive. The Jain concept of self-mastery involves learning to live within material limitations, whilst aiming to transcend spiritual and intellectual boundaries. However Jainism is far from being a quietist philosophy. It values social engagement, participation in politics, culture, business and the professions. All of these paths can enrich spiritual understanding, as well as improving the lot of fellow men and women, or by important extension, animals, plants and ecosystems. Jains have a powerful tradition of philanthropy, of campaigning for global justice, for the environment and animal welfare – or what has come to be known to some Westerners as 'animal liberation'. But they are guided in these activities by a sense of proportion, an ability to stand outside their immediate selves that acts as a brake on fanatical impulses and power hunger. Jainism will never solely be a 'green religion', and it would be facile either to view it as such or try to turn it in that direction. Nonetheless, the influence of Jainism could have an at once broadening and deepening effect on the evolving green awareness, in the West and elsewhere, making it more holistic, less explicitly adversarial, but as result more radical and far-reaching in its critique.

At a spiritual level, the Jain quest for individual enlightenment is a challenge to the authoritarian and hierarchical structures often associated with organised religion. Jainism, like the modern scientific world view, accepts the idea of different levels of consciousness among life forms (including supernatural beings) and different levels of ability among humans. However these differences are not viewed in terms of a pyramidal structure with humans or the divine principle at the top and elementary life forms, such as insects, at the bottom. Instead, Jains see creation as a pattern in which all points of light are interconnected and so of equal importance in the overall scheme. If anything, Jainism is about finding and understanding that pattern of creation, and this means ceasing to think in hierarchical terms which denote limitation and attachment. In the same way, there are in Jainism *acharyas* or spiritual teachers, and there are also munis and *sadhus*, ascetics and wandering philosophers who impart their wisdom to devotees, act as role models for younger Jains or, for most of the laity, represent an ideal to aspire to in a future life. Such individuals are seen as guides or preceptors, rather than leaders who can compel obedience. They are sources of wisdom, not indoctrination.

Every Jain aspires to become an ascetic, if not in this incarnation, then in the next, and Jains may take ascetic vows in at any stage in their lives from early childhood through to old age. But in Jainism, ultimately everyone is his or her own guru. Hierarchy and power relationships are irrelevant and distracting, because of the irrational attachments they generate, which weigh down the soul. They also bear no true relation to Jain principles, which are based on the premise of spiritual equality. All Jains are committed to achieving whatever they can for themselves in the spiritual arena, without either competing with others or submitting uncritically before external powers. Uncritical submission is the opposite of Jainism, because clear-mindedness and detachment from external influence is a prerequisite of moksha.

Only a small minority of Jains can succeed in achieving moksha within their lifetimes. They are prevented by circumstances, by their own limitations as human beings and by karmic bonds inherited from previous lives. Nonetheless, they have the power to work towards more auspicious future incarnations, which offer clearer paths towards spiritual progress. In Jainism, every level of existence, each incarnation, each form of life is linked by a cosmic thread and is part of a sacred pattern of existence. This insight of an ancient faith is reflected once again in modern scientific investigations, which show us that the life forms we describe as elementary are in fact highly complex and often have a vital, irreplaceable role in nature's grand design. When we dismiss such elementary forms of life as unimportant or primitive, we are showing a lack of advancement, just as we show our lack of sophistication when we dismiss indigenous or tribal societies as backward or undeveloped.

Jains are very modest about their faith tradition, preferring to live it out as best they can rather than proselytise or blow their own trumpets. For this reason, they can at times seem content enough to be mistaken socially for Hindus, and this stance has misled many commentators, including academic researchers, into treating Jainism as a branch or offshoot of the Hindu dharma. This modesty, even reticence, has been a necessary survival mechanism for Jains, who have been a perpetually small minority in an overwhelmingly Hindu Indian society and who have adapted in turn to Muslim Emperors and Christian colonialists.[1] It is also a highly attractive trait that denotes true humility. Jains are aware, both individually and collectively, that they lead imperfect lives, like other human beings of all faiths and none. The high standards of behaviour enjoined by Jain teachings make laypeople and ascetics too aware of their imperfections to be self-righteous or arrogant about their beliefs and the conduct of their lives. They do not presume, therefore, to impose their ideas on others, because they are too preoccupied with trying to lead ethical lives themselves, and so live up to the example of Mahavira and other Jinas.

To assert the superiority of Jainism would be in itself un-Jain and conducive only to negative karma. Yet Jains with an interest in their own history will sometimes reveal a certain amused surprise that ecologically minded Westerners, in particular, are only now beginning to arrive at truths that Jainism understood millennia ago. Such Jains will remind us, gently, that they have been vegetarians for three thousand years, indeed much longer, and that their diet arose from an archaic ecological consciousness, coupled with a strong awareness that animals possessed souls and so were spiritually alive. Jainism recognised thousands of years ago that all life is interconnected, whether human or non-human, on Earth or anywhere in the cosmos. This is an idea that Western science is only really beginning to appreciate, and to which Western society is feeling its way with very great difficulty and resistance.

The linear world view, which sees history, science and time itself in terms of an inexorable forward motion, a route march of inevitable 'progress', has long prevailed in the West and reached its zenith at the height of the industrial era. Yet it is increasingly clear that technological advancement does not necessarily civilise human beings. It is a double-edged sword that can make life more pleasurable and humane, but is equally capable of contributing to new forms of barbarism. The continuous pursuit of economic growth is based on the idea that progress is inevitable and always desirable, coupled with a sense that resources are infinite. The Earth is seen as a form of gigantic, constantly self-replenishing larder, to be raided at will. This approach, although avowedly rationalistic, quickly lapses into a form of magical thinking. Market economists speak superstitiously of the 'hidden hand' and Marxists talk of 'historical inevitability', albeit less so in these post-Communist times, as they re-evaluate and modify their assumptions in the light of twentieth century history. Many

Marxist – and erstwhile Marxist – thinkers have come to understand better than their liberal counterparts the pitfalls of 'progressive' dogma. They can see that the linear view of progress and growth has proved to be at variance with observable truth and lived experience. Resources can now be seen to be finite and the impact of uncontrolled development is impoverishing large areas of the globe, environmentally and culturally. As well as the ecological crisis, linear thinking has contributed to immense global iniquities, to political turbulence and war, and to a growing sense of moral and spiritual vacuum.

One of the green movement's original aims was to replace the linear view with a more holistic consciousness, re-embedding humanity in the web of life. This holistic sense has always existed in Jainism. Jains have never held a linear view of time and history, seeing them instead as a limitless series of cycles, akin to the downward and upward movements of a wheel, called *avasarpini* and *utsarpini* respectively. The present encounter and increasing dialogue, between the philosophies of East and West, would therefore seem obvious, elementary even, to a Jain. For as well as questioning the certainties associated with 'progress' and growth, thoughtful Western men and women are drawing increasingly upon Eastern wisdom in a constructive critique of science, health care (physical and mental), politics and economics. They are seeking a change of consciousness, a 'paradigm shift' as it is sometimes called, in which pure reason is balanced by intuition, giving it new depths, or to return to the neurological metaphor, the direct and linear left side of the brain is reconciled with the vaguer but more rounded right. Father Bede Griffiths, the British Benedictine monk who devoted much of his career to dialogue between Christianity and Hinduism, spoke of this process as the 'marriage of East and West'. His respect for Indian philosophy extended beyond what he called 'the Vedic revelation' to encompass parallel traditions such as Jainism. He expresses reverence for Mahavira, the privileged young man who 'left everything to wander naked in search of liberation'.[2] Father Bede described his departure for India in 1955 as a quest to 'find the other half of his soul' and believed that the East's 'intuitive wisdom' would refresh Western thought, which had become rigid and inflexible in its patterns. The idea that there is something lacking in the West, despite its immense technological and artistic achievements, is central to the movement loosely known as the New Age, and underlies ecological awareness as well. For Jains, the marriage of East and West is a matter of no surprise at all, for it shows that a wheel of history has come full circle.

The entire structure of Jainism is cyclical and holistic. It is a rational faith based on intellectual insights familiar to the Western humanistic tradition, reflecting the conclusions and speculations of the most recent generation of physicists. Jains take it as a given, for example, that energy can neither be created nor destroyed. The universe is itself eternal and so does not have a creator. Jainism is, therefore, a non-theistic religion, which does not depend on a Creator God as the originator and point of return. Gods and goddesses, or heavenly beings (and hell-beings) exist in Jain folk practice. Often they have local associations, or represent principles within nature. Deities from the Hindu pantheon, such as Ganesh and Indra, have been drawn into Jain mythology and ritual. Jains hold to their own vision of the truth, but practised 'inter-faith dialogue' many centuries before the phrase was coined. As such, they see no harm in accommodating and responding positively towards the wider Vedic tradition, with which they share a common Indian heritage.

Jain cosmology envisages the universe as being in a state of permanent flux, at one level eternal, at another constantly evolving and renewing itself. The principles of continuity and change complement each other, rather than being in opposition as in the adversarial culture of the West. Equilibrium, be it personal, social or cosmic, depends on a balance of these two principles. Thus Jainism has an intellectual and scholarly aspect, but it also assumes devotional forms through temple worship and, as in Hinduism, the ritual or *puja*. Many Jains worship images, intricate sculptures or paintings with an iconic status. Most of these images are of the Twenty-four Tirthankaras, as outstanding human beings that have evolved into Jinas, exalted souls who have escaped the cosmic wheel. Jains regard the Tithankaras as role models rather than divinities. They are exemplars of ideal conduct, and so ascetics and lay men and women draw inspiration from them as they meditate.

Jainism's strength is that it combines themes of direct appeal to modern, or even the post-modern mind, with insight and intuition of a profoundly ancient character. A complex, sophisticated philosophy, easily reconciled with modern science and at home with all the concepts of the Enlightenment, the Jain path also perceives souls in all life forms, as well as mountains, streams and rock formations. The universe is full of souls, all of them conscious, independent yet connected to each other and as real as gross matter. This aspect of Jainism calls to mind the earliest forms of human spiritual awareness, the so-called archaic belief systems of animism and shamanism, or folk religions shaped by landscape and local memory' like Shinto in Japan, or the Native American reverence for the land, or the religious customs of ancient Greece. Modern ideas of individual freedom, human equality, animal welfare and scientific reason coexist with archaic concepts of nature and the universe, which inspire a primitive sense of wonder and a perception of humanity's smallness within the cosmos rather than potential mastery of it. These two approaches complement and reinforce each other, rather than finding themselves in conflict.

Jains do not seek converts, at least in the sense that Christians, Muslims and Buddhists understand the term. These are missionary faiths, in their own very different ways, which seek to impart to non-initiates a universal message of salvation and enlightenment. They differ in that respect from Shinto, which is associated with Japanese uniqueness, or the traditional belief systems of the Native American or Inuit, based on the connection between specific peoples and the lands they inhabit. Monotheistic faiths, such as Judaism and Sikhism, are also closely linked to specific cultures, histories and landscapes and the Hindu dharma, although all encompassing, is bound inextricably with Indian experience. Many of these traditions have produced missionary – and usually mystical – offshoots: from Judaism, the Kabbalah, the Radhosoamis from Sikhism and Hindu-derived revivalist movements like Krishna Consciousness, or the more cerebral Ramakrishna Vedanta, to which Western intellectuals like Christopher Isherwood were drawn. In his memorable book *My Guru and His Disciple*, he recounts his partially successful experiences with this philosophy in action and his inability to discard Western culture. Had he been studying Jainism, he would not have been required to turn his back on the West.[3]

One can distinguish, at least approximately, between those faiths that look for converts and seek to reshape humanity according to a new pattern, and those that focus on the inward path and set for themselves limited cultural boundaries. As is so often the case, Jainism straddles a delicate cultural divide, this time between the missionary and exclusive expressions of faith. Jains, as already noted, are intensely reticent about their spiritual practice and can seem private and guarded to the outsider. Yet they see their dharma as a cultural resource, a body of ideas, principles and practices from which humanity as a whole can draw. The Jain approach is to lead by example, rather than by preaching to the outer world or, as with some missionary campaigns, using force to impose an interpretation of the truth. The example of an ethical life successfully led will, it is hoped, lead to Jain principles being gradually absorbed by the surrounding society, the customs of which are respected and – except in extreme circumstances – the laws obeyed.

This strategy would seem to have failed, when measured in competitive Western terms, which value quantity over quality, and so would note that Jainism is a numerically small religion, dwarfed overwhelmingly by Hinduism and Islam. At a deeper level, the Jain approach of diplomatic but dogged perseverance has nonetheless paid off. Against overwhelming numerical odds, mere survival is an achievement in itself, but Jainism has done much more than survive. Its success can be glimpsed visibly in the quiet confidence of Jain communities around the world, as well as in their wealth and their educational or professional achievements. More importantly, it is reflected in the high esteem in which Jains are held, even by people who know little about them and have no conscious curiosity about the world's religions. Sometimes that high esteem is dangerous for Jains, because it leads to their doctrines being misinterpreted or twisted to serve inappropriate ends. The violent wing of the animal rights movement, for instance, sometimes claims Jain inspiration, although there is nothing further removed from Jain practice than the distorted, self-righteous anger and of the single-issue fanatic, which leads to authoritarian impulses and harmful acts.

By setting itself up as a spiritual resource, rather than openly proselytising or attempting to make others submit, the Jain path inoculates itself against fanatical distortions and the notorious zeal of the convert. At the same time, the Jain path has had a powerful but subtle influence on the ideas and conduct of non-Jains. Remarkably for a non-theistic religion, Jainism won the support and patronage of Muslim Emperors. Nearer our own time, it powerfully influenced Gandhi, affecting his politics and causing him to revise his interpretation of Hinduism and look for the essence rather than caring about the outward forms or literal interpretations of doctrine. Einstein's recognition that the Jain ascetics were in touch with eternal truths was unprecedented in a mid-twentieth century scientist, and the endorsement of this icon of scientific progress affirms Jainism is a rational faith. Jains and Hindus have for many centuries borrowed from and enriched each other in thought and practice. Rather than acting as spiritual salesmen, peddling their religion in the global marketplace of ideas, Jains are the judicious bearers of a sacred flame, kept alive over many generations for inquirers to seek out, as and when they are ready. It is likely that there will be many more such inquirers in the ensuing years. For this is proving to be an age when barriers between peoples and cultures are breaking down, when political and religious orthodoxies can no longer explain, let alone resolve, human problems, and where technologies surge forward, but the future of the planet itself is called into question.

Jains are natural internationalists, who are forming communities with relative ease across the world and preserve their culture whilst integrating unobtrusively. The very success of Jains in this regard has led to their being largely overlooked by Western commentators. Although – or rather because – they are one of the greatest success stories of the multi-cultural society, they are generally treated as an invisible 'minority'. This invisibility has been in many ways a strength. There is nothing politically or socially controversial about Jain communities in the West. They do not evolve into pockets of deprivation and disaffection, or voice political demands and threaten to silence their critics. They share with the Western mainstream broad aspirations towards democracy and equality, a belief in the value of education for all and a respect for the individual.

As such, Jains have avoided both the malicious narrowness of the political right, and the patronisingly 'enlightened' despotism of the political left. They have not produced self-styled 'community leaders' who arouse hostile opinion and at the same time oppress their own people. Although it is easy to see Jains as a self-contained or enclosed society, because their tradition of self-help is so strong, the idea of a Jain ghetto is a contradiction in terms. Jain social activity, including charitable giving and voluntary work, is aimed at non-Jains as much as at the faithful. Indeed in their purest form, Jain ethics extend the principle of equality to all conscious life forms, which is why as much time, energy and resources are devoted to animal as human welfare. The principle of inclusion is extended, without simplistic slogans or fanfare, across the barriers of species as well as human cultural boundaries.

The same process could well take place with Jain ideas. They could spread, unobtrusively enough, through different levels of Western society, until they become widely accepted. As an enduring tradition, Jainism is an unbroken thread connecting Eastern and Western patterns of thought, insights shrouded in myth and antiquity with concerns that increasingly preoccupy us today. The Jain dharma unites the ancient and modern worlds in a critique of violence in all forms, physical, mental and ecological, and above all violence towards the self through false values, such as unnecessary acquisitiveness and gratuitous aggression.

In this age of weapons of mass destruction (real or imagined), resurgent fundamentalism and nationalism, environmental despoliation and a global economy that appears to be spinning out of control, there is a growing tendency to make connections. Links are increasingly perceived between private aggression and public militarism, exploitation of the environment and exploitative human relationships, false human pride and cruelty to animals, neurosis and the separation of human beings from nature. A century of psychoanalytic practice and thought has contributed to this process of questioning received assumptions and making connections between areas of life that were once treated as separate compartments. The underlying rationalism of Freud, the spiritual insights of Jung and the more recent emergence of transpersonal psychology, which looks beyond the immediate self, all in their own ways emphasise connectedness. This is couched either in terms of psychological integration – the reconciling of various areas of the human personality – but often as the integration of individual well-being with the health of the larger society.

The phrase 'the personal is political', somewhat hackneyed by now and subject to frequent misuse, expresses a sense that the division between private self and public self has in the past been a convenient illusion. Coined by feminists in the 1970s, it was intended to have a significance beyond the relationship between men and women and challenge the dominance of abstract theory over direct experience of life. More recently, an awareness that the spiritual is political, or that the scientific is spiritual, has begun to gain ground. Politics and science have become too disconnected, too left-brained, because they have ignored or denigrated the emotional life, and beyond that the sense of the sacred and the reverence for life that stems from it.

Wholeness, integration and interconnectedness are some of the buzzwords of an emerging, but as yet not very coherent new consciousness. At one level, there is a wish to look beneath surface impressions created by the media and their news agenda, and by received opinions about human nature and how society should be organised. There is a desire to gain deeper insights and a sense that the superficial is not enough and is frequently dangerous. At another level, there is an urge to refashion and reinvent, to renounce tradition in all its forms and cast off the injustice and prejudices of the past. There is a wish to take the long view, rejecting short-term solutions and stopgap reforms, but it contrasts with a desire for change 'now', as if transforming society and human consciousness was but another form of instant gratification.

Aspirations towards inner change compete, and sometimes

openly clash, with demands for social justice. Many feel forced to choose between personal growth and political campaigns, constrained by pressures from each side to make that choice. The new consciousness exalts the individual, set free from repressive convention and taboo, or spiritually awakened, or 'in touch' with natural forces, in the environment or within him or her self. Yet at the same time, it elevates communal activity, based (in theory at least) on spontaneous connections and free association, rather than traditional ritual, old-fashioned etiquette or shared cultural inheritance. Individual freedom is sacrosanct, but so are group rights, which classify people by race, or gender, or sexuality, and so promise them freedom but quickly come to obliterate their individuality and deny the complexity of their lives. This is how the attempt to balance male and female principles degenerates into a 'battle of the sexes', or the movement for racial justice becomes a struggle between races, rather than a release of individual creativity.

The new consciousness, as part of the wider movement towards a New Age, is at once an acknowledgement of complexity – human, spiritual and ecological – and a desperate search for simple solutions. It is a negation of ideological rigidity, but at the same time a search for a 'theory of everything' that provides an intellectual comfort blanket, like simplified Marxism for a previous generation, or the equally simplistic 'economic liberalism' of our own time. In other words, the new consciousness is still based on polarities, conducive to conflict rather than emotional or intellectual balance, let alone spiritual development. This is because, although it aspires towards a holistic world view, it is still rooted in specifically Western obsessions with domination and submission, power and rebellion, struggle and victory – either/or in contrast to both/and. The very repudiation of Western values by some New Age aficionados, frequently with violent rhetoric and ritual denunciation, is proof of the hold that Western ideas of power still have over their imagination. In this, they resemble political activists who uncritically embrace Third World 'liberation' movements, or peace campaigners whose banners whose banners seem to burn with hatred and anger. Even the quest for wholeness in human relationships founders on the reef of competition and conflict. Indeed the pursuit of equality, which should be an emancipating experience and a release of creativity for all human beings, has become a source of anger, grievance and oppression, both for those supposedly being 'made equal' and those who are held collectively to account for past wrongs.

Why this culture of conflict? A starting point might be to consider the emphasis Western society places on the word 'choice'. Choice has become as much of a fetish in New Age circles as it is for free-market economists and the politicians who implement market ideology. Viewed superficially, the idea of continual choice appears to be liberating and empowering to the individual and socially good as well, because it leads to greater diversity, greater interest and more possibilities. This is why politicians speak of 'extending choice' and why the New Age all too often becomes a form of mix-and-match spirituality, where we 'choose' those aspects of a religious or cultural tradition that suit us best and discard the inconvenient aspects. Yet there is an aspect of the Western approach to choice that is highly restrictive, because it demands exclusive selection and, as a result, the exclusion of other options and possibilities. One 'chooses' not only a bank or an insurance policy, but a belief system or ideology and the various 'lifestyle options' that go with it. Our 'choices' often imprison us or weigh us down because they lock us in to ways of living and modes of thought that do not always suit us, but which we cannot easily escape without making equally restrictive choices and forming equally closed allegiances. We can observe this phenomenon in former religious believers who become atheists and in political thinkers who move dramatically from 'left' to 'right' – or vice versa.

In such situations, the clinging to doctrinaire certainty remains the same, as almost always does the internal dissatisfaction and conflict. Almost invariably, Western choices of belief and lifestyle need to be 'defended' against other choices, and so are proclaimed more zealously than inherited ideas or loyalties. Thus the cult of choice can be as narrowing an experience as the absence of all options, just as the unfettered market produces chain stores and supermarkets in place of small businesses and local variety – private monopoly that mirrors state monopoly. Western 'choice' is the application of either/or to all areas of life. It creates the illusion of freedom, but shuts off a multitude of possibilities in the process.

When it is elevated to an absolute principle, instead of one aspect of human experience, the idea of choice becomes an obstacle to the search for wholeness. Restrictive, adversarial choice is linked inextricably in the Western mindset to ideas of conflict and competition. The New Age is influenced by these patterns of thought as much as any Western social movement or ideology, indeed probably more than most, precisely because it is avowedly new. Therefore, it finds it more difficult to draw upon centuries of accumulated wisdom, or gain the flexibility that history and tradition can allow. This helps us to understand why some New Age movements evolve into oppressive personality cults. It also explains why horizontal or non-hierarchical structures, associated with environmental or 'anti-war' campaigns, adopt conventions at least as rigid and conformist as those of mainstream politics. For such movements, to embrace a new idea or adopt a new way of living is not enough. Instead, that idea or way of life must score victories over, or suppress any possible alternative – by moral pressure and, where necessary, coercion.

In similar vein, the 'empowerment' of one human group is taken to mean the 'disempowerment' of another, whilst the granting of 'rights' to some involves the removal of rights from others. Thus the emancipation of the poor implies the humiliation of the rich, whilst economic freedom implies the removal of social provision. In both these (apparently opposite) cases, the system of adversarial choice fails abysmally: poverty is intensified rather than abolished by punitive measures, and instead of economic liberty, a free-for-all policy becomes a policy of smash-and-grab, from which stultifying corporate monopolies quickly emerge. Under the system of adversarial choice, power of whatever kind is to be captured at the centre, rather than dispersed, so that victory becomes an end in itself and overshadows the idea being 'fought for' in the first place. The search for truth is portrayed as a 'battle of ideas', to be 'won' at all costs, even intellectual honesty. It is assumed that those ideas that triumph, and so dominate public discourse, possess an inherent superiority and strength. Such intellectual triumphalism translates into the processes of power politics. It is expressed physically in the subjugation of peoples and territories, the domination of animals by humans and the 'conquest' of nature, so that the environment is treated as an unlimited resource, over which we believe we have the 'right' to exercise unlimited control.

For Jains, the battle of ideas is a form of intellectual 'himsa'. It is harmful to the ideas themselves, which are destroyed when they become instruments of the will to power and control. It is harmful to their proponents, for whom the desire to dominate and oppress, or even to stand out as victorious, does grave spiritual damage. And it is harmful to human consciousness as a whole, because it erects artificial barriers between human beings and reinforces divisions between humanity and nature. The pursuit of ideological or intellectual 'victory', to the Jain, disrupts spiritual development, because it prevents individuals from grasping larger truths, or to rise above arguments rather than merely to 'win' them. The Jain path draws little distinction between intellectual 'himsa' and the actual damage inflicted by violence, domination of others and the arbitrary exercise of power. After all, the thought is precursor to the deed and the so intention is at least as important as the outcome. If anything, intellectual himsa has worse consequences for the individual than blind obedience to orders, the implications of which are not properly understood. This is because intellectual himsa is based on conscious decisions, on a surrender to lower instincts rationalised by false ideals.

Jainism is quite often caricatured as quietist, because of its unobtrusive quality that seeks to influence subtly rather than assert direct control. But if we dismiss the Jain path in this way, we overlook its most challenging message to Western humanity. For as a philosophy, Jainism takes us beyond the movements for pseudo-liberation, be they spiritual and political. To Jains, there is no difference between the harsh judgements of the evangelical Christian, who seeks to impose his beliefs on others, and the bitterly anti-Christian stance of a certain type of New Age enthusiast, who vents her anger on Christians in a deliberate attempt to cause hurt. There is no profound difference between male and female sexism, or between the West-knows-best mentality and the furious anti-Western rhetoric of (among others) radical Islamists in the Middle East. In Jainism, the desire for victory and conquest, and the attempt to vanquish and destroy perceived opponents, is destructive whether in the purely intellectual realms, or whether it is put into practice, whether it is individual or collective, based on purely moral pressure or the recourse to physical coercion. Hatred, anger and resentment exert a heavy psychological burden, to the extent that we often speak of affected individuals as weighed down by hatred, or burdened by resentment. In the same way, anger and the will to power exert a spiritual burden. They weigh down the soul, the true self, trapping it in the material realm and adding layers of negative karma to obscure the way to enlightenment. The desire for victory – political or moral as well as physical or military – is a form of attachment. Therefore, it must itself be overcome by restraint and spiritual practice. That is the Jain idea of conquest: inmost spiritual victory over the pursuit of material or competitive victory.

The Jain approach to these questions might at first glance seem severe. Surely, as Jains themselves acknowledge, some ideas have greater human or universal value than others, and so they deserve to 'win' over inferior or destructive ideas. Surely the establishment of democracy is more valuable than the entrenchment of dictatorship? Is the righting of historic wrongs not nobler than the preservation of beliefs and practices that discriminate and repress? Is not social conscience worth more than gross materialism and greed? Jainism does draw such distinctions, indeed it emphasises them. This is why Jains attribute such a supreme importance to intention. If the motive behind a deed (or thought) is spiritual rather than material, or the pursuit of social justice instead of mean-spirited bigotry, then the karmic weight will probably be less intense. Yet it is precisely because Jainism acknowledges complexity that it adopts a rigorous stance against intellectual himsa, and avoids the distinctions taken for granted in the West. Jains are less concerned with low or debased aims than they are with the corruption of high ideals, the mixing of motives and the vengeful impulses that turn idealists into fanatics, or liberators into oppressors. Their position is vindicated by twentieth century totalitarianism, which combined idealism and romantic notions with the will to power, appealed to mythologies of race and class and was based on collective punishment of excluded groups.

Secular totalitarianism is either/or logic pushed to its most extreme point, but we are also often reminded today of the cruelties that can be inflicted in the name of faith. In the modern West, the rise of single-issue politics, including faith-based campaigns, is generating new forms of intolerance. Animal rights protesters who intimidate and threaten human beings epitomise this trend, but the single issue way of thinking is increasingly taking hold of Western discourse and influencing moderate campaigners as well. As the world becomes more visibly complicated, the search for simple solutions gathers momentum. Jainism is aware of these dangers, not least because as a minority tradition it has had to learn, over centuries, the art of survival through diplomacy, negotiation and blending in. The Jains have chosen not to expand like their Buddhist and Christian counterparts. Living out their philosophy of non-violence, guiding others by example, and working quietly towards self-conquest, they do not mind being members of a perpetual minority and often see it as an advantage.

Expansion and conversion – certainly forced conversion – can be viewed as forms of himsa, and therefore to be rejected as corrupting to Jain ideals. Some, especially those attached to Western adversarial modes of thought, might see this approach as risk-averse, or as a retreat into intellectual purity and holier-than-thou moralism. The latter suggestion is certainly misconceived. Jains are far too aware of their own imperfections as human beings to compare themselves favourably with others or impose on them 'their' way of thinking and doing. They are also far too concerned with their own internal spiritual growth than with spreading their spirituality externally or holding it up as an ultimate truth. Yet the Jains have also made a considered decision about their faith and the direction their community should take. For they have chosen indirect influence over direct power. Such influence is wholly non-violent, subtle rather than overt and, ultimately more powerful than overt authority. Thus Jains aim to achieve not only victory over the very idea of victory, but also the primacy of spiritual over worldly power.

Jainism, as indicated above, is frequently portrayed as a harsh religion, placing austere spiritual discipline above the celebration of life. It has been castigated as such by critics from the early Buddhists onwards, and this uncompromising quality is often held responsible for the sangha's small size, as well as the lack of apparent interest or observance on the part of many Jains. Ironically, it is Jainism's coherent approach, widely depicted as harsh, that is attracting a younger generation of Jains and arousing the increasing interest of non-Jains. With its emphasis on interdependency, Jainism addresses modern, Western and urban concerns, but unlike the many transient 'theories of everything' has a strong and stable historical basis. Jain doctrines can be applied to all areas of life, but contain a flexibility that makes them an attractive alternative to fundamentalism, or to the mass political movements of a more or less totalitarian nature.

The flexibility of Jainism arises from its ability to recognise paradox and come to terms with it. Jains accept the possibility of being ecologically conscious whilst seeking liberation from worldly concerns, of pursuing professional or business goals whilst eschewing crude materialism, of valuing personal freedom whilst leading a well-ordered life. Jainism emphasises discipline, but a discipline that comes from within, an internal conquest, rather than an authoritarian structure imposed from above or outside. Being a 'religion without God', it does not force its adherents to choose between the scientific and the spiritual, to make uncompromising leaps of faith and submit to an unseen but all-powerful Creator. Jains recognise the equivalent value of intellect and intuition. Unlike the New Age, and its evangelical shadow, their dharma does not impose a series of rigid choices: between East and West, the ascetic and the erotic, equality and freedom, patriarchal and matriarchal wisdom. For Jains, all these points of reference have distinct value, but also distinct limitations, all of which are recognised and accepted. At the same time, the Jain tradition avoids that other great pitfall of New Age thinking, the cultural relativism that shrilly proclaims all beliefs as 'equally valid'. It does not shrink from uncomfortable truths merely because these might be too inconvenient or too 'difficult' for most to grasp.

In short, the very foundation of Jainism is that holistic approach to the human experience and the natural world for which New Age seekers in the West are striving, but which they cannot arrive at because they are trapped in adversarial patterns of thought. Although in many ways strict, and nowhere stricter than in its insistence on non-violence, the Jain dharma is far more inclusive and tolerant than those movements that trumpet their inclusivity. The combination of rigour and latitudinarianism is a paradox central to this ancient doctrine. It challenges the West to throw off the adversarial mindset, which narrows consciousness so tragically and dangerously. In a comparable Western philosophy, the contrast between equanimity as an ideal for the individual and the commitment to promote and practise non-violence would be a continual source of tension, conflict and schism. In Jainism, the two principles depend on and constantly reinforce each other.

The Jain pursuit of equanimity, of becoming 'beyond good and evil', is interpreted by critics as other worldly, life-denying or at worst a prescription for apathy in the face of oppression. After all, the Jina or conqueror is so-called, according to the *Tattvartha Sutra*, 'because he has liberated himself from karma by over-coming love and hatred'. The *Tattvartha Sutra* does not discriminate between spontaneous intuition and intellectual insight in attaining enlightenment, thus overriding the distinctions between human and animal perceptions that were as con-ventionally accepted in India as in the West. Even in Jainism,

rebirth as a human is usually viewed as the only way to enlightenment, but the dharma is always ready to admit of exceptions:

The enlightened world-view may arise spontaneously or through learning.

*The worldly life of a soul has no beginning. The soul transmigrates
from one birth to the next according to its karma, which determines
its destiny. Nevertheless, each unique soul possesses the inherent
knowledge and intuition which can empower it to destroy the
beginningless deluded world-view tormenting it. The enlightened
world-view can arise at the appropriate moment in any form of life
– infernal, subhuman, human or celestial – when the painful nature
of life is realised, a vision of the Jina is seen, the teachings of the
Jina heard or a past life remembered. Sometimes this enlightened
view breaks through spontaneously without outside assistance.
Sometimes it arises through tuition or study.*

This description of the life of the unfettered soul could easily be
portrayed as an ideal of floating above, of aloofness or abstention
from the normal preoccupations of life, including moral dilemmas.
To an extent this is true, for the goal is both transcendence of
worldly desire and escape from the cycle of birth, death and
rebirth, with all the responsibilities that are part of that cycle. All
actions, all experiences are ultimately karmic, weighing down the
soul and so becoming obstacles to self-realisation. The Jain
conception of bliss involves the absence of all sensation and
release from the 'choices' that bind ordinary mortals, at ordinary
levels of consciousness. However the picture becomes more
complex when we remember that there are positive as well as

negative forms of karma. While the former still weigh the soul down, they bind with less intensity and they also provide pointers towards enlightenment. Positive karma is often referred to as 'auspicious', because it provides the framework for a harmonious and responsible way of living, which is the springboard to liberation. Among the causes of auspicious karma are 'purity of world view', 'persistent cultivation of knowledge', 'establishing harmony and peace' and 'proper practice and learning of the spiritual path'. These principles are more than compatible with positive actions to promote peace and social justice. They impel such actions, which are seen as important steps on the path of spiritual evolution, pointing towards release from self-centred and short-term attachments.

Of more importance, ultimately, is that the Jain ideal of equanimity, of the Jina as above and beyond sensation, gives a sense of proportion to all human desires, including the desire for a more just society. Used properly, this perspective ensures that the prevailing vision of justice will not be too abstract or impersonal and that the pursuit of justice – and peace – will be free from the single-minded fanaticism that has destroyed so many individuals and movements with idealistic goals. The Jain influence on Gandhi was political as well as spiritual, in that it helped to anchor his anti-colonial movement in the principle of non-violence and retain a sense of the human scale, favouring the village over the city, craftsmanship over mass production and ecological balance over relentless economic expansion. Furthermore, the emphasis on inner motivation as much as explicit aim allows a clear distinction to be drawn between power-hungry politicians or activists on the one hand, and on the other those who work sincerely to improve society and the environment. Whereas the former frequently use the language of equality and justice as a means to oppress and dominate, the latter work without ambition or noise, and remain largely oblivious to any acclaim that accrues to them. The former tend towards abstract and lofty visions of the good society, the latter are more local and more modest in their goals, but in reality they are closer to universal truths. Leading a peaceful and compassionate life is as important as pursuing non-violence and compassion as social goals – more important, in fact, because those who are hypocritical, or governed by their attachments, do not produce positive changes in society. The spiritual discipline of Jainism instils an understanding of complexity, as well as a sense of the interconnectedness of all moral and spiritual issues, large and small. It emphasises shades of meaning, subtlety and nuance, the search for unity in place of fragmentation and deconstruction.

This is the relevance to the West of the Jain idea of conquest. The ideal of the Jina as the ultimate non-partisan reminds us of how one-sided our culture of acquisitiveness and 'winning' at all costs has become. For the Jina has not only triumphed over material longings and transient attachments. He or she – or, more precisely, it – is neither 'for' nor 'against', above 'right' and 'wrong' and, in secular political parlance, well beyond 'right' and 'left'. From the Jain standpoint, even the prevailing Western concept of objectivity is one-sided, because it is based on the banishment of the spiritual dimension. It is therefore both an illusion and an attachment, as much so as those cults and sects that deny the value of reason, or those movements that deny the value of the individual. The pursuit of reason in the West has led us to see that narrow, linear thinking presents a fractured view of the human experience, that a morality of either/or is a morality of division and violence. The Jain path emphasises wholeness and rejects fanaticism. It can therefore act as a useful guide to those in the West who wish to re-evaluate our own rich cultural tradition, freeing it from those aspects which have become distorted or exaggerated and so, like karma, weigh us down.

The Jain path seeks neither to dominate the West, nor to replace the Western cultural tradition. That form of intellectual expansionism would be laughed at as absurd by any thoughtful Jain. Instead, we are invited by the Jains to reflect that true conquest involves much more than victory over opponents. It means learning to organise society, and our own thought processes, on less conflict-ridden lines, and so becoming broader and more rounded in our thinking process. To understand how the Jain path can guide us out of our current impasse, we should look more closely at the spiritual system it has elaborated over millennia. And for this, the best place to start is the Jain view of karma, by which we are presently bound but from which we have the promise of freedom.

CHAPTER FOUR

A MATTER OF KARMA

A hungry person with the most negative black karma
uproots and kills an entire tree to obtain a few mangoes.
The person of blue karma fells the tree by chopping the
trunk, again merely to gain a handful of fruits. Fraught
with grey karma, a third person spares the trunk but
cuts off the major limbs of the tree. The one with red
karma carelessly and needlessly lops off several
branches to reach the mangoes. The fifth, exhibiting
white karma, merely picks up ripe fruit that has dropped
to the foot of the tree.

JAGMANDERLAL JAINI, *THE OUTLINES OF JAINISM*
(CAMBRIDGE: CAMBRIDGE UNIVERSITY PRESS, 1916), P.47

'before i became a cockroach, i was a free-verse poet.'
e.e. cummings

Karma is at once the most alluring and elusive aspect of the Eastern spiritual paths. Literally meaning action, it is interpreted broadly as the law of cause and effect. Or, at a less abstract level, karma is understood in terms of the relationship between motive and action, and the assigning of just rewards or just deserts. In the moralistic West, this last interpretation strikes a chord, but leads to many misunderstandings as ideas of punishment, sin and guilt are superimposed on more reflective, less crudely judgemental, longer-term approaches. For the doctrine of karma takes the long view, unlike religious or secular concepts of salvation in one lifetime. Cause and effect, it assumes, unfold over many lifetimes and so transfer from one existence or incarnation to another and through the many cycles of history and evolution.

This sounds a relatively straightforward idea. But because it has such wide, indeed universal ramifications, it is used and abused in a vast number of ways and has, to put it mildly, many unforeseen consequences. It is as if the concept of karma itself generates its own karmic patterns. In the East, karma lends itself readily to a pedantic and rigid interpretation of human destiny. At best, this results in excessively scholastic speculation that is too abstract for most people to engage with actively and so contributes little to an understanding of the cosmos and still less to practical attempts by individuals to lead more ethical lives. At worst, it becomes a justification for inequality and extreme social injustice, including the supposed inevitability of caste stratifications, the primacy of men over women, or discrimination based on race and colour.

Lest we judge these aberrant interpretations too harshly, or dismiss them as 'Eastern' errors, we should recall that notions of preordained salvation have taken many centuries to fade from Christian doctrine, and have still not entirely vanished. Similarly, Christianity itself arose in large part as a response to an excessive, inhuman emphasis on rules and structures for their own sake, rather than as a benevolent ethical framework or as pointers towards a more morally enriching way of life. Just as the Scribes and Pharisees deserved to be reminded that the Sabbath was made for man, not man for the Sabbath, so today's doctrinaire, inflexible gurus need reminding that karma is a potential tool of liberation rather than a mere instrument of control.

In the West, karma is subject not only to misunderstanding, but to gross forms of sensationalism. It is depicted in terms of retribution, revenge, punishment or righteous reward by those who, whilst trying to break loose from intellectual bondage, are still locked into dualistic patterns of thought. It is also portrayed in coarsely reductionist terms, best exemplified by the claims of a British football player in the late 1990s that people with disabilities were paying the price for bad behaviour in previous lives. These, and similar claims from ill-informed sources, have received wide coverage throughout the British and European news media. Although intellectually lightweight, such commentaries have contributed to the belief that karma is an arbitrary force, cruel and exacting, reinforcing instead of challenging human injustices. The reduction of karma to this level arises from an attempt to superimpose on an ancient idea the more recent Judaeo-Christian concepts of sin – and the punishment of sin – and its corollary of salvation and reward.

These concepts have themselves been simplified, for the benefit of a media age in which slogans have become substitutes for thought. However in such dismissals of karma there is also a strong element of projection. It is Western ideologies, after all, that have shown themselves, in recent years especially, to be inflexible and unresponsive to human and ecological concerns. The Western approach to economics, in particular, is more constraining to humanity and nature than the karmic web. As well as rationalising social iniquity and global imbalance, it subordinates all living systems to the law of supply and demand, the profit motive and the cult of economic expansion. These restrictive ideologies are spiritually corrosive as well as destructive of the environment and human relations. They are therefore part of the karmic cycle, from which an understanding of karma provides the possibility of escape.

There is, nonetheless, no escape from the fact that karma is difficult. It is subtle and liberating in its message, but it can also be restrictive and uncompromising in its approach. As such, it poses problems for those who seek instant emancipation, or who reject (instinctively or by conditioning) the idea of reincarnation of continuity between lifetimes. Yet perhaps the best way to approach such problems is to cut to the essence of karma, peeling away the layers of mystification – karmic layers themselves – that have adhered to karma over many generations of thought and practice. When we do this, it is possible to see in the idea of karma an intuitive sense of connectedness. Karma, in other words, presupposes that there are intimate links between human beings in the social sphere, between past, present and future generations, between humans and the environment, and, most importantly, between all forms of life, human and non-human. The Jain view of karma is particularly explicit in its emphasis on connectedness. In Jainism's karmic web are absorbed all creatures from the higher primates to micro-organisms, as well as all vegetable and mineral life, the self-created, self-perpetuating universe and the invisible world of deities and hell-beings.

As such, the Jain conception of karma encompasses the ancient Indian cosmology, based on intuitive understanding, and the highly 'modern' scientific insights (coming from East and West alike) about the nature of ecosystems and the structure of the universe. In Jain karma, the jiva or unit of life can move through its incarnations between species, or from animal to vegetable or mineral and back again, as well as from male to female, or from one social class to another. Moreover, it can move between the visible and invisible world, natural and supernatural worlds and different levels of reality. This is the most flexible and holistic version of the doctrine of karma, but it is also the most challenging and demanding. It offers unlimited possibilities for spiritual advancement, but also includes the risk of falling from great heights before liberation is achieved and having to begin the journey from a lower plane of consciousness. Embedded in Jain karma is an awareness of the evolutionary process, including stagnation or regression as well as advancement, along with understanding of complicated relationships between living systems, the connections that are subtle rather than explicit, underlying rather than overt.

In the cosmology of Jainism, there is even the possibility of parallel universes, as represented by the worlds of the devas, the hell-beings and the blissful higher state in which enlightened jivas live. Through the karmic process, these parallel worlds can interact and overlap with our own reality. It has become fairly commonplace to speak of the web of life, when considering the links between ecosystems and the importance of biodiversity. Similarly, karma has often been likened to a web, and this image enables us to view it as a network through which all of life is linked in intricate patterns, through which the destinies of all beings are brought together.

Karma therefore provides a unified theory of consciousness and interdependence. Although its application is principally spiritual, it offers practical insights into the true relationship between humanity and the natural world, the convergence of spirituality and science, and the reawakening of spiritual awareness in a secular, rational and moral framework. In karma, barriers are eroded, concepts and belief systems overlap and paths to the truth come together.

Within most Indic traditions, including Jainism, karma is linked to the notion of *samsara*, the idea of the cycle of death, birth or rebirth that entraps the soul until it achieves liberation, known as moksha or sometimes *mukti*, through which it transcends the material world and reaches a higher level of consciousness. In most Hindu traditions, this involves the realisation of the individual soul's true identity with the divine, of the Atman with Brahman. In Buddhism's original form, it means recognition of samsara, and hence individual identity, as illusory and distracting, with liberation implying a loss of identity, a melting away into pure, undifferentiated consciousness. For Jains, the jiva retains its individuality when it escapes the karmic cycle. Indeed moksha is seen not as the negation of individual consciousness but as the true realisation of individuality, not as escape from life, but as life in its highest and purest form.

In Jainism, the jiva is not a soul in the way that Western (and many Eastern) traditions understand the term, but a life monad, which gives life-energy and individuality to each human being, or animal, plant and microbe – or supernatural being. It is also, as we have seen, a unit of pure consciousness, uncluttered by material preoccupations and limits, set free from the restricted understanding that karmic bondage imposes. Jiva means that which is alive, and the immediately perceptible material world is *ajiva*, 'not alive'. Ajiva does not mean the same as illusory. The material world exists, as does the karma that binds the jiva to it. However it is a lower level of consciousness, a lesser reality than that which is achieved through moksha. This is why all worldly preoccupations, be they material or spiritual, disciplined or dissipated, loving or hate-filled, are ultimately karmic. Whatever their merits or demerits, they involve the individual in samsara, rather than pointing towards escape from karma. But Jainism compensates for this apparent harshness by acknowledging that there are positive and negative forms of karma. That is to say, there are entirely negative emotions, ideas and deeds, and there are those which, although still karmic, place the individual in conditions where higher consciousness, and perhaps liberation, might be achieved.

On the karmic continuum, there are many colours between black and white, indeed many shades of grey and places where 'good' and 'bad' karma might intersect or merge into each other. The individual jiva is indeed trapped by karma, but has the possibility of working its way, consciously, out of the cycle of birth, death and rebirth. Far from being a passive pawn or captive of destiny, it can avail itself of a range of possibilities, and this range widens, for good or ill, as it evolves through different stages on the journey to liberation. Thus the greater the level of evolved consciousness, the greater the possibility of growth, but also the greater the dangers of regression. The path that can lead to liberation should be seen less as a straight line, pointing forwards or upwards, but more as a spiral pattern of winding and intersecting loops, a string that unravels constantly through space, time and consciousness. There is no guarantee at all that higher spiritual insight, let alone moksha, will be attained through the work of a single lifetime. Such prospects are so unlikely that they are not seriously contemplated, in part because overconfidence would itself be karmic and counter-productive. Therefore, Jains are used to planning for innumerable future incarnations as well as present reality, a truly 'proactive' approach to spiritual development!

The Jain idea of karma is thus bound up, literally and metaphorically, with the belief in the primacy of the individual. This belief in individual autonomy provides a useful point of contact between Jainism and Western thought, because the latter sanctifies the human individual as one created in the divine image, or as the secular possessor of political rights. In Jainism, individuality is equally important, which is why unlike other Eastern paths it does not seek the obliteration of individual consciousness, or merger with a universal self. Yet its conception of the individual is flexible and moves freely between sexes, species, forms of life and dimensions of reality. Beyond that flexible form, there is an inner core of consistency and stability, an essence that transfers between lives and circumstances, accumulating or shedding karmic baggage in transit. This aspect of the Jain view of karma displays an understanding that all life forms (visible or otherwise) are intricate systems. Therefore, there is no reason to suppose that an insect, or a micro-organism, is any less complex or 'developed' in its structure than a human being merely because it lacks the human capacities for reason, moral choice and spiritual growth. There are differences of kind in Jainism, based on the intellectual and spiritual capacities that beings or species possess. At the same time, however, all beings are equal in that they all serve a karmic purpose and that there is a thread of continuity – the jiva or life force within – that binds them together from one cycle of existence to another.

Here there is a further parallel between Jainism and the primal religions. For these also contain an awareness of the connections, parallels and overlaps between human and non-human species, as well as their mutual dependence. The shamanic traditions of Siberia and the Americas both include the concept of shape shifting, whereby the shaman acquires mystical powers, including the ability to travel between worlds, from assuming the attributes of another species. Shamans also work with 'power animals', such as wolves or bears, which inhabit parallel spiritual realms and confer power and wisdom. In Shinto, the most ancient spiritual tradition of Japan, there is a concept known as '*mono no aware*', or 'sympathy with all creatures', which is a strong echo of Jainism as well as the more familiar Buddhist thought.[1] According to one commentator, this ancient Shinto teaching confers on the Japanese the capacity for 'feeling vividly a consanguineous kinship with plants and animals', which are therefore not really separate species, or life forms, in separate compartments, but 'of the same blood' and therefore ultimately as one.[2] This idea is contained in the Jain doctrine of ahimsa, for the relationship between humans and other creatures is the principal reason why the latter should not be harmed.

In most ancient faiths, an awareness of the life's intricate web arises from direct experience as well as intuition. It emerges out of the struggle for subsistence and from the need to submit to natural process or at least work with the grain of nature rather than actively oppose it. Crucially, it is linked to the dependence humans have on animals, as companions or beasts of burden, spiritual guides or sources of food. Arctic peoples, for example, have traditionally revered or worshipped the animals they hunt and kill, seeing in the hunt the expression of a cycle of creation, or an early understanding of the karmic cycle. Jainism includes this form of primal understanding, but combines it with a scientific approach to living systems and an ethical responsibility to avoid damage to all forms of life. These three aspects – the intuitive, the objective and the ethical - meet and merge in the Jain approach to karma. It is a recognition of continuity within change, and of the existence of spiritual qualities in the most obscure recesses of a universe filled to the brim with life.

Karmic particles are themselves minute life forms. They have a physical existence, albeit at the level of subtle rather than gross matter, and they combine to form powerful spiritual ecosystems, somewhat like coral reefs around the soul. Karma in Jainism even has colour. Mahavira taught that there are six *lesyas*, shades or tints of karmic colour: *krishna* or black; *neel* (blue); *kapota* (grey); *tejo* (red or yellow); *padma* (pink) and *sukla* (white). The subtle body of karma fluctuates constantly between these shades of colour, which shade into each other and overlap on all points of the spectrum between the 'black' and 'white' souls. At the moment of transmigration, the colour of the karmic matter indicates the health of the soul and so has a bearing on the next worldly existence. In a curious form of spiritual synaesthesia, karmic colours can be tasted and smelled as well as being visible at the subtle level. Colour as a metaphor for mood or moral state is well-known in the West, where it has become an increasingly popular form of therapy. Some Western clairvoyants are able to see the colour of a client's aura and draw profound conclusions from it about that client's health and future prospects. They are working within an ancient Jain system, although in most cases they probably do not know it.

For Jains, karma is more than a mechanical process in which the individual soul becomes enmeshed. Karma is seen in terms of a web, or a pattern, or a thread that connects all living beings in the universe. But it is also seen in direct and explicitly material terms. In Jainism, particles of karmic matter attach themselves to the soul and in a literal sense weigh it down by causing it to become embodied in matter. Karmic matter obscures the soul's clarity of perception and so stands between it and enlightenment, which is pure consciousness. This spiritual and intellectual entrapment is linked to a process of physical entrapment, whereby the soul is imprisoned in the body and its pure life energy corrupted by physical processes, the cycle of birth, death and rebirth.

The physical and the spiritual aspects of *bandha*, or karmic bondage, are indistinguishable, and so Jains interpret the struggle for liberation in physical as much as psychic terms. This accounts, at least in part, for the emphasis that Jainism places on austerities that can seem exaggerated to outsiders. For souls at advanced stages of spiritual progress, withdrawal from the body is as much a part of the process of seeking liberation as withdrawal from concerns for wealth or transient ambitions. Yet at another level, the perception of karma in material terms is evidence of Jainism's flexibility. For as always, it is equally concerned with direct experience as with abstract speculation and values particular experience as much as general principle. Each life form is working its way through the karmic cycle, but doing so in its own way, at its own pace, its specific situation as significant as that of any other living being. The karmic web is therefore seen less as a grand design and more as the sum total of individual experiences – the experiences of souls embodied in karma and seeking freedom from it.

Moksha, liberation from karma, is therefore pure energy as well as pure consciousness, immortality as much as omniscience. Far from being 'life after death', moksha is 'life after life', or rather the achievement of genuine life, as opposed to the temporary and at best only second-rate existence conferred by karmic bondage. The idea of casting off a 'mortal coil' is easily understood by a Jain, for the mortal coil is karma. However it would be too simple to see the Jain process of spiritual liberation exclusively in terms of renunciation, or demanding unconditional withdrawal from social concerns. Its logic points in that direction, but Jainism acknowledges shades of meaning, individual circumstance and what is compatible in the long term with spiritual growth. Thus there are positive, or auspicious, forms of karma, which although they involve worldly concerns can guide the corrupted soul towards more favourable conditions for spiritual development.

Karmic particles are invisible to the naked eye. They are also spiritually invisible to un-awakened souls who do not recognise their presence and their effect. Their invisibility does not make them any less real, for Jainism presupposes that the inhabited or 'occupied' universe, the *lokakasa*, is teeming with life and that sub-atomic particles, or *anu*, are all-pervasive, the basic units of material existence. Karmic particles are but one of a variety of *anu* and they are drawn to incarnated souls by a process of physical attraction. The early Jains had an intuitive understanding of sub-atomic particles thousands of years before their existence could be verified by scientific observation. This means that they lacked the technological paraphernalia available to modern science and the immense advantages this confers. At the same time, they lacked the prejudices associated with technology-based societies, in which hyper-rationalism itself becomes a superstition. Their use of reason encompassed processes, beings and phenomena considered magical or supernatural by the modern and hyper-rational consciousness. And so in the same way as Jain thinkers were able to speculate on elementary life forms and the links between all living systems, they were also able to conceive of subtle matter, parallel worlds and different levels of reality.

In an age of string theory and dark matter, when the mechanical models of the modern era are increasingly called into question, and a holistic science admits of infinite possibilities, the Jain approach does not seem quite as 'primitive' a cosmology as the hyper-rationalist critic might assume. Indeed there are many ways in which the Jain perspective makes more sense to our present level of consciousness, in the West especially, in which we are subjecting the principles of the Enlightenment to enlightened questioning. The Jain conception of karma offers a possible point of intersection between the concrete and rational, on the one hand, and on the other the ethereal and intuitive. For without the other, each is incomplete.

The devout Jain believes in the reality of karma, and the existence of karmic particles, as literal truths, no less real than a book, or a computer, or a political party. In an important sense, they can be seen as more real, for they represent higher truths than we can discern through lived experience alone. However this

literal belief in karma should not be seen as a form of fundamentalism. It does not contradict modern scientific insights into the
nature and structure of the universe. On the contrary, it seeks to
complement them, or give them a more rounded and spiritual
perspective. By contrast, certain types of hyper-rational approach

can take on the appearance of secular fundamentalism. This narrow
view of reality is also coming to seem increasingly outmoded,
increasingly 'primitive' as a form of cosmology, although like
similar mechanistic dogmas in economics, it retains a vice-like
grip on many areas of intellectual and public life. And yet, in
our questioning of the narrow interpretation of Enlightenment
principles, we must remain (in relative terms) 'enlightened' and
rooted in reason. An over-emphasis on the ethereal can be as
counter-productive as hyper-rationalism, if not even more so. It
can give rise to an irrational and mystical approach to spirituality
which lacks discernment, subtlety and strong cultural roots, and
so makes the spiritual seeker vulnerable to fraudulent gurus or
cults based on mind control. The Jain view of karma is part of a
spiritual framework. Far from being removed from the lived
experience, and reasoning, of human beings today, it includes and
encompasses that experience. Every human action, individual or
collective, is karmic, as is every thought or idea, however
apparently significant or trivial, however subjectively 'good' or
'bad'. In Jain karma, ideas are a form of action, as are emotions,
feelings and unconscious responses. The mind-body dichotomy is
as artificial irrelevant as the separation of humanity and nature.

For non-Jains, the process of accumulating – and sloughing
off – karmic matter can be seen as a metaphor for the various
stages of consciousness. Those who are spiritually dormant, the

un-awakened souls, are highly receptive to karmic particles. They usually accumulate them through seeing material goals as ends in themselves, instead of transient concerns, or at best stages on a journey through many lifetimes. Those who are spiritually more conscious build up immunity to karmic incursion. After this, they are able to shed layers of karma, as their perception becomes clear and they become spiritually healthier and more whole. We can see karmic matter as a dead weight, holding us down and limiting our ability to move. By shedding it we find in ourselves a new agility, strength and lightness of spirit.

Equally, karma is seen as a mask, a blindfold, or a form of restricted vision, perhaps a spiritual cataract. When we grow spiritually, our vision ceases to be opaque and becomes accurately focussed. Interpreting karma as metaphor fits within the Jain frame of reference as much as the literal acceptance of its existence. The two approaches do not contradict each other, but peacefully coexist. Yet none of the popular descriptions of karma, as infectious agent, deadening weight or visual impediment express more than an element of the underlying truth. For there are positive as well as negative karmic influences, there is light as well as heavy karma and there are karmic experiences that enrich an individual's vision or benefit others. Release from karma does not mean acquiring vision in the limited human sense, but being able to see into realms of consciousness invisible even to the most highly developed human beings, as well beyond the divisions of past, present and future. And, in karmic terms, a little learning is a dangerous thing. The spiritually half-awake are more vulnerable than the spiritually dormant to perverse or misdirected forms of consciousness, including fanaticism and extremist ideologies.

These, and the actions to which they often lead, attract vast quantities of karma because they result in intellectual and physical violence. Karma, for Jains, is an all-inclusive system, existing at literal and metaphorical levels, at once a spiritual and physical process. Only through moksha does jiva separate itself fully from ajiva and the soul cease to be involved in karma. Outside the karmic cycle, the jiva returns to true role as a unit of pure consciousness. It thus becomes fully alive as the 'supreme self' is realised. This retains its unique individual identity, and yet, as the *Acaranga Sutra* tells us:

> [The true self] is not long nor small nor round nor triangular nor quadrangular nor circular; it is not black nor blue nor red nor green nor white; neither of good nor bad smell; not bitter nor pungent nor astringent nor sweet; neither rough nor soft; neither heavy nor light; neither cold nor hot; neither harsh nor smooth. It does not have a body, it is not born again, has no attachment and is without sexual gender. While having knowledge and sentience, there is nonetheless nothing with which it can be compared. Its being is without form, there is no condition of the unconditioned. It is not sound nor form nor smell, nor anything like that.

The belief in moksha as a return to true life can, like the belief itself, be viewed at literal and metaphorical levels simultaneously. Through moksha, the enlightened jiva comes back to life in the sense that it is reawakened from worldly confusion and achieves a totality of perception that is impossible in a state of human bondage. We have already presented moksha as spiritual

synaesthesia, in which the divisions between the senses break
down, no detail is obscured, no idea unknown. At the same time,
the enlightened, all-seeing soul has a forensic grasp of detail. It can
discriminate with ultimate precision, unavailable to the incarnate
soul, confused by karma, and can see beneath the surface of
conventional reality to the subtle connections at work in the
universe. Enlightened humans, visionaries, gain only a fleeting
impression of what moksha can be like. Jainism is other-worldly
in that, like the Hindu and Buddhist paths, it regards the karmic
cycle as something to be transcended, or overcome by spiritual
discipline. There is a sense in which Jainism goes further than
these parallel Indic traditions, in its description of karma as a
material impediment that holds the soul down. Furthermore, it
characterises material existence and the lokakasa or observable
universe as ajiva, or not truly alive. The jiva as a life monad
passes between one incarnation – one temporary life – as another.
When it is liberated the soul does not pass beyond life, or 'attain
eternal life', but is recalled to its true existence.

Nonetheless, ajiva does not imply complete non-existence,
or the Vedantic view of material existence as little more than
illusion. Ajiva is false consciousness, or more accurately limited
consciousness, but it is better expressed as a lower level of reality
than as something unreal. Spiritual evolution for Jains, within one
lifetime or many, implies progress to higher visions of reality.
This principle operates along much the same lines as secular
knowledge, which should confer a wider understanding of life.
Ajiva can therefore be seen as a lesser reality, or a reality obscured
by karma, rather than a mere illusion. Moksha, however, is viewed
by Jains as a material process, like the build-up of karmic particles.

It is seen in terms of physical release from karmic bondage and equally as the liberation of the soul from the constraints of ajiva. The method by which karmic particles attach to the soul is also interpreted in physical terms. They attach themselves by a process of attraction, manifested through the activities of the embodied jiva, whether physical or mental. Conscious or otherwise, the actions of humans, or other life forms, create cosmic vibrations that lead to an inflow of karmic particles towards the embodied soul. These adhere to the soul, and their presence in turn increases the likelihood of further karmic activity. In seeking freedom from the karmic cycle, an individual attempts to gain control of his or her own life and looks for a deeper understanding of the truth, beyond superficial impressions of reality. The search for enlightenment in Jainism is a conscious altering of priorities and perceptions. It requires a balance of intellect and intuition, a sense a sense of ultimate purpose and a sense of ultimate release.

The Jain view of karma is therefore distinctive in two crucial respects. First, it sees karma in terms of subtle matter that adheres to the soul, a direct personal and physical experience rather than merely an abstract process. The concept of karma as subtle matter, particles invisible to the naked eye, is part of the Jain intuition that sub-atomic particles exist and pervade the known universe. Secondly, Jains believe that through breaking the karmic cycle, the true self is realised, not by merging with any larger entity, or dissolving, but achieving the full autonomy that is seen as part of pure consciousness. Thus we have a view of karma that diverges from the Vedic and Buddhist traditions, both in stressing the physical aspect of karma – the literal truth of karmic bondage – and in its powerful emphasis on the jiva as an autonomous individual, the fulfilment of the true self.

This stress on personal autonomy and the importance of the individual soul is easy enough for those immersed in Western civilisation to absorb. The role of individual conscience is, after all, a powerful theme in Western thought, connecting Classical Antiquity with Judaeo-Christianity and its various secular rationalist successors. It is a concept equally pervasive in Jainism. The Jain view of the self is at once more starkly minimalist and more inclusive than the prevailing Western model. It is minimalist, because in its realised form it has shorn off all the attributes we associate with individual identity. Characteristics such as shape, size and gender are shed and do not persist even in illusory or representative form, whilst the enlightened being, the Jina revered by Jains, is devoid of anything that we would recognise as personality, character or temperament. This is a radical difference from, for example, Christian saints or their counterparts in Shi'a Islam. Realising the self is a process of internal conquest, in which the lower, sensual self is mastered and the higher self fulfilled. This is quite different from self-fulfilment as it is understood in the post-Christian age, where self-realisation is often equated too simply with the expression and enactment of desire, and where personal autonomy is reduced to a myriad 'choices' of limited lasting value.

The Jain sense of the self can easily sound elitist and puritanical, and these elements undoubtedly exist in Jain doctrine and practice. Yet it is also profoundly inclusive, because the process of self-development takes place over many lifetimes and crosses all recognised biological barriers and the division between 'natural' and 'supernatural' beings. Self-realisation in Jainism is therefore an all-encompassing experience, reflecting the connections between all living systems within the inhabited universe, and even the parallel universes inhabited by deities. Awareness of the shared quest for enlightenment, and common experience of the karmic cycle, intensifies the Jain commitment to ahimsa. If all life is seen to be connected, then it becomes all the more imperative for rational, evolving beings to avoid injuring life in any possible way. Jain self-realisation is about achieving omniscience, but it is not about attaining power or exercising control. The liberated jiva has progressed beyond the karmic ambitions that give rise to the will to power in human beings and the Tirthankaras, worshipped by Jains as symbols of omniscience, do not intercede on behalf of their worshippers, or indeed act for humanity in any way. Instead, they provide inspiration to living men and women as they struggle to free themselves from karma and so realise their potential. This is why they are known as ford-makers or pathfinders. They are not active agents of change, which can only come from within, through thought and practice. However they can act as spiritual role models, pointing the way to self-liberation. The following, typically Jain prayer says much about the prevailing attitude towards the Tirthankaras, and towards enlightened souls in general:

Him who is the revealer of the path to salvation, who is the remover of mountains of karmas, and who is the knower of all reality, him I worship, in order that I may realise his qualities within myself.

The path to salvation is revealed by the example of ethical living, the mountains of karmas refer to the Jina's achievement in overcoming karmic patterns in his own life and carried over from previous existence. Worship takes place as part of spiritual development, not in obeisance to a more powerful force or in the hope of intercession. It is not an invocation, nor is it intended to pacify, for the Tirthankara is already defined by its passivity. Worship of Jinas is at once a mark of respect for those who have completed the process of liberation, and an identification with enlightened souls in the hope of emulating them and ultimately joining in a state of pure consciousness. It is not 'worship' in the sense of obeisance or surrender. Instead of submitting, the Jain worshipper views the Jina or Tirthankara as something he or she could become, a state that can be attained. Worship, therefore, is a reminder of the potential to overcome karma. Although it has freed itself from the mundane world, the liberated jiva is not something separate, but part of a continuum that includes all species, all living forms, however basic they might appear, and even supernatural forces such as devas. For just as a rational human being can achieve liberation, so he or she can 'revert' to the animal, plant or mineral world, or be isolated as a supernatural being. Likewise, a primitive or supernatural life form may spiritually evolve to human rebirth, which is normally one of the pre-conditions of moksha.

In this sense, Jainism can seem hierarchical and human-centred. Many supporters of the green movement in the West might call it 'anthropocentric' or 'speciesist' because it acknowledges different levels of consciousness and with them different possibilities. From a Jain standpoint, it cannot be said that 'all animals are equal', because moksha requires rebirth as a human being (or, with the

Digambaras, specifically as a human male). Yet this Jain hierarchy is not a fixed pyramid or chain of being but a karmic spiral, in a state of constant motion. For the Jain view of karma takes as its starting point the relationship of all living beings and the continuity between one life form and another. Thousands of years before Darwin, Jain seers intuited the evolutionary continuum. Jains also realised that animals, indeed all sentient beings, can think for themselves, experience pleasure, pain, and powerful emotions, that they are (at least) as biologically complex as humans, and are spiritual beings as well. These are conclusions with which Western science and theology are still coming to terms, and with which politics have not nearly caught up.

Furthermore, the karmic cycle differs from the cycles of creation found in shamanic societies. These resemble Jainism in that they are based on interconnectedness, but their view of interconnectedness sanctions hunting, killing and trapping. In Jainism, by contrast, awareness of our kinship with other beings imposes responsibilities on rational men and women. Because we are aware of our connections – biological or karmic – with the animal world – we must reduce our exploitation of animals – and the natural world – to the barest minimum.

Despite superficial appearances, the Jain perspective slots neatly into modern, and especially Western debates on animal rights, the sentience of non-human species and restoring the connection between humanity and nature. Its approach is less about hierarchy and more about fluidity and diversity. The Jain view of karma is based on reincarnation, and there are auspicious and inauspicious rebirths, with human-to-animal rebirths invariably inauspicious. However it is radically egalitarian in its acceptance of non-humans as spiritual beings and promoting an ethic of non-exploitation. Similarly, a spiritual discipline that often appears harsh, uncompromising and elitist also points towards spiritual equality. The Jina is 'superior' only in the sense that it has reached a higher level of consciousness, but it can neither frighten nor compel. There are no dieties in Jainism that can punish, or rescue human beings and worship is based on respect instead of subservience. In Jainism, all souls are equal in the sense that they are all on the karmic journey. They go forwards, they regress, they move sideways and then they advance once more. Karma is a great leveller as much as it is an instrument of liberation. It is also a physical process in which all beings are caught up.

The Jain view of karma arises out of a wider interpretation of reality, which divides the universe into two distinctive but interdependent parts, jiva, that which lives, and ajiva, the non-living. All that we would conventionally interpret as a sign of life is ajiva. This includes the entire physical world, our emotional and intellectual lives and all those characteristics that define and so restrict us: species, gender, physical prowess or weakness, social status and the limits of our intelligence and understanding. Even our innermost thoughts are ajiva, although through spiritual practice we can hope to realise the life within, the jiva which is formless, all-knowing, 'beyond good and evil', or any other worldly constraint.

At first glance, this seems a life-denying doctrine, or indeed a denial of life as we would understand it. For a philosophy that stresses the significance of the individual, the aim of eliminating all characteristics identifying the 'self' seems paradoxical. On both counts, a more subtle explanation can be discerned. Whilst it is true that Jainism has a profound and powerful renunciatory tradition, and that ajiva does literally mean 'non-living', the ajiva universe is, as we have seen, not a pure illusion or a dream, but a lower level of reality in which only lesser forms of consciousness are possible. Jainism stresses the individual, but its view of individuality is more inclusive than the human person, which is merely a stage of spiritual development. The true individuality is the jiva, the unit of pure consciousness which is obscured by karma. Karmic matter encases the un-liberated soul, but the process of karma connects the parallel universes of jiva and ajiva. Through the process of karma, the soul rises from one universe, one level of consciousness, to another, rising gradually as it sheds karmic layers.

Since karma is conceived as matter, as 'actual physical material which makes the soul impure'[4], the karmic process is viewed by Jains in descriptive terms that are both intricate and highly practical, and which can seem more material and physical than spiritual in character. The Jain explanation of how karma works arises from the 'Nine Reals', the *tattvas*, which are recognised as underlying cosmic principles. These principles can be summarised as follows:

1   *Jiva*: the 'soul' as a unit of pure consciousness, a life monad.

2   *Ajiva*: all that is 'non-soul' or material in nature. This includes everything in the known universe, or lokakasa. Crucially, it includes karmic particles which attach themselves to the jiva and impose physical and spiritual limits.

3   *Asrava*: the inflow of karmic particles to the soul, making it lose its self-awareness.

4   *Bandha*: the 'bondage' of the soul, or process by which karmic particles attach themselves and exert a long-term influence.

5   *Punya*: the principle of auspicious karma. This can be understood as 'good' karma, or positive actions which, although karmic, can point the way towards liberation.

6   *Papa*: the principle of inauspicious karma. This can be understood as 'bad' karma, or negative actions which point towards a downward spiral of spiritual regression.

7   *Samvara*: the stoppage of karmic inflow. This process eventually counters asrava. It is achieved through intellectual and spiritual discipline, which eventually repels karmic particles.

8   *Nirjara*: the shedding of karmic particles. This can take place through spiritual discipline and austerities (tapas). There is also a natural process by which karmic particles 'bear fruit' and fall away, since like other aspects of ajiva, they are finite.

9   *Moksha*: spiritual and physical liberation. In attaining moksha, the true self is realised, pure consciousness is achieved. The jiva is released from the karmic cycle and becomes omniscient. For Jains, this is the highest possible

spiritual goal.

Spiritual development is therefore a cyclical process, beginning and ending with the jiva. This matches the Jain view of time and history as cycles, as opposed to mere linear progressions. The karmic process is one of continuous development, and its inevitable corollary, regression. Yet there is also an important continuity, the jiva, which in attaining moksha, quite literally returns to its self. The fully evolved soul, which has achieved liberation, is the nearest that Jainism comes to a divine power. For the non-theistic Jains, the highest form of life is not a 'god', but a fully realised individual in a state to which any human being can aspire. It is worshipped and revered as something we can all become, eventually, when we have conquered our material selves.

Within the Jain cosmos, there are manifold souls, pure and impure, free and embodied. Only a soul in human form is usually capable of achieving moksha, because only humans have the intellectual and spiritual ability to make conscious moral decisions, even though other species are able to think and feel. Souls are trapped within all beings because karma encases them in four forms, also known to Jains as the 'four destinies': human or *manushya*, animal or plant *(tiryancha)*, hellish *(naraki)* and *deva* or divine (but not a deity in the Western sense). Nirjara, the shedding of karma, aids the process of evolution from tiryancha to manushya, but negative choices in the latter phase can trigger a regression, or rebirth as a hell-being. Rebirth as a deva, a divine being, is not so much an advancement as a diversion, a form of spiritual siding. A deva is a spiritual being, and might well embody a moral or natural principle, but it is not a pure soul. It is still within samsara, the cycle of birth, death and rebirth, still caught in the karmic web, still ajiva. Thus the deva in Jainism is of a lesser order than, for example, the Shinto *kami* and is not an archetype of the divine, like the Hindu image of god or goddess. A soul embodied as a deva or a hell-being must reincarnate in human form to progress. It achieves this largely through the passive form of nirjara because its scope for moral choice is limited. In other words, becoming a deva can delay liberation and these supposedly supernatural beings are part of the lokakasa. Therefore, they are governed by karma rather than existing above or outside it.

Karma is therefore a physical process, studied by scientific method, as much as it is an ethical system, understood by meditation and austerity. Given that Jainism draws no distinction between moral and physical realms, this approach is quite logical. Karma, in Sanskrit, means 'action' or 'activity' and in Jainism, action is all-inclusive, so that thoughts are as important as deeds, private emotions as significant as public behaviour. This again is quite reasonable in the context of Jain dharma, for the goal is escape from both physical and intellectual limitations. As such, Jains make no distinction between 'mind' and 'body'. Both are equally relevant in the short term, equally irrelevant in the long term. The jiva itself is at once infinitely strong and infinitely vulnerable. The freely floating soul does not choose to come into contact with karma, and only acquires the ability to free itself when it develops as a human being. Freed from karma, it is omniscient, but when in direct contact with karma, it loses its pure essence and attracts karmic particles. This inflow (asrava) has been compared to water leaking into a damaged vessel. The analogy works only partially, however, because such a vessel will inevitably sink, whereas an impure soul has the possibility of eventual escape.

Jainism can seem vague about why, let alone how, the jiva first comes into contact with karmic particles. In a sense, the 'why' is irrelevant, because life and the universe, despite their strong ethical foundations, have no first cause. The jiva, as pure energy as well as pure consciousness, is neither created nor destroyed, but eternal. So is the universe itself, and the individual soul's journey mirrors the continuous upward and downward cycles through which the universe moves. For Jains, each soul is individual and unique, although equal, whereas all karmic particles are identical. They differ only in the effect they have on the souls they come in contact with, which is determined by the way the soul initially reacts, and by its future incarnations.

In its pure state, the soul is inactive, but when it comes into contact with karma, it begins to move and its vibrations, or *aura*, attract karma. To Jains, all actions, all aspects of the ajiva universe, generate karma. This is true whether they are conscious or unconscious, good, evil or morally neutral, even spiritual acts such as prayer or necessary physical functions such as breathing. The soul, when it is not involved in samsara, has four outstanding characteristics:

- Infinite knowledge
- Infinite perception
- Infinite energy
- Infinite bliss

The concept of 'bliss' (*ananda*) means more than total happiness – a worldly emotion, after all – or even the total absence of pain.

Instead it implies a benign understanding of everything in the universe, a state of inner and outer calm that comes through freedom from all violent and passionate impulses. The state of bliss, therefore, is a synthesis of the other three characteristics of the soul, but contact with karma undermines all these properties. When karmic matter attaches itself to the soul, it therefore:

- Obscures knowledge
- Erodes perception
- Obstructs energy
- Corrupts the state of bliss

This is how the soul, entrapped by karma, loses its pure consciousness and has to begin to find a way out through many rebirths. Until consciousness is properly awakened, the inflow of karmic particles is unstoppable. The particles do not necessarily do harm. They can be neutral, or indeed auspicious, in which case they will be shed 'naturally'. In the long run – and everything in Jainism is in the long run – they will not be impediments to moksha, and might hasten the onset of liberation in some circumstances. Yet the process of asrava is polluting when the embodied jiva makes the wrong choices. The effects of karma are shaped by five main influences:

- *mithyattva*: one-sided or perverted world view
- *pramada*: carelessness or indifferences
- *avirati*: lack of self-discipline
- *yoga*: activity
- *kasaya*: passions

Needless to say, *virati* or self-discipline, has a positive effect on karma, helping to block its inflow and reducing its ill-effects. Likewise, passions can be controlled or overcome, and activities can have good or bad spiritual outcomes, according to their nature. In bandha, the process by which karmic particles bond, or attach themselves to the soul, the strength of the adhesion depends on the four factors cited above. Passions, felt or enacted, lack of discipline or inner resolve, destructive activities or the infliction of harm, callous indifference towards others and a perverted world-view, including extremism or fanaticism: all these intensify the bonds of karma. Equanimity, benevolence towards others (human and non-human) and disciplined, measured conduct lighten the karmic burden. The Jain scientist Kanti Mardia explains bandha in terms of 'karmic fusion'. Karmic particles, which he calls 'karmons', recompose into 'heavy' or 'light' karmic matter:

> Heavy karmic matter implies that the karmic bondage is strong, whereas light karmic matter implies that the karmic bondage is light and it is easier to remove this karmic matter from the soul.[5]

This interpretation of bandha illustrates well the continuities between Jain doctrine and the methods of modern scientific analysis, which helps us understand why Jains take such a positive view of Western science. The Jain path balances this almost clinical approach, however, with the concepts of auspicious and inauspicious karma, whereby actions are measured according to their ethical outcomes. Punya, or auspicious karma, arises out of 'good' actions, such as philanthropy, papa, or inauspicious karma, from cruelty or immorality. The liberated soul is free from karmic influence. Yet to attain moksha it is essential not only to stop accumulating karmic particles, but to be able to shed them, through conscious actions. Thus although the ultimate Jain ideal is non-action, simply deciding not to act can never be enough. It is not possible to short-circuit samsara, to escape the karmic spiral before acquiring the necessary level of consciousness. And to acquire that level of consciousness, it is necessary to undergo karmic experiences.

Before beginning to escape from karmic bondage, one must learn to discriminate between punya and papa, between positive and negative acts. To escape from mundane morality, one must learn to make moral choices. The notion of auspicious karma squares a circle within Jainism, resolving an apparent contradiction between the ideal of non-action and the ethic of service to all beings. To the Western mind, which has become uncomfortable with contradictions, this is important. It provides a strand of consistency, connecting benevolent worldly goals, such as social reform or voluntary charitable work, with the ascetic ideal of renunciation and non-action. As is usual in Jainism, there is nonetheless an overlap of consciousness in which the two ideals and practices meet. For one of the paradoxes of Jainism is that *because* it is such a precise doctrine, it allows for areas of vagueness. Because it seeks to explore all areas of existence, it admits of infinite possibilities, exceptions and shades of grey.

Furthermore, the doctrine of punya and papa, auspicious and inauspicious karma, addresses an intellectual paradox for thoughtful Jains, the problem of choice. Thought, in Jainism, is a type of activity, a yoga, as much as decisions and actions that result from that thought. Karma itself is action, whether conscious or unconscious, mental or physical, and so encompasses all human experience. Therefore, the decision to focus on Jain principles, such as the Five Vows, is itself karmic, as is the conscious decision to shed layers of karma. Even the experience of living as an ascetic is based on conscious action as much as spiritual intuition. The *Tattvartha Sutra* takes account of this by providing for a series of 'careful actions', or *samiti*, all of which derive from the Five Vows. The most important of these, *iryasamiti*, or 'care in movement', enjoins concern for the natural world in all the ascetic's movements and actions, reducing his human impact on the ecosystem to a bare minimum. Others relate to avoidance of careless speech, excessive or mocking laughter, which distort the senses, judicious acceptance of alms and the well-known ascetic Jain practice of avoiding harm to tiny life forms. Thus even the life of the ascetic, who is at the pinnacle of Jain practice, is enmeshed in karmic actions, but such actions put him in a position from where he can aspire to liberation.

The actions that attract karma are themselves grouped into three categories: *kaya* (physical), *vachana* (vocal) and *mana* (mental or psychic). In karmic terms there is no difference between these categories, no notion that something is 'only in the mind' and so less important. Indeed a negative thought or twisted fantasy is less auspicious, and generates more karma, than an indifferent or mildly malicious deed. Actions of all three types create the vibrations that bond karmic particles to the soul. There are degrees of vibration, strong and weak, and these influence in turn the solidity of the karmic bondage. Actions of little consequence or impact on others generate lesser form of bondage, known as *dravya karma*. When passions that distort the consciousness are involved, the karmic bondage is stronger, and the vibrations are known as *bhava* - intentional – *karma*. Both types of karma are cumulative and stand between the jiva and its self-realisation. Both interact and contribute to the karmic cycle that passes from one existence to another. But it is bhava karma that presents the most complex moral and spiritual dilemmas for Jains, and which acts as the most powerful obstacle to moksha. Bhava karma is divided into eight broad categories, the first four of which are defined as *ghatiya* (destructive) karma, the last four *aghatiya* (non-destructive) because they represent mere facts of mundane existence, rather than mistaken actions or choices that keep the samsaric cycle in being. The eight karmic categories are as follows:

1 *Jnanavarniya* – Knowledge Obstructing karma

This karma is generated by the refusal to learn, or to be open to ideas. It is brought about by the closing of the mind, the spreading of false or one-sided information and by ridiculing and undermining those who pursue knowledge. In other words, this is a very broad type of karma that encompasses philistinism, anti-intellectualism, indifference, self-centred materialism or the vociferous advocacy of fanatical and prejudiced opinion.

2 *Darsanavarniya* – Intuition Obstructing karma

The second karmic category is a more subtle form of 1.), in which the capacity for spiritual insight is not only denied, but held up as an object of ridicule, and visionaries are either unrecognised or dismissed without thought. Hyper-rationalism can fall into the category of *darsanavarniya,* because it lacks the sense of balance that is so important to Jains, focusing on only one area of consciousness and refusing to be guided by intuitive wisdom as well as 'pure' reason. Intuition obstructing karma is the denial of anything transcendent and a stubborn clinging to the material and mundane.

3 *Antaraya* – Energy Obstructing karma

This type of karma obstructs the flow of positive energy from the soul and so encourages the flow of karmic particles *into* the soul. The characteristics, or symptoms, of antaraya, include meanness of spirit, lack of generosity of outlook and the absence of charitable or nurturing instincts. It encompasses the absence of kindness as well as active unkindness, passive indifference to suffering as much as exploitative acts that induce suffering. It includes laziness and contempt for those who seek a more just social order, or improving the lot of those around them, or pursuing a spiritual path. Antaraya is a karma that carries its own punishment with it, for those affected by this type of bandha are incapable of enjoyment of life, let alone addressing their spiritual needs. Even if they are materially successful, they are never satisfied with their wealth and are incapable of using it constructively for themselves or others. Antaraya creates a condition of bitterness, pessimism and misanthropy that affects the individual's behaviour towards others and imprisons him or her in a negative pattern of thinking that attracts fresh formations of karma.

4 *Mohaniya* – Deluding karma

In many ways the most dangerous type of karma is that which is associated with self-delusion and the conviction of absolute truth. Mohaniya is the karma of fanaticism, intolerance, fundamentalism and the blinkered mentality that leads to acts of cruelty and violence. It is the karma of authoritarianism, rigidity and contempt for all forms of life, of megalomaniac experiments, totalitarian social engineering and the reduction of the individual to a cipher, a mere 'element' in an 'historical process' or grand narrative. The logical consequences of mohaniya are best expressed by George Orwell when he speaks of totalitarianism – right-wing or left-wing – as 'a jackboot stamping on a human face forever'. The person affected by deluding karma is consumed with hatred and anger. This can be directed at convenient targets, such as supposedly 'inferior' races, cultures or ways of life that are reduced to grotesque stereotypes. Yet it can also be expressed on behalf of human groups – 'the working class', 'women' or 'ethnic minorities', for instance – that are reduced to abstract collectives and are rarely consulted by those who claim to be liberating them.

Thus in today's Western context, deluding karma cuts across the alleged left/right divide on the political spectrum, affecting progressives and conservatives, religious fundamentalists and radical feminists, racists and anti-racists, homophobes and gay rights activists, pro-life campaigners as well as defenders of 'choice'. The holding of strong opinions, however mistaken they might seem to the liberal consensus, is not necessarily an indication of mohaniya. There are many who cling to narrow-minded prejudices who are still generous and positive in their treatment of fellow human beings, just as there are enlightened liberals who are, in thought and action, hypocritical and mean. But mohaniya is the karma of rigid 'political correctness' as much as it is the karma of fascism or imperialism.

Some ideologies point inherently towards destructive – and especially deluding – forms of karma. Racial or caste prejudice, for example, violates every principle at the heart of Jainism, as do militaristic movements in any form, except for strict self-defence or the prevention of a greater wrong (although such defensive movements would still generate high levels of karmic inflow). Yet other political doctrines, which seek the emancipation of all or part of humanity - or non-human life - can be just as much the magnets for destructive karma when they turn into *mithyattvas,* or perverted world-views, when compassion and idealism turn into fanatical hatred. When justified opposition to racism turns into reverse racism, when feminists turn away from healing wounds between the sexes and becomes hostile to men, then they and their movements develop negative karma as well as losing their original power of emancipation. When abstract love of humanity is not matched by compassionate engagement with fellow human beings, the result can only be hatred, oppression and the accumulation of destructive karma. The same danger can affect the animal rights movement, in those situations where it strays from the idea of universal compassion, when anger against injustice and cruelty give rise to unjust and cruel acts.

Mohaniya goes beyond overt and extreme examples of fanaticism and bigotry. It includes in its remit any closed system of values that excludes other possibilities and refuses to accept complexity. This extends to rigid economic models, into which human beings, other species and the environment are expected to fit. The neo-liberal cult of market forces as a universal panacea is, therefore, just as much an example of deluding karma as the idea that liberation is gained through total state control. There is destructive karma in the dehumanising and denatured approach to science that treats animals as objects of exploitation and torture 'for the greater good', or the environment as a resource to be consumed instead of a series of living systems to be conserved. And just as inflexible political ideologies generally produce only human misery (and ecological crisis), so the inflexible ideology of *scientism* generally produces bad science.

More important than the ideology itself is the attitude that goes with it and the effect it has on the individual's actions and spiritual development. This explains why there are two broad concepts of deluding karma, *darsana* mohaniya (karma that deludes the world-view) and *chatriya* mohaniya (character-deluding karma). They are interdependent, because fanaticism and rigidity extinguish all spiritual insight and any opportunity for critical reflection. It is important to note as well that amorality is as destructive, karmically, as moral fundamentalism, whilst know-nothing relativism that acknowledges no truth is as deluded as declarations of zealous certainty. This is because Jains recognise that both extremes of opinion point in the same direction. Fanaticism is amoral in its contempt for life and its dismissal of the consequences of actions. Relativism quickly transforms itself into a narrow and vociferous dogma, in which the absence of truth is asserted as an absolute in itself. Mohaniya is the karma of self-righteousness, of one-sided conclusions about life inflamed by passion and translated into physical and psychic violence.

5 *Vedaniya* – Pleasure and Pain-Causing karma

The karma of pleasure and pain straddles the border between the ghatiya and aghatiya karmas, being either wholly destructive in form, or benign and therefore either neutral or beneficial, depending on the level of activity. All actions are to a greater or lesser extent karmic, but those actions which bring pleasure or positive gain to others – and not only humans, of course – are defined as *sata-vedaniya* or pleasure-giving karma. Those which create unhappiness, pain or violence create *asata-vedaniya* karma, literally the karma of displeasure or sorrow. Pleasure-giving karma does not impede the soul's journey towards liberation, but for obvious reasons its opposite perpetuates the cycle of samsara.

6 *Ayus* - Life Span Determining karma

Ayus is the karmic pattern that determines the individual soul's place in the lokakasa, the occupied universe, in its next incarnation. There is a natural fruition or falling-off of spent karma, and this unconscious nirjara brings a measure of release for the bonded soul. Nonetheless, the soul's journey to liberation is determined almost entirely by the choices it makes when embodied in human form. Human beings are endowed with a moral conscience and an ability to act autonomously, two of the most important pointers towards moksha. There are therefore infinite possibilities for human beings to make spiritual progress and, in a few cases, manage to break free of the karmic cycle. But along with these possibilities come the dangers of regression. It is easy for human beings to use their intellectual powers unwisely, to deflect their capacity for reason towards negative and destructive goals, or to become consumed with worldly or material concerns that suppress the soul within.

Those who use the power of their intelligence to act cruelly (and worse still justify this on ideological or pseudo-moral grounds) are likely to reincarnate in a lower form, so that they lose their power of reasoning and can be cut off for aeons from any spiritual consciousness. A 'lower form of life' can mean a microbe or an insect, a sub-atomic particle or, at worst, a naraki, or hell-being. In such cases, the cruelty and violence of a previous lifetime is quite literally directed inwards. A passive and supine figure, the naraki experiences the pain and suffering that it inflicted in previous human existences. An accumulation of inauspicious karma, in one or several lives, can lead to rebirth as a hell-being, but escape from naraki status is more difficult. The capacities for action are limited and so the hell-being is largely dependent on the natural, passive form of nirjara, as, for opposite reasons, is the deva. Therefore, the goal of practising Jains is to retain a human incarnation and, if the opportunity to become an ascetic is not possible in this lifetime, to seek an auspicious rebirth in which it is possible. Living within Jain principles, in particular the Five Vows, will increase the probability of an auspicious rebirth. Such possibilities are determined by the build-up of non-destructive karma and the absence of destructive karma. Needless to say, the ascetic who achieves liberation has succeeded in freeing himself from all karmic influences, positive or negative.

7 *Nama* – Birth and Physique Determining karma

This karma determines the destiny (gati) of the re-embodied soul, or jiva: as a human (manushya), a hell-being (naraki), within the plant and animal kingdoms (tiryancha) or as a deva, a 'shining' spiritual being that is still an embodied soul. Nama also defines the species or type of organism into which the soul is embodied. The gati is crucial for the soul's spiritual journey, determining the immediate, and sometimes long-term, prospects for progress.

8 *Gotra* – Status Determining karma

Status determining karma determines the social status of a human incarnation. It does not follow from this that reincarnation need be seen as a form of cosmic social climbing. In its pure form, Jainism eschews caste divisions. The ascetic, who is the spiritual role model for all Jains, lives outside the conventional social framework, with the ambitions, obligations and preoccupations that go with it. The concept of the liberated soul goes further, being placed beyond gender as well as caste or class – 'it', rather than 'he' or 'she'. In keeping with these principles, ascetics are recruited from both sexes, all social backgrounds and even all ages, youth and age being no more a barrier to spiritual awakening than social status. Nonetheless, in practice most Jains who contemplate a spiritual life are relatively privileged and well-educated, with the time, the intellectual resources to consider a radical change in their way of life. The last two Tirthankaras, Parshva and Mahavira, were born into high castes and renounced privilege for self-sacrifice in the pursuit of truth, as did the Buddha who emerged from a parallel tradition of Indian spirituality. Jains regard their dharma as preceding caste distinctions, because it is pre-Vedic, but it is safe to assume that the pre-historic path finders were also from privileged groups, at least in terms of education or scholarship.

Social status, therefore, can still play a powerful role in determining spiritual progress, even in an egalitarian tradition like Jainism. But like the privilege of human incarnation, high social status brings with it ethical duties, and the dangers of regression to a lower plane of consciousness are very high. A 'high' birth is auspicious, but from the karmic point of view it is akin to a double-edged sword. This is because, like superior intelligence or knowledge, a privileged background brings with it responsibilities of a spiritual nature, along with social obligations to fellow human beings and creatures. At the same time, an auspicious birth presents the greatest opportunities, and temptations, to abuse power and to use superior knowledge to deceive or oppress. Such a birth, therefore, demands of favoured individuals that they take especial care to practice samvara, or self-restraint, the mechanism by which karma is reduced. Auspicious birth brings with it crucial opportunities for spiritual growth. But it also brings the greatest possibilities for spiritual confusion, because it presents the widest range of superficial choices and the greatest potential for cruelty, venality and exploitation of others. Although Jainism is at one level hierarchical in its approach to karma, it is also egalitarian because an auspicious birth demands more self-restraint and higher degrees of renunciation, as well as presenting more possibilities for karmic misadventure.

In a sense, it is probably misleading to speak of favoured individuals or, for that matter, auspicious birth. Jainism has a strong spiritual work ethic, despite its ultimate goal of non-action. In keeping with the principle of karmic reward, a rebirth in positive circumstances is based on spiritual endeavour in previous lives, which has led to the loss of negative karma and the accumulation of positive karma. The 'fruition' and falling-off of previous karmas assists the soul's journey, but this process is impeded by destructive actions or thoughts. Karmic particles combine to form

a subtle body, known as *karmana sarira*, which encases the jiva
and grows or shrinks over an earthly lifetime. When the earthly
body dies, the karmana sarira survives and adapts itself to the next
incarnation, as a reminder of past lives. Such lives are not, in the
vast majority of cases, consciously recalled. They are, nonetheless,
part of an individual's spiritual inheritance, linking him or her with
other circumstances and other beings.

Even by the standards of Indic traditions, the Jain view of
karma is rigorous and exacting. To the modern and
especially Western mind, it can seem almost impossibly harsh,
uncompromising and other-worldly. What then, does it have to
offer to Western men and women, trying to make sense of the
spiritual, social and ecological problems that affect us,
individually and collectively? Can Jain karma, and the seemingly
archaic cosmology that goes with it, help us make sense of
our world?

In approaching these questions, it is worth noting the areas of
overlap between the Jain view of karma and ethical approaches
more familiar from a Western perspective. In the Judaeo-Christian
tradition, sin is often presented as an evil that defiles the soul, by
which the 'sinners' are oppressed at least as much as their victims.
Accordingly, repentance is likened to a cleansing process, by
which the soul is purified. In Jainism, the shedding of karma is
seen equally in terms of purification, in which the soul throws off
contaminating matter and becomes pure and 'luminous', and
thus able to realise its true identity. Moksha is a reawakening
into a state of pure consciousness. It is therefore a state of grace.
In Jainism, as in the West's Christian, Jewish and Classical
inheritance, the individual is the starting point as well as the final

point of reference. The individual in the Western tradition is created in the divine image and works for reconciliation with the divine. In Jainism, the individual aims to become divine, in achieving immortality and omniscience. In the Western tradition, the material world is often depicted as a place of suffering and darkness, and those who inhabit it are seen as 'fallen', but with the possibility of salvation through faith and good works. In Jainism, worldly existence is part of samsara. It is a lesser existence and the incarnated soul is corrupted and defiled – fallen into karma – with the possibility of escape through good works and pure thoughts. In its emphasis on individual salvation, Jainism is radically different from other Indic traditions, but finds common ground with the mentality of the West and so closes a spiritual divide.

Viewed in this light, the Jain view of karma is far from deterministic and is not the set of rigid formulae that it appears to the initial inquirer. Instead, it is an almost infinitely flexible system. Quite unlike most interpretations of karma, it is based on free will and individual choice, genuine choice, as opposed to the illusory choices currently offered by consumerism and politics. Yet the Jain interpretation of the individual is broader than the conventional Western view. Individuality is rooted in the *jiva*, which passes through many cycles of mundane existence, rather than narrowly confined to one lifetime and a single set of experiences. The Jain 'individual' therefore spans many lifetimes and many varieties of living organism. Karma is also a wider concept than sin, because it includes all worldly activities, good and evil, creative and destructive. Karma is action, and so in this respect it is (to use a fashionable Western phrase) 'non-judgemental'. It is not really *about* judgement at all, but the spiritual journey of the individual and the eventual discovery of the true self.

The spiritual journey, or hero's journey, has been a powerful theme of Western literature and philosophy since Homeric Greece. In the Western tradition, the spiritual development of individuals takes place over one lifetime. During that lifetime, they might, on more than one occasion, 'reinvent' themselves, radically changing their opinions about politics and spirituality, or altering their priorities, goals and behaviour towards others. Sometimes, these changes take place suddenly, but more often they are subtle changes, moulded by experience. It is the same in Jainism, except that the journey is that of the individual soul through many versions of existence, human and non-human. And whereas in the West the individual is judged and measured against a divine or secular ideal, in Jainism individuals take control of their own salvation. There is no First Cause and no collective judgement, only the chance to work towards release from karma. Thus, despite its many strictures and the puritanism of its ascetics, Jainism is not about harsh moral judgement but about providing an ethical framework for self-realisation. Looked at in this way, the Jain conception of karma can be seen as a broad and accommodating doctrine, taking account of the immense variety of life and experience and the hidden or subtle points of connection between all living systems, finding complexity in the most apparently primitive and simplicity in the most seemingly intricate. It is well suited, therefore, to our present age of dissolving boundaries, in which we are more aware than ever of complexity and difference, but at the same time searching harder for reconciliation and wholeness.

Jainism can seem to outsiders to be a legalistic tradition,

obsessed with rules and regulations. This response is especially prevalent in a Western world that it obsessed with the dismantling of rules, the deregulation of every aspect of life. The doctrine of karma refutes this interpretation, because it shows that Jainism is about personal spiritual responsibility and self-realisation: the discovery of the true self by moving beyond superficial desire. But Jainism can also seem to be a religion of extreme self-denial and, in the case of its ascetics, self-mortification. Again, this is especially true of the West, where in its post-Christian (some would say 'post-everything') phase hedonism has become a substitute for religion and asceticism is dismissed as repressive or neurotic. The Jain view of karma once again gives the lie to this simplistic interpretation, which is based on the outward manifestations of Jainism – strict diets, naked or white-clad ascetics – rather than the quiet devotional practice of most Jains and the beliefs that inspire them. For the avoidance of karma is about moderation of behaviour, the reduction of all acts that have impact on others. This takes place first by restriction only to benevolent acts, then to the pursuit of a contemplative inner life, through which the true self may be revealed. In this context, Jain ascetics can be seen as extreme moderates, men and women who have taken the principle of restraint to its logical conclusion and reduced to the barest minimum their social impact and their ecological footprints. As such, they have come as near as is humanly possible to purging themselves of karmic matter.

The Jain view of karma reaches well beyond overt actions. It encompasses thoughts, which are themselves classified as actions, and the entire organisation of the mind. For Jains recognise that the way in which thoughts are projected affects the way they take life as concrete acts. Thus a benevolent thought, or an ideal, becomes destructive when it is corrupted by fanaticism and inflexibility. The minimising of destructive passion is therefore as much a part of the Jain path to release from karma as the reduction of ecological impact. Passions, or kasaya, are one of the main influences on karmic development and bhava karma, the karma based on deliberate choice, is compounded by passions, especially fanatical zeal, which gives rise to mohaniya, the karma of delusion which is the most destructive karma of all.

For Western society, this is perhaps the most powerful message of the Jain view of karma. As we lose our sense of certainty about the merits of our form of civilisation, a certainty that was itself often deluded and karmic, we are paradoxically more rather than less prone to fanaticism. The rise of the 'Single Issue Fanatic', who 'concentrates on doing us good, by *his* definition of *our* good' has been a clearly observable feature of our political and social landscape for a generation.[6] Many of the single issues in question are benign in themselves and in keeping with the spirit of Jainism, notably animal rights, minority rights, concern for the environment and opposition to war and the increasingly monstrous, homogenising tyranny of multination corporations. Yet in karmic terms, as well as in terms of the effect on human, life, there is almost nothing worse than idealism corrupted by the deluded conviction of certainty.

Mohiyana taints idealism and turns it into a hunger for power and domination, making idealists themselves acquire the worst characteristics of their opponents. We are reminded of this truth by the experience of twentieth century totalitarianism, by the more recent rise of fundamentalism in various religious traditions and, of

NB also Revolutions eg French + Russian

greatest relevance in the context of Jain values, the transformation of benevolent campaigners into intolerant zealots, rigid and fanatical at best, and at worst totalitarian and violent. Jainism provides a useful reminder to those who work for social and environmental justice that equanimity is a more powerful instrument for social good than the descent into vengeful anger. Even where passionate activists 'win', their victory is a delusion, because its fruits are poisoned by negative karma.

To Jains, emergence from the karmic cycle involves shedding, or stripping away, layers of unwanted and irrelevant matter, the 'stuff' of karma that bonds the soul. Karma is a form of spiritual clutter. Like material clutter, it is accumulated to satisfy deluded desires and does not bring satisfaction, but creates a sense of inner emptiness. The Western way of life is intensely cluttered, with material goods, information and a seemingly endless range of possibilities, many of which lack substance or depth. Quite apart from the impact of material accumulation on the planet, its pursuit has singularly failed to provide human beings with even basic contentment, let alone happiness. Similarly, the age of mass media has if anything increased the sum total of human ignorance rather than knowledge, whilst the cargo cult of consumer choice has produced confusion and a sense of captivity rather than freedom. The Jain view of karma can guide us, intellectually and spiritually, as we seek to de-clutter our civilisation in keeping with ecological imperatives, chief amongst which must be survival. The purification of the mind is balanced by Jainism's doctrine of aparigraha, the limiting of possessions or 'to each according to need'. Aparigraha is the first of what we shall call the Three A's of Jainism, which have particular relevance to the West. The others, which will be considered in Chapters Six and Seven, are *Anekantvada*, the doctrine of many-sidedness and Ahimsa, non-injury, the foundation stone of the Jain path. Aparigraha is also one of the Five Vows, on which Jainism is lived out in practice. It is to this ethos of voluntary simplicity that the Jain view of karma should take us.

CHAPTER FIVE

LEARNING TO LIVE LIGHTLY: JAINISM'S ECOLOGICAL VISION

*Abstinence from violence, falsehood, stealing, carnality
and possessiveness – these are the vows*
TATTVARTHA SUTRA

Viewed superficially, Jainism's Five Vows (*vratas*), with the exception of the ban on stealing, can look thoroughly negative and off-putting. A hedonistic society does not like prohibitions, and those who live in it tend to equate self-fulfilment, 'being oneself', with the removal of restraint. This is the case even with those thoughtful men and women who oppose materialism and struggle against it. All too often, the struggle itself becomes a form of attachment, their opposition a form of self-righteousness and sometimes falsehood. Jainism's 'don'ts' often fail to attract the spiritual shopper. That, in itself, is not a problem for Jains, because they do not regard their dharma as a saleable commodity, are uninterested in making it fashionable, for fashion's sake, and do not seek to convert, but to exercise subtle influence. In this approach, Jainism differs markedly from the style and methods associated with the 'New Age'. The varied cluster of movements that work under that umbrella appeal to a widespread hunger for spiritual truth and are often sources of knowledge and insight for the West. Yet unlike an ancient philosophy such as Jainism, such movements project outwards rather than cultivating the inward way. Inevitably, they are as much a part of the consumer society as a reaction against it.

Jainism, unlike much of the 'New Age', does not campaign overtly against consumerism or the cult of continuous economic growth. Nor do Jains, collectively, identify themselves with political movements that directly challenge materialistic society, although Jains might choose to do so as individuals. This apparent lack of engagement, indeed conservatism, can give the impression that Jainism is a quietist faith. However this misses a crucial point about Jain doctrine, and about the way that Jains choose to live in the world. Both for philosophical and pragmatic reasons, Jainism does not make direct challenges to existing authority structures and prevailing patterns of thought. At the philosophical level, such challenges contain the dangers of attachment, possessiveness and worldliness. In particular of accumulation of *mohaniya*, the deluding karma that becomes a powerful impediment to spiritual progress. At the pragmatic level, the accumulated wisdom of thousands of years has taught Jains that the survival and effectiveness of their world view is best ensured by outward conformity and subtle methods of influencing others, so that Jain ideas do not spread but percolate gradually through the wider society.

These two facets, philosophical and pragmatic, can be seen to overlap when we consider the tendency of protest movements to be co-opted by the society and values they challenge, and to adopt their most extreme characteristics. The example of Communism in the Soviet Union and Eastern Europe springs readily to mind, for not only did that social experiment quickly slide into bureaucratic totalitarian terror, but it produced a society more radically unequal than that which it replaced. Or, to take an apparently very different example, the evangelical Protestantism of North America, now associated principally with a 'religious right' based on retrenchment and extreme social conservatism, was less than a century ago a force associated with rural populism and urban social reform. In the West today, many of us are searching for approaches to political organisation and spiritual organisation. Jains have long been aware, through both experience and intuition, of the dangers associated with confrontation and the imposition of ideologies, dangers both for society and for the individual, and alike at spiritual and material levels. Once again, this should not be taken to mean that Jainism is quietist, or that it is wholly conservative. Its critique is more radical than that of many who identify as such, for it contends that truth lies beyond either/or choices, beyond absolutes. True knowledge is absorbed slowly, through the ways we organise our outer and inner lives. False knowledge, by contrast, is that which is grasped, hung on to and imposed on others.

As is usual with Jainism, we must draw a distinction – but not an either/or division – between the outward appearance and the inward reality. The outward appearance of quiet conformity conceals, from the Western observer, an alternative view of reality. According to the Jain world view, the goals worth striving for are spiritual rather than material, in which enlightenment is pursued patiently through many lifetimes, in which withdrawal from the world is the eventual goal, yet individual acts of compassion matter more than abstract ideals of perfection, which are impossible to achieve in a world infused with karma. This philosophy is, by any standards, a radical critique of materialism and consumerism, and the values and practices associated with them. Its power, however, lies in its indirectness, its oblique rather than overt challenge. We can see it, therefore, as an equal critique of conventional forms of opposition, which confront one absolutist assumption with another and use weapons, whether verbal or physical, to state their case.

The outward conformity is therefore just as much a part of the Jains' alternative vision of reality as the rejection of material goals. Whilst the ultimate aim is withdrawal from the world and its concerns, the ascetic's goal, it is also possible for the lay man or woman to live satisfactorily in the world and act as an unobtrusive force for good. By doing this, the lay Jain accumulates positive karma, which whilst imperfect points him or her towards enlightenment – in this incarnation or more probably the next one. But the lay Jains, by living consciously and successfully in the world, also exercise a profound spiritual power. For their Jain values are reflected in their daily lives and actions, less dramatically than in the case of ascetics, but in ways that are more likely to have an impact on the wider community, both in practical ways and in gradually changing hearts and minds. The successful lay Jain is therefore very likely to be a philanthropist and very unlikely to be a rebel. The philanthropy is not – as some left-wing activists might claim – a means of shoring up privilege or cushioning inequality. It is part of his spiritual journey as an individual, and it is also a way of introducing Jain practice and values to a sceptical world.

In assessing the Jain vows, the same distinction should be drawn between what is obvious and what is beneath the surface.

The study of Jainism can seem at times like a process of spiritual excavation, in which the researcher must dig ever more deeply, but always with extreme care, meeting all obstacles with gentleness and assuming an almost eternal patience. For like an archaeological site, Jain philosophy reveals itself slowly, not always willingly, and seekers of insight must, like archaeologists, expect to revise their assumptions and keep their minds open or risk being caught out. But Jainism is more than an archaeological site. It is a living tradition, which encompasses some of the most ancient and the most modern aspects of human thought. As well as helping to explain our past, it can contribute directly to our understanding of the present and future, whether we are Jains or not. The archaeologist is often faced with physical or climatic barriers.

Likewise, the spiritual inquirer often faces the barrier of silence when attempting to come to terms with Jain doctrines. This is especially true if he or she comes from the Western cultural tradition. The reason for this is not anti-Western bias among the Jains. Far from it, for as we have already noted, there are Jain ideas about the centrality of the individual that correspond with Western ideas in a creative and positive way. Instead, it is traditional Western methods of inquiry that are misleading and which create intellectual – and spiritual – barriers. The adversarial method, based on direct questioning, confrontation and the imposition of labels is quite ineffectual when it comes to a holistic philosophy such as Jainism. Whereas the Western seeker tends to expect 'answers', Jainism merely raises further questions. Where the Westerner expects clear positions, Jainism offers overlaps and shades of meaning. Jains think of circles, spirals and abstract shapes, whilst the Western mindset tends towards squares and straight lines. The Western mentality is focussed on immediately achievable goals, whether of personal salvation or material satisfaction. Jains, by contrast, think in terms of cycles, whether at the level of the individual – the samsaric cycle of birth, death and rebirth – or at universal level, with the utsarpini and avasarpini, the upward and downward movements of the cosmic wheel over countless thousands of years. The discrepancy between the adversarial and the multi-layered, the short term and the long term, has affected Western understanding of other Eastern paths, along with the philosophies of indigenous peoples such as Native Americans and an increased scientific emphasis on interconnectedness, as opposed to separation. In our awareness of these developments, it has proved both possible and necessary to uncover the suppressed holistic dimensions of Western thought, and we should do the same if we are to learn more about, or indeed learn from, the Jain dharma.

With this in mind, we can look at the Five Vows of Jainism through a more optimistic lens. For just as Jain communities can outwardly conform to materialistic ways, yet privately pursue entirely contrasting aims, so their structures of prohibition can conceal a sense of ultimate freedom. The method of both/and, rather than either/or, is key to an understanding of Jainism, and of the Five Vows or vratas that are central to the way it is lived out. As a series of 'don'ts', the vratas can give the impression that Jain philosophy is based on constraint and prohibition, and so is ultimately life-denying. This is the conclusion that many Western observers have come to, from Christian missionaries to secular rationalists who observe the extreme behaviour of ascetics, or as in the famous bird hospitals of Ahmedabad, the effects of ahimsa carried to its logical conclusion. Similar conclusions have been drawn by Indians, including some Jains themselves: Bhagwan Shree Rajneesh, for example, came from a Jain family, but abandoned Jainism because he considered it too puritanical for the modern world. Yet to dismiss either ascetic or lay Jainism as life-denying is to fail to grasp the Jain concept of life, which is realised in full by liberation from samsara. That which seems life-denying to the outsider, the Jain ascetic experiences as working towards the elimination of karma, and so realising his or her true self and experiencing life at its fullest. The ascetic aims to practise the vows in as absolute and literal a way as possible. They are the *mahavratas*, the Greater Vows, which mark ascetics off from the majority and point them towards moksha.

To become an ascetic, or to be reborn as one, is an important goal for practising Jains. Most do not expect to attain this straight away, and so do their best to live out Jain principles in a positive way so that they shed as much malign karma as possible and accumulate only benign karma. They do not hope to free themselves completely, but to build up credits for an auspicious rebirth. Lay Jains therefore live by the *anuvratas*, the Lesser Vows, the same five negatives as the ascetics. The aim of these 'negatives' is less to constrain and forbid and more to free the lay Jain from the possibility of harm or self-harm, from the possibility of hurting others and of inflicting spiritual damage on him or herself. More important even than that, they aim to set lay Jains free from the destructive, karmic energies associated with passion and attachment. These, after all, give rise to a vicious circle of confrontation, ranging from war over territories and resources to emotional and physical abuse, encompassing prejudice and discrimination, and finding its ultimate expression in the rape of the Earth. The Jain dharma recognises that all these negative areas of human existence are intimately linked, as are their positive counterparts, such as friendship and love, creativity and reason, which form virtuous circles, karmic but benign. Negative thoughts and acts of oppression, whether 'political' or 'personal', are part of a continuum. They connect with each other, rather than falling conveniently into discrete compartments.

Viewed from this perspective, the negativity of the vratas becomes liberating. The vows allow the practising Jain to live in the world but maintain a sense of proportion about worldly priorities. The values associated with the spiritual path hold up a critical mirror to those of the material world. They represent a higher level of consciousness than the mundane and provide an alternative set of aspirations, which are of ultimate importance, whereas materialistic aims are only short-term. The Jain layperson is thereby psychologically and spiritually equipped to survive and prosper at the mundane level, whilst pursuing parallel spiritual objectives that have lasting value. He or she becomes aware that competition and accumulation, and all the struggles of the worldly plane, are of superficial significance and have no ultimate meaning. The *vratas* give Jains the chance to avoid the attachments, emotional and material, that result in accumulation of destructive karma, and all the accompanying bitterness, disappointment and pain.

Ascetics are empowered by the Five Vows towards radical withdrawal from the world. Lay Jains, in turn, are freed from spiritually distracting anxiety and stress by the pursuit of higher,

non-material ambitions. At the same time, they are given a framework that enables them to balance their materialistic impulses and
needs with the requirements of the spiritual path. Acceptance of the
vratas is a process of learning to live with minimal attachments, be
they to material possessions (and by extension territories or states),
ideas and beliefs, the desire to 'win' at any price, be it in argument
or in the commercial sphere. Attachment to people, being a source
of karma, is problematic as well. Although it is overwhelmingly a
source of positive karma, it can also mutate very easily into possessive entanglements, in which commitment to others gives way
to narrow egoism. The fact that Jains regard human ties as
potentially dangerous attachments is grist to those who argue that
theirs is a pessimistic and negative philosophy. But they forget that
the highest forms of love, and friendship, and the ones which
survive the best, are those which are offered without selfish strings
attached, without jealousy or expectations that are unrealistic and
unjust. In the Jain approach, there is an awareness of emotional
complexities, of the pitfalls of selfish attachments and the value of
unconditional love – for those we know and care for, and beyond
that for all forms of life.

The Jain ideal of ahimsa encompasses unconditional love, as
well as a more abstract affinity with all other forms of life. This
affinity is not the same as the 'oneness' emphasised by Vedanta and
other Hindu schools that have become popular in the West, nor the
absence of individuation that is the Buddhist ideal. Jains perceive
each life form as existing in its own right, with its own innate
value, yet connected to every other living organism by the
experience of living and the possession of a soul. The ascetic aims
to withdraw from human attachments altogether, seeing them as

worldly and so impeding spiritual progression. Even the order of ascetics becomes an attachment, and the monk or nun cultivates total detachment, that lofty equanimity which Jains regard as the key to enlightenment. Lay Jains, however, are enjoined to manage their human relationships in the same way that they organise the rest of their lives on the material plane. This involves minimising harm to others, exercising compassion and care at all times, awareness of complexity (and simplicity), and the pursuit of truths, however subtle and elusive they prove to be. Within lay Jain communities, there is a powerful commitment to 'family values' expressed in strong ties to the extended as well as the nuclear family. There is also a projection of compassion outwards, through an emphasis on public works, philanthropy, a bias towards 'caring' professions such as medicine and a respect for scientific research when it improves the lot of humanity and the planet.

Rather than being seen as prohibitions, the Five Vows are more constructively viewed as parameters, or as broad brushstrokes, leaving a canvas that can stay plain or be filled with shapes, colours and forms of the individual's choosing. The vratas provide what political scientists in the West have termed 'negative freedom', clear boundaries that exist to ensure the survival of liberty rather than rein it in. Their terse, minimalist framework reminds us, in an age of noisy demands and over-regulation, of the value of what remains unsaid over what is explicitly stated. That distinction is increasingly regarded, in the West, as one of the chief components of 'emotional intelligence', a concept that would perhaps have appealed to Mahavira. Each negative injunction conceals an almost infinite range of positive possibilities. Each removal of freedom provides a wealth of opportunity for other freedoms to emerge. To the Western spiritual seeker, the Five Vows have the virtue of being baldly and unequivocally stated, with little apparent room for argument or demur.

Yet as usual with Jainism, simplicity and complexity interact. The vratas are simple, and despite their initially forbidding appearance are comparatively easy to obey. And yet each of them has multiple meanings, or to return to our archaeological metaphor, multiple layers of meaning which we can gradually attempt to unearth. Violence – himsa – means far more than acts of force, or overt cruelty. It exists at the intellectual and even spiritual levels as well, with the assumption of absolute truth and the consequent urge to impose one-sided arguments on others. It exists in the desire to dominate, whether that means 'conquering' instead of working with the grain of nature, the emotional oppression of those close to us, or the forms of philanthropy and social activism that assume a patronising form and so become a form of self-centred attachment. Since, according to Jain practice, the intention is at least as important as the outcome, it follows that acts of superficial benevolence will generate destructive karma, when the true motive behind them is self-promotion or hunger for power. This corresponds well with human experience, because attempts at intervention or reform always turn out to be destructive when the motive behind them is corrupt. The opinionated 'do-gooder' and the activist who loves humanity but shows contempt for real human beings are alive in our consciousness as stereotypes, but like most of these they reveal in simple form certain underlying truths. Jainism is alive to these truths and accepts that corrupted benevolence can be just as great a form of himsa as the unapologetic forms of domination, that emotional cruelty is as destructive as physical violence.

The emergence of twentieth century totalitarianisms of 'left' and 'right' – and the symbiotic relationship between them – is of little surprise to those who understand the Jain view of himsa. False consciousness produces the greatest violence of all, because it derives from mohaniya, the karma of self-delusion. Abstention from violence therefore requires the avoidance of self-delusion. It is a continuous intellectual challenge as much as it is a moral and political stance or an injunction for right living.

Similar analyses may be brought to bear on the other four injunctions. The strictures against falsehood, stealing, carnality and possessiveness are just as straightforward, and just as multi-faceted, as the prohibition on violence. 'Falsehood', for instance, covers self-delusion equally if not more than attempts to deceive others. We have all experienced the effects of megalomaniac polit-ical leaders who believe their own lies and draw their populations into war or economic collapse. Even the highest forms of truth can turn into falsehoods when they are applied in rigid, one-sided ways and interpreted so literally that they lose their inner meaning. This is how spiritual insights turn into fundamentalist shibboleths and programmes for social reform become dogmatic and inhumane. Jains also cite 'despicable comments' intended to discredit or wound others as falsehoods, even if their basis is true. For the value of this truth is undermined by the harm created by its expression and the hurtful intention behind that utterance. In other words, the Jain view of truth includes a form of cosmic libel law in which denunciations leading to mental or physical violence are regarded as falsehoods whether their superficial 'truth' can be proved or not. Jainism regards truth as a precious and rare quality, of eternal strength and yet eternally vulnerable to human manipulation and distortion. The abuse of truth, or the use of it as a weapon, makes it corrupt and worldly, and so it becomes a falsehood.

Likewise 'stealing' in Jain ethics does not simply mean taking what does not belong to you, in legal and moral terms. It is also defined as 'taking anything that is not given'. For the ascetic, that is to be interpreted in literal terms. Ascetics work towards a situation in which they possess nothing except that which is the common property of all human beings, or even all creatures. The *Tattvartha Sutra* cites the open road as an example of common property and enjoins Jain ascetics not to take 'even a blade of grass' that has not been offered. Ascetics operate on a different level of consciousness as well as practice. For lay Jains, the concept of asteya, abstention from stealing, is linked intimately to the ideal of minimising possessions, or aspiring to values beyond the material. Benefiting materially from the misfortunes of others, earning excessive profits by exploitation and meanness, or the frivolous and unconstructive use of wealth all fall within the Jain definition of stealing. As can be expected, the motive is important. If the legal acquisition of possessions causes harm – direct or indirect – or the 'contamination of the mind', then it is counted as an act of theft. We shall consider later Jain sexual morality and its relevance, or otherwise, for the West. However it is worth noting here that 'carnality' means much more than mere sexual promiscuity. It means lack of respect for others, the reduction of other human beings (of either sex) to the level of objects to be possessed and conquered, and the 'conduct-deluding karma' associated with lust, which is the polar opposite of love.

It has become a convention amongst those who write about Jainism, be they Jain or non-Jain, to take the ideal of ahimsa as a starting and finishing point, the 'Alpha and Omega' of this ancient doctrine. This is correct, of course, because without non-violence, none of the other four vows can be lived out. Or, as Umasvati explains in his commentary on the seventh chapter of the *Tattvartha Sutra*:

> Non-violence is mentioned first, because it is the principal vow, the basis of all other vows. In the same way that a fence is meant to protect a field the last four vows are meant to protect the primary vow of non-violence.

The primacy of non-violence in Jain philosophy is incontrovertible, and the ideal of ahimsa is its main gift to the wider world. Ahimsa is the primary vow and the point at which all the vratas connect with each other. Falsehood, stealing, carnality and possessiveness are all sources of himsa, violence or harm, for all those affected by them, perpetrators as well as victims. We can therefore, if we find it helpful, see the vratas less as a series of injunctions, separate yet philosophically linked, and more as different expressions of the same truth. When viewed in this way, each vrata becomes a point of entry for those seeking enlightenment. At the same time, each of the vows is dependent on each of the others to form part of a coherent doctrine or practice. This combination of individual value and interdependence symbolises Jainism.

Similarly, the vows reflect the coexistence of complexity and deep simplicity within the Jain dharma. For ascetics, they present a series of complex problems in living, for the achievement of total withdrawal is nothing if not complicated! Yet the complex and apparently arcane rules that they must obey produce lives that are free from material and emotional clutter. For lay Jains, the Five Vows provide an eminently practical code of conduct for life in the material realm, whereby they can function effectively within it, but at the same time protect themselves against its negative influences. They are guidelines for a balanced way of living that reduces or minimises harm, and combines a large degree of freedom of action with the possibility of ethical choice: the Three Jewels of 'Right Faith, Right Conduct and Right Livelihood'. Under the ascetic regime, Jainism's vows are to be literally interpreted and applied. For lay people, they may be interpreted flexibly, not on a pick and choose basis, but adapted to circumstance and controlled by individual conscience or judgement rather than by priestly hierarchy or threat of divine retribution. Thus it is not always true that Jainism is about 'shades of grey' instead of 'black and white'. Subtle as it is, it encompasses both. Truth is absolute as much as it is relative, as simple as it is complicated, as naïve as it is nuanced.

Ahimsa is the primary and the ultimate Jain principle, the first and most encompassing of the vows. But because the vows are interconnected, the primary vow is not the only point of entry to the Jain world view. For the Western inquirer, the most relevant starting point could well be the doctrine and vow of non-possessiveness, or aparigraha. To ascetics, needless to say, this means the literal abandonment of worldly goods. To the lay man or woman, it means the minimisation of possessions to those which are necessary and useful. It means learning to live lightly and breaking the addiction to materialism and consumption. Violence and possessiveness, the first and fifth prohibitions of the vratas, are also the most directly connected. Possessiveness is a form of violence, at both social and psychic levels. Violence in all its forms originates in the desire to possess, dominate and control. Possessiveness limits consciousness and blunts awareness, whether it involves consolidating existing possessions or expanding to acquire ever more. And yet only ascetic Jains seek to eschew possessions altogether. Lay men and women have duties, to their families, their friends and to the wider community, that make total renunciation impossible. If all Jains became ascetics, the Jain population would disappear and with it many ideas that have universal validity.

It follows that the lay Jain who makes a positive contribution to society, and who uses his or her wealth for the public good, is as valuable to Jainism as the wandering monk or nun who refuses to possess anything. Such a lay person is a repository of Jain ideals and ensures the survival of Jainism, both as an ethical force and as a way of life. The dignified and self-restrained behaviour of lay Jains has won the respect, over the centuries, of people of all other faiths as well as non-theistic humanists. For the outsider, in particular the Western outsider, they provide an effective and discreet introduction to the Jain path, as opposed to ascetics whose practices can seem baffling and bizarre. Ascetics are not interested in persuasion or propaganda but in the achievement of enlightenment and the realisation of their true selves. The wider Jain community, by contrast, whilst refusing to see itself as 'superior' to others, seeks to set a quiet example of ethical conduct. And central to this is the minimising or wise use of possessions, for attachment is the origin of violence.

In the Western context, Jean-Jacques Rousseau, the eighteenth century philosopher, wrote in his *Second Discourse on Inequality* that the man who first enclosed an area of land, said 'this is mine' and found others simple enough to believe him was the true founder of civil society. He hankered after a 'state of nature' without man-made laws and coined the phrase 'Noble Savage', which is considered patronising and racist by many today, but was radically anti-imperialist two centuries ago. The Swiss-born thinker – who still profoundly influences Western thought – did not regret the foundation of civil society, because he saw it as essential to human development and the human good. His aim, however, was to resolve the tension between the natural and spontaneously creative on the one hand, and the well-ordered life of the community on the other. In the same way, he sought a middle path between the religious and spiritual world view that had prevailed until recently and the materialistic rationalism of the Age of Enlightenment. Whereas the former had become repressive and doctrinally rigid, the latter was already assuming the character of orthodoxy, as blind to questions of faith as faith had been to questions of reason.

At the political level, Rousseau was also searching for a way to reconcile the principles of freedom and equality. These questions predate Rousseau's era, but they have been at the centre of Western thought ever since. In the modern era, much of political and philosophical debate in the West has revolved around these core issues. This is perhaps especially true of the United States. In the mid-nineteenth century, Alexis de Tocqueville wrote of Americans' refusal to choose between freedom and equality, although the two principles were often in conflict. Today's 'culture wars' also centre on the perceived conflicts between faith and reason, free choice and social restraint, equality and liberty. To a greater or lesser extent, these Western controversies are all bound up with the idea of possessiveness. They are familiar to Jains, because their philosophy is essentially about resolving these tensions, transforming them from pairs of opposites, to aspects of an integrated system of values. That is why, in an age of increasing polarisation, engaging with Jain ideas can offer us useful perspectives on reconciling apparent opposites and moving beyond either/or.

In Jainism, the concept of possessiveness encompasses equally the desire for possessions and the ownership of possessions themselves. Desire is, if anything, more important than actual ownership. We have seen that the ownership of possessions is acceptable to the non-ascetic Jain, and indeed they are indispensable to the duties of the householder. For lay people, the critical issues are the use to which possessions are put and the reasons for holding them in the first place. If the motive is to provide for family and friends, as a means towards good works, then possessions are karmically neutral or even benevolent. If the motives are self-centred, then they get in the way of realising the true self. Desire, moreover, is a potent form of attachment that binds the soul, and so interrupts the spiritual journey. It creates false values and priorities, corrupts relationships between human beings. Therefore it generates himsa, and leads to the infliction of harm. The principle of aparigraha, non-possessiveness, requires the minimising of desire to possess as a first step to the minimising of possessions. Aparigraha is therefore about inner transformation before changes in outward behaviour. It is a principally a psychological process and so it is part of the underlying goal of self-realisation through the conquest of egoism, which is in fact the conquest of desire.

The reduction of material desire is a theme that is common to most spiritual paths and very familiar to the Western tradition. St Paul's words to Timothy, popularised in English literature by Chaucer, were *'radix malorum est cupiditas'*. This is often mistranslated as 'money is the root of all evil', but the Latin word 'cupiditas' really means greed or desire for money, or love of money. It is this that violates the Christian principle of love of God, and love of one's fellow human being as the image of God, creating debased, exploitative relationships and corrupted souls. In Hinduism, the ideal of karma yoga, or soul-realisation through work and action, is realised through learning to work for the common good without seeking material reward or social accolade. As Swami Vivekananda tells us:

> He works best who works without any motive, neither for money, nor for fame, nor for anything else; and when a man can do that, he will be a Buddha, and out of him will come the power to work in such a manner as will transform the world. This man represents the very highest ideal of Karma-Yoga.[1]

Vivekananda chooses Gautama Buddha as his example of the ideal of karma yoga. In a sense, he could also have chosen Mahavira, or any of the Tirthankaras, although as we have noted the Jina is one who ultimately transcends even good works. Many Hindus identify Buddhism and Jainism alike as manifestations of karma yoga. This is part of the inclusive approach of Hinduism towards other Indic traditions. It is also true, as far as it goes, because both the Jain and Buddhist paths lead beyond karma yoga, beyond action to a quiet state of peace with the universe. Karma yoga is a practical expression of aparigraha. The man or woman who becomes oblivious to material reward or personal acclaim is capable of casting off negative karma as well as living in balance with him or herself and with nature – living 'sustainably', as we now like to say.

Like Christianity, Jainism requires that we love our neighbour 'as our self', but the idea of 'neighbour' extends more explicitly beyond humanity to encompass all beings. To the Christian, the human being is made in the image of the divine. To the Jain, the universe does have 'begin' or 'end' but is self-perpetuating and self-renewing. Therefore, all living beings within it are connected. They arise from, and return to the same source. More importantly, they all have souls, which – unlike the Christian idea of soul – can transfer from one being to another, from the seemingly primitive to the seemingly advanced, or vice versa. We are back to e.e. cummings and the image of the cockroach who was once a free verse poet. Possessiveness and love of money – cupiditas – hinders the path of Christian salvation. In Jainism, it obstructs the progress of the soul by enmeshing it further in the karmic web.

Renunciation as a symbol of purity is also part of many spiritual traditions besides Jainism. The Hindu *sadhu* renounces possessions in order to achieve union with the divine. In Buddhism, the monk or *bikkhu* leaves behind worldly concerns in order, ultimately, to renounce the self. Christ enjoined his followers to abandon their worldly goods, and all material ties, including family ties and this conception of right livelihood informs monastic communities today. Daoist hermits withdraw from the world and practice austerities to cultivate simple virtue, gain insight into the true workings of nature and perhaps ultimately achieve the highest prize of physical immortality. In shamanic cultures, the holy man or woman often leads an austere lifestyle or undergoes periods of austerity as part of spiritual training. The apprentice shaman, in particular, is likely to be subject to periods of fasting, or celibacy, as a means of learning the spiritual discipline required to use his powers wisely.

Such austerities are quite similar to the tapas practiced periodically by lay Jains, to remind them of the importance of the Five Vows. Austerity is central to the lives of ascetics and sets them apart from their lay brethren. The idea of a man – or equally a woman in some traditions – who cultivates spiritual power through being set apart from his contemporaries is part of many religious systems, whether modern or archaic, universal or indigenous. Jainism, which encompasses the archaic and the highly advanced, sets great store by asceticism as a route towards moksha and as an aid to insight or scholarship. In his pursuit of austerity, Mahavira goes well beyond the 'middle way' laid down by the Buddha. His renunciation, as we have seen, assumes some of the characteristics of self-torture associated with the trainee shaman, including isolation, fasting and altered states of consciousness. This is aparigraha pushed to its logical conclusion, so that it goes beyond renunciation of possessions to renunciation of the whole material plane.

Renunciation, however, is not in itself enough. For Jains, the point of Mahavira's austerities was that they served a larger purpose, namely self-realisation. Had they been undertaken as a means of controlling others, or to inspire fear or even reverence, then they would be worse than worthless. So, in turn, is renunciation for its own sake, as a means of testing oneself, or appearing virtuous. This is where Jain doctrine goes beyond the yoga of action. While it is true that, as in karma yoga, meritorious are part of the process of acquiring merit, in Jainism the process is not an end to itself. Attitude of mind is the starting point, and so a householder of substance who uses that wealth responsibly or creatively is infinitely superior to a false ascetic. For Jains, as in many other spiritual paths (including Christian monasticism), the idea of renunciation is bound up with celibacy or chastity, brahmacharya in Indic cultures. This is of course a vow in its own right, but it is closely connected to the idea of restraint and non-possessiveness. The ascetic is committed to total celibacy, the lay Jain to responsibility in relationships, to trying to avoid those impulses to control and possess that can corrupt and destroy love and friendship. Aparigraha requires the avoidance of sexual promiscuity, not for puritanical reasons, but because it is seen as a variant form of possessiveness. Whilst it is not possession in the sense of clinging, it involves the treatment of the human person as a commodity to be traded and exchanged. The treatment of living beings, endowed with souls, as objects of transient worth is considered spiritually degrading, a form of emotional and psychological himsa.

There is a strong sense in which the Jain critique of promiscuity mirrors modern feminist critiques of 'objectification', although the principles of brahmacharya are of equal relevance to men and women who undertake the Five Vows. It relates closely to the Jain ideal of regarding all living beings with dignity, which informs attitudes to animal welfare and ecology. To treat any being endowed with a soul as an object, to be fleetingly possessed and cast aside, is to show a profound lack of spiritual awareness. Transient possessiveness is a form of attachment and is based on one-sided relationships of exploitation of power, rather than unconditional love and equanimity.

The concept of non-possessiveness is as applicable to relationships between human beings as it is to our attachments towards material goods. It also applies to human relationships with other species, one of the reasons why the exploitation of animals is so disapproved of by Jains. Even seemingly benign forms of exploitation are frowned upon. Jains are aware of some of the problems with the keeping of animals as pets. They are critical, for instance, of the way in which 'owners' (the term itself a giveaway) project human emotions and sentiments onto 'their' animals and so can fail to meet their genuine needs. The widespread redefinition of pets as 'companion animals', with different thought processes from humans, might be more compatible with Jain precepts, if it marks a genuine cultural shift. At the human level, it is a truth now more or less universally acknowledged that possessiveness is the origin of most problems in relationships, personal or social. Much psychological harm is inflicted, for example, by parents who pressurise their children towards superficial 'success' and so measure them by their exam results – and how they 'compare' with others – instead of their moral qualities, wisdom, compassion or worthwhile activity. This can be as dangerous as overt emotional neglect, because it breaks the natural ties of affection and puts in their place what is essentially an exploitative relationship of possession. In this instance, children are not loved, for themselves, but judged like commodities, by criteria of efficiency and performance. Possessiveness and attachment make the relationship of love and trust mutate into a material relationship, built on measurement and result.

Jains understand karma as that which obstructs or obscures true understanding, and which converts the spiritual into the material. Possessiveness distorts relationships in exactly the same way, reducing them to the level of material transactions or attachment without feeling or understanding. Therefore, the reduction of possessiveness is part of a wider process of reducing karmic influences and realising the spiritual self. Possessiveness distorts direct relationships between human beings, be they parents and children, friends, employers and workers, men and women, religious authorities and lay people. It has similar effects on the relationship between the human and animal world, or two-leggeds and four-leggeds, to use an appealing Native American term that Jains would readily understand. The idea of possessiveness, of human ownership of the four-legged world, leads to animals being exploited as throwaway resources to be consumed or experimented upon for human convenience. This leads us, quite logically, towards the concentration camp conditions of factory farms and vivisection laboratories. Jainism's critique of this form of domination and possession is uncomfortable for many Westerners, because it links these forms of animal abuse with other forms of domination and cruelty.

The distortions created by possessiveness find their clearest expression, perhaps, in humanity's relationship with the Earth, and in the belief of modern Western humanity, in particular, that the natural world is a limitless resource to be controlled and exploited, rather than something that we are part of and with which we need to co-operate to survive. The mounting ecological crisis, and the dehumanised, denatured nightmare of so much of urban life, are products of this misconception about our relationship with the rest of nature, a misconception born out of possessiveness.

Likewise, bellicose nationalism is a distortion of basic and natural impulses based on cultural and linguistic ties, loyalty to people and places, and a spiritual affinity with the local environment, be it the mountains and forests that inspire works of art and romantic verse, or vast plains that afford space and freedom. Such feelings need not imply aggressive attachment or an illusion of superiority over other peoples and cultures and a wish to conquer or enslave them. But nationalism, as a form of possessiveness, turns a simple love of 'country' or region into an ideology of economic competition and physical aggression, which finds its logical expressions in colonialism and war. Negative karma, therefore, has direct material consequences for humans, and our world, as well as imposing spiritual burdens on us. False understanding leads to physical destruction along with psychic disturbance and Jainism does not distinguish the two processes. Possessiveness is false understanding writ large. Its reduction is necessary to increase clarity of perception. Its abolition is necessary for total enlightenment.

Looked at in this way, Jain doctrine can be seen to resemble the certain aspects of the Western ideologies of socialism and anarchism, expressed in their purest forms. For like Jains, ethical socialists and non-violent anarchists view possessiveness as the origin of discord between human beings, including inequality. Those of 'green' sensibility extend this analysis to the relationship between humanity and nature. False understanding, in Marxist language 'false consciousness', creates and perpetuates exploitative relationships, but through clarity of vision (or correct 'analysis') society can be transformed from its roots. The parallel between this feature of Jainism and the politics of the radical left is attractive in many ways. It links an ancient doctrine with modern ideals and connects what is often seen as a non-engaged philosophy with practical programmes for social change. At the same time, it lends a spiritual authority to radical political demands. Therefore it is tempting to place Jainism under the radical umbrella, in a manner akin to 'engaged Buddhism' or Liberation Theology within the Christian tradition. There is an element of truth in this view, given that Jainism is radical in the true sense of examining problems from their roots upwards, whether those problems are social or spiritual. However it is very far from the whole truth. Jainism, after all, balances radicalism with conservatism, again in the original sense, for it values continuity as much as change, stability as much as flux, the eternal as much as the impermanent. This approach is one of the ways in which Jain doctrines differ from those of the Buddhists, who believe in permanent change as the underlying principle of the universe. Unlike political ideologies, Jainism provides ethical guidelines for living, as expressed in the five vratas, but its principal aim is not the perfectibility of human beings. Christ's 'kingdom' was 'not of this world', and Jain enlightenment is an individual experience which transcends worldly concerns.

In Jain terms, political ideology is a form of possessiveness. Ideologues, be they of left or right – or inspired by fundamentalist interpretation of religion – work under the illusion that they possess the whole truth, whereas at most they have only a fractional understanding. This illusion, like other illusions generated by possessiveness, results in alienation and the corruption of high ideals into instruments of tyranny. Political or ideological possessiveness creates an intolerant mindset and the desire to impose ideological conformity on others, rather than cultivate virtue in ones inner self. Nonetheless, Jainism can influence political thought and action in a positive way, and give spiritual inspiration to those who seek practical changes. And, as Mahatma Gandhi recognised, if Jain principles were disseminated more widely, then millions of individual human lives, and human life collectively, would change in dramatic ways as priorities shifted. Jainism encompasses the political, but it cannot be reduced to the level of a political ideology, and nor can any secular belief system co-opt it or claim ownership of it.

Ascetics live by principles that would be recognised in many respects by anarchists, especially, but also by ethical or utopian socialists. They renounce possessions of all forms, they answer to no human-imposed authority structure except for their own consciences and the corpus of spiritual wisdom accumulated over millennia. They break with artificial ties such as country, family and the social conventions of a settled population. But their disengagement from the world, rather than conscious activity within it, differentiates them from political radicals or activists. In Jainism, charitable works, philanthropy and activism, as generators of beneficent karma, fall within the remit of the lay man and woman.

The ascetic seeks to shed karma, rather than merely reduce or block off karmic inflow, and so he or she aims for non-action. The ascetic ideal is neutrality in human and worldly affairs and an austerity that reflects inner discipline. Ascetic self-realisation is quite different from the possessive forms of 'self-fulfilment' that have become popular in the West over recent decades, including those sections of the New Age movement that adopt a consumerist and *laissez faire* approach to spirituality. Jain ascetics, like members of some Christian and Buddhist mendicant orders, are recipients of charity. But unlike monks or nuns from these two other great traditions, their principal aim is not charitable work, although some ascetics do perform charity towards humans, and the acharya, or spiritual leader, can be active in promoting ascetic values. The advanced ascetic takes the concept of aparigraha to its logical conclusion, which is total non-possession and, ultimately, complete withdrawal from the world. It is in the lay approach to aparigraha that the Jain dharma shows its flexibility and its practical dimension. Through lay discipline, it provides insights for a Western civilisation in a state of high anxiety and lack of balance. The Age of Anxiety is, after all, an age of possessiveness.

For ascetics, therefore, non-possessiveness is carried, ideally, to its ultimate conclusion: total non-attachment, which means detachment from ordinary human reality. Lay men and women, by contrast, live in the world and indeed are required to do so by the responsibilities of family and community. The Jain householder cannot abandon his or her responsibilities on a whim to lead a mendicant lifestyle. Becoming an ascetic is a gradual process, not to be undertaken lightly, and cannot involve the neglect of others, or a flight from commitment. Most Jains, in any case, do not expect to become ascetics during their present lifetimes, which is why they take the 'Lesser' version of the Five Vows. But from a Western standpoint, at least, the anuvratas are a subtle and complex, yet refreshingly simple, code for living. Through the vow of aparigra-

ha, an ancient doctrine of the East interacts with an ecological consciousness that is awakening in the modern West and is beneath the
surface of much political discussion and philosophical speculation.

Aparigraha, in short, is Jainism's green vision for the West. It is
green in the broadest sense, which need not mean partisan loyalty
or the recital of fashionable activist slogans. Jainism's green vision
means respect for nature as an extension of respect for oneself. It
means restraint, in relation to the natural world, as an extension of
restraint in relation to fellow human beings and material possessions. Aparigraha for lay Jains means working within a framework
of responsibilities, towards oneself, one's family and friends, the
wider community – Jain and non-Jain – and the environment, the
collection of ecosystems that make our lives possible. It is a rebalancing exercise, a change in values which involves the relinquish-
ing of a sense of 'ownership' of fellow humans, creatures and
things in favour of acceptance, calm and unconditional love.
Aparigraha is interconnectedness, a sense of oneness with all
beings without the arbitrary lines of possessiveness to interrupt the
flow of positive energy. Possessiveness is about separation, whereas aparigraha is about unity within diversity.

The goal of minimising possessiveness can strike powerful
chords in the West. It has found, and still finds, a variety of expressions, from the orders of St Francis or St Benedict to the ascetic
poet and thinker, Henry David Thoreau, who rejected nineteenth
century materialism and, anticipating the greens of today, admon-
ished us to 'tread lightly' as we conduct our lives on Earth. To the
great religious orders, collective action by groups of conscious
individuals could make a difference to society and have a positive
spiritual effect on humanity as a whole. To Thoreau, who practiced

voluntary simplicity and non-violence, the choices made by individuals were paramount. Both positions are recognised by Jains, and the practice of aparigraha need not require the withdrawal and austerity that it implies. The doctrine of non-possessiveness is as important to the conservative householder as the radical ascetic.

For lay men and women, therefore, the vow of aparigraha is part of the householder's spiritual progress. The Five Vows confer on the householder a network of responsibilities, which include the familial, the communal and the ecological.

In this last context, especially, there is no contradiction between the ideal of non-possessiveness and the fulfilment of worldly obligations. A feature of Jainism is that concepts do not present themselves in convenient pairs of opposites but overlap at many different levels. Aparigraha and its fulfilment can be seen as part of the householder's spiritual path. As he or she moves through life's journey, priorities alter subtly and worldly ties are loosened. Material responsibilities gradually yield to spiritual responsibilities, one of which is working towards an auspicious rebirth. The sense of continuity from one life to another provides a sense of perspective on the life currently experienced. But the karmic cycle also offers a cosmic incentive to live according to the principles of the Five Vows, and to consider spiritual responsibilities as well as material or familial. Karma is seen as a physical trap, a dead weight impeding progress, but the possibility of lightening the weight of karma, and eventually escaping it, motivates the practising Jain. The practice of aparigraha is therefore closely connected to the process of samvara, the stoppage of karmic inflow by the reduction of passion. Possessiveness is both a passion in itself and the origin of much of the 'passionate intensity' that leads to anxiety, exploitation and bloodletting. Nirjara, the dissociation of karma, comes through the practice of non-possessiveness. The loosening of material bonds, and the attachments that sustain them, result in the stripping away of karmic layers.

Non-possessiveness begins with an attitude of mind, a conscious turning away from the material and a growing indifference to worldly considerations. This is accompanied by the cultivation of the mind through meditation and working towards that state of calm that is the highest form of human consciousness. Having adopted that frame of mind, the lay Jain aims to reduce his or her dependence on possessions, by reducing the number of those possessions or using wealth – large-scale or modest – for the benefit of others or for a specifically spiritual purpose such as temple building and education in Jain values. In this context, a think tank, an environmental organisation or a hospital (animal or human) count as spiritual purposes as well. Mere austerity is not enough. Simple living is not necessarily proof of non-possessiveness if the motive behind it is self-righteousness, self-delusions or mere flight from the world. It must be a conscious process by a spiritually empowered individual. Likewise, the frivolous disposal of possessions is not proof of non-attachment. Like promiscuity, it is viewed as evidence of a self-centred and trivial outlook, a throw-away mentality which is just as materialistic as overt greed. The practice of aparigraha does not involve the use of material possessions in grandiloquent gestures. It is a subtle form of illumination and a gradual shift of consciousness reflected in structured rather than sudden or extreme change. Aparigraha is a process of inner transformation, reflected in outward behaviour and values. It is a transition from the fast mode of life to the slow, from the dynamic to the reflective. The vow of aparigraha is a way of rebalancing one's life, a shift of emphasis from change to continuity, from what is shifting and transient to what is of permanent value. As such, it parallels the cosmic tension between continuity and change, within a universe overshadowed by karma.

For ascetics, non-possessiveness is total. They are the cutting edge, the dharma's logical conclusion but also its radical extreme. For lay Jains, by contrast, there are no absolutist rules for how to practice aparigraha. In a sense, that is true for the ascetic as well, as his or her discipline comes from within and is an inborn quality. Householders might use written texts as guidelines, but they work largely according to intuition and where their abilities, experiences and interests direct them. Attachment to rigid rules can be a form of possessiveness, which is another reason why there is no such thing as 'Jain fundamentalism'. It might also help to explain why some of the great spiritual teachers of humanity, such as Socrates, Jesus and the Buddha, as well as Mahavira, never put anything directly into writing. In Jainism, there is no real distinction between thought and action. Non-possessiveness is a world-view and can be practiced by small gestures as well as large, by comparatively minor decisions as well as major life-changes. This is not to underestimate the importance of aparigraha, but it should be seen as an integrated system, the sum total of individual parts rather than a set of prescriptions and prohibitions. This fifth vow can be applied with imagination and flexibility. The educator, the medic, the artist or the patron of the arts, the charitable volunteer, the ethical entrepreneur, are all potential practitioners of non-possessiveness if they approach their work with clear minds, conscience and compassion.

There is a parallel here with the practical aspects of the environmental movement in the West, those men and women who choose to live out their ecological consciousness. Practical environmentalism encompasses everything from the recycling of household goods by urban professionals, through organic farming and permaculture to more radical changes in lifestyle, such as communal living or the growing phenomenon of 'down-shifting'. Like the vow of non-possessiveness, down-shifting involves the casting off of unwanted possessions along with ambitions that generate anguish and passion, rather than calm. Also like aparigraha, it is based on a change of priorities, and usually this involves a movement towards ecological concerns. Often involving relocation from urban areas, down-shifting is associated with the creation of alternative structures based on less materialistic values. Based on working with, rather than in defiance of, natural rhythms, it is still far from opposed to technology, but on the contrary embraces the internet as a tool for lighter living and wider choice. Emphasising local roots and sense of community, it nonetheless embraces global communication and cross-cultural insights. This approach encompasses politics but it also goes well beyond the political. Its basis is not a mass movement or party, but the individual conscience. Yet the cumulative effect on the way society is organised is potentially immense.

In the Western context, it might be helpful for us to view aparigraha as a form of spiritual down-shifting. It gives coherence and a spiritual underpinning to the sense that something has gone profoundly 'wrong' with our system of values, and that this is reflected in our relationship with the environment and with each other. The ecological imbalances evidenced by climate change, deforestation and atmospheric pollution are mirrored by an increasing breakdown of the human ecosystem: the destruction of communities and cultures, the loss of the extended family, the absence of shared values and the rise of violent extremism. These developments, human and ecological, are part of a larger spiritual malaise, which like most illnesses is based on imbalance. The idea of aparigraha, living lightly upon the Earth and minimising our desire to possess, takes us back to the dilemma of Western, or any urban-based, civilisation – that of reconciling natural impulses and affinities with the constraints of civil society.

Jainism has never been a simple 'back-to-nature' movement in the sense of resisting technologies and attempting to thwart scientific advance. As an ancient, almost timeless faith it contains deep reverence for nature, its concept of the soul extending to rocks and streams as well as animal or vegetable life. As a living tradition it encompasses philosophical speculation and rational thought, along with the highest respect for scientific progress. These two strands are united by the holistic principle of the Jain dharma that all living systems in the universe are mutually dependent and interlocked, and therefore we must behave towards them with restraint and respect. Aparigraha is the living out of this principle, so that we free ourselves from the dead weight of accumulated desires, and clear our minds of the obsessive attachments that create anxiety and separation from our spiritual selves and from our fellow beings.

The movement towards non-possessiveness is related to the karmic journey, in which we seek to lighten our burden in preparation for future lives and hopefully, the ultimate awakening of moksha. It is also related to the individual's journey through one lifetime, in which responsibilities are discharged but material attachments are progressively sloughed off as spiritual considerations take precedence. From the Western standpoint, another parallel could be drawn with the collective human journey. Our civilisation contains many possibilities for decline and collapse. But equally, there are reasons to look forward positively. To balance the rise of extremism, there is a groundswell of tolerance and understanding that was unthinkable even a short generation ago.

In response to our violent assault on the Earth, there is a rising ecological consciousness and a desire for a more satisfying, less materially demanding and stressful way of life. Just as the individual Jain can choose the paths of secular decline or spiritual awakening, and choose to reinvent him or herself by forsaking materialism, so our civilisation can mature beyond the idea of relentless economic growth and ever-increasing affluence, matched by relentless environmental destruction and ever-increasing inequality. The culture of economic growth is one of attachment and possessiveness, in which the natural world is violated and the spiritual dimension dismissed or ignored. Through the example of Jainism, we can see that ecological and spiritual awakening are one and the same. Collective aparigraha offers the possibility of redemption and renewal.

In the commentaries on the *Tattvartha Sutra*, possessiveness is defined, somewhat crisply, as the act of clinging and the instinct to hold on:

Possessiveness is clinging to the animate and inanimate. It may refer to clinging to something in the external world or to feelings within the self. [Possessiveness is] desire, coveting, craving, longing, yearning, greed, clinging. ... Nourishing the passions of the mind is also a form of emotional clinging.

This beautiful and subtle commentary resonates also with the next of the Three As, anekantvada, the non-violence of the mind. It also evokes the discomfort and unhappiness associated with possessiveness and its disastrous results both for that which is clung to and those who cling. Aparigraha is the possibility of liberation through letting go. And in letting go, destructive and poisonous attachments fall away like the layers of malign karma they represent. In letting go, we feel a sense of connectedness rather than competitiveness, a limitless compassion and unconditional love. Surely this is an ecological wisdom that we can learn to live by.

CHAPTER SIX

NON-VIOLENCE OF THE MIND: THE DOCTRINE OF MANY-SIDEDNESS

'Think it possible that you may be mistaken',
OLIVER CROMWELL

The assumption that we have privileged access to truth is the most powerful engine of conflict between human beings. It destroys relationships between friends, within families and communities and between one larger group of human beings and another, at the level of tribe, nation or continent, or the clash of civilisations, ideologies and faiths. The belief that 'our' version of the truth is superior to that of others, and that we have a right, divine or secular, to impose it, finds logical expression in war, oppression and enslavement, in authoritarian, faceless bureaucracies and the persistence of those prejudices, overt and insidious, by which one human group defends its right to dominate or despise another. More than that, this idea serves as a rationale for our assault on nature, based on the notions of human superiority and separateness. The exercise of power in this way is the negative aspect of human energy, the flip side of our creativity and intelligence. And it is invariably justified by dogmas, which whil st seeming to differ, closely resemble each other both in theory and practice.

One of the clichés of political science, which is no less true for being a cliché, is that there is a meeting place between extremes of left and right. Certainly the followers of communism and fascism resembled each other in their actions. Their closed belief systems mirrored each other in their worship of the collective, their contempt for individual life – and their assumption of absolute truth through racial destiny or historical inevitability. During the Cold War years, left-wing critics of capitalism and Soviet-style socialism alike pointed to sinister resemblances between the two systems, such as dehumanising bureaucracy and mechanistic 'models' of economics. 'Capitalism is the exploitation of man by man. Communism is the opposite,' was reported as a *samizdat* (underground) slogan found in Eastern Europe, pre-1989. In our own time, fundamentalist movements often seem much closer to each other than their liberal co-religionists, in their mentality and practice. Sometimes, they sink their differences and work across the boundaries of denomination and faith, usually in support of censorship of plays, films or works of art, or to control the sexual behaviour of others.

The more such dogmas, religious and political, resemble each other the less they resemble the truth. This is not because they are necessarily untrue. Indeed they are likely to be part of a larger, less discernible truth that cannot be reached by dogmatic belief, still less by the assumption of certainty. However when they are asserted as the whole truth, or used as instruments of control, they are transformed into dangerous delusions that stand between humanity and the pure consciousness and enlightenment for which humans have always searched. Jainism has always recognised the dangers inherent in assumptions of absolute truth or ultimate knowledge, and the disastrous results of attempts to impose such 'truths' by force on others. This awareness arises out of several tendencies in Jain philosophy. First, there is the sense of humility in the face of a mysterious cosmos. There is a sense that the human condition creates innate barriers to absolute knowledge and full understanding of the truth. Those who achieve pure consciousness, after all, have ceased to be human and become Jinas or conquerors, liberated souls that have moved beyond human limitations. Humanity's place within the universe is limited and as human beings seeking knowledge we must learn to live within limits instead of subduing all before us. That is the basis of aparigraha, or non-possessiveness, and it is also part of every Jain's commitment to ahimsa, the abstention from anything that causes harm to other beings.

Jains, therefore, believe in working within ecological limits and in respect for all life. These practical guidelines – valued increasingly by the modern world, but too rarely lived out in practice – are mirrored by an acceptance of intellectual limitations. From this we should not infer that it is in some way seen as 'wrong' or 'sinful' to ask questions, or to seek knowledge. On the contrary, it is the task of all Jains to do everything they can to pursue an elusive truth and live in ways that reflect it. Yet this is balanced by the sense that humanity is not a fully evolved species and that spiritual liberation is not of this world.

The sense of inherent limits would seem to contrast with a second strand of Jain thinking, grounded in values that are familiar to liberal humanists in the West. Being a non-theistic creed, Jainism holds that there is no point of origin or ultimate source, in which the universe is eternal and that time is cyclical rather than linear. There is therefore no 'First Cause', although the laws of karma pervade the universe, giving coherence and structure to its material and spiritual beings. With its non-theistic basis, and its sense that the universe, like energy itself, is neither created nor destroyed, Jainism leaves a large area in which there is room for doubt, inquiry and intellectual speculation. In a sense, the cosmology of the Jains precludes dogmatic certainty and is based on the almost agnostic proposition that there is much we do not know and cannot yet fathom. Therefore, it follows that every idea must be called into question, justified and evaluated, every proposition must be tested as much as is humanly possible. That way, ideas acquire intellectual and moral authority and so our individual and collective understanding evolves.

This is also the founding principle of the European Enlightenment, the basis of scientific and philosophical speculation in the West's modern era. Yet unlike the post-Enlightenment West, there is no division in Jainism between reason and faith. Far from being separate principles, they are complementary and continuously interact. Right Faith and Right Knowledge are two out of the Three Jewels. Neither can stand alone, and through the third Jewel, Right Action, they attain their true worth. There is no true contradiction, therefore, between the intuition that we must live within limits and the process of constant questioning in pursuit of knowledge. The first principle recognises that humanity is fallible and dependent on the natural world, of which it is part. The second recognises that human beings have the capacity to pursue knowledge and acquire at least an approximation of the truth. In acquiring knowledge, we make spiritual progress, and the more we know the more ethical obligations we have.

Both tendencies in Jain thought, the sense that there are limits to human knowledge and the possibility of pursuing knowledge, militate against dogmatic absolutism. But in considering Jain attitudes towards certainty and doubt, we must take account of two further intertwined principles that influence all aspects of Jain thought: samsara, the cycle of birth, death and rebirth, and karma, the law of cause and effect that governs our existence within that cycle, and from which we must aim to free ourselves. For it is through an understanding of samsara that we become aware of our limitations as human beings, that our connections with other life forms arise as much from shared imperfection as the virtues we hold in common.

In samsara, the soul is impure, corrupted by matter and weighed down by karmic particles. Yet each individual soul, or jiva, is on a journey towards liberation and so the possibility of progress and spiritual evolution exists. The intuitive sense of the spiritual and the sacred, the cultivation of the inner life and the rational pursuit of knowledge can help us as individuals to make spiritual progress, or even break free. However neither pure intuition nor pure intellect are in themselves enough, and they will not work well together without the attempt to apply them in daily life and in the way we relate to other beings. This is a philosophy that is at once highly abstract and eminently practical, at once free from theological dogma and replete with rigorous injunctions for living.

Jain opposition to dogma can therefore be understood in rational, intuitive and karmic terms. Rationally, it is founded on the awareness that human knowledge is not complete, but that our creative intelligence compels us to attempt to know more and to ask constant questions. Intuitively, it is based on the idea of innate limits to human capacity, along with the sense that we are part of the lokakasa, the inhabited universe, not above or beyond it. Therefore, it is our duty as humans to co-operate with all beings, and to work with the grain of nature rather than engaging in disastrous attempts to dominate it. At the karmic level, doctrinaire certainty is a form of attachment that generates passion and delusion and so presents a powerful spiritual barrier. This approach is shaped, at least in part, by the historical experience of the Jains as a minority tradition whose members had to protect it from persecution or forced conversion by Muslims or Christians, or absorption in the inclusive Hindu pantheon. The Jain dharma was seen, necessarily, as rare spiritual knowledge to be nurtured and kept alive through a strategy of non-obtrusiveness, subtlety and living according to a strong ethical code. In that way, the values of Mahavira and the Tirthankaras would be lived out through example, their influence reaching beneath the surface of the dominant culture. Therefore, Jains do not seek converts to their faith, but merely hope that people of all spiritual traditions, or none, will absorb their example of non-violence and ecological concern.

This quietly dignified approach has been successful, in that it has granted a large measure of freedom from persecution by followers of missionary religions and preserved Jainism from full assimilation in surrounding cultures, whether Hindu or secular. As a philosophy and way of life, it earned the acceptance as well as the tolerance of first Muslim, then Christian rulers. It has influenced Hindu reformers, and has enjoyed a constant creative tension with the larger tradition of the Vedas. Jainism enjoys a large measure of

respect in modern, secular India, which is proud of the commitment to peaceful living that is the hallmark of Jain communities, as
well as the contribution of many individual Jains to commerce,
politics and science. The Jain sangha is not only alive and well, but
also flourishing, having survived centuries of profound and often
traumatic change in the surrounding society. In this respect, its fate
contrasts with Buddhism, which became one of the world's great
faiths but almost perished in its native India. Jain success on
the subcontinent has been replicated in a series of Diaspora
communities around the world, which are noted for their cohesion,
their preservation of underlying principles and the success of their
members in the mainstream world.

The tradition of tolerance can therefore be seen in the context
of cultural survival. It is part of a broader response to minority
status. Yet this is a less than satisfactory explanation in itself, for
many religious or cultural minorities respond by closing
themselves off to the outer world, adopting an aggressive-
defensive posture towards it and a purist or fundamentalist
standpoint within their own subcultures. Jains, by contrast, have an
attitude of openness that combines cultural preservation with an
emphasis on integrating and participating in the societies around
them. We can see in this ancient survival strategy an application of
the principle of non-violence to the mental process, to the way in
which human beings form their thoughts and respond to the
thoughts and beliefs of others. The result is an intellectual ahimsa,
a non-violence of the mind that recognises that truth cannot be
imposed on others by physical force and nor can it be understood
through a one-sided thought process based on narrow definitions
of what is true and what is untrue. There is a psychological

understanding that fanaticism, absolutism and rigid thinking are harmful to mental and spiritual health as much as they are detrimental to society. As well as leading to repression and violence, they generate within the individual an inner violence, a psychic civil war that gives rise to neurosis, repression and a sense of separation from fellow-humans and the natural world. Non-violence of the mind moves us beyond mere tolerance towards a radical critique of the way we relate to each other, and our environment, and a prescription for living in ways that avoid conflict.

The recognition that thoughts and actions are one and the same underlies the commitment to intellectual ahimsa. This mentality equips Jains well for living in a pluralist society and gives the Jain philosophy a new resonance in the multi-cultural West – as well as an increasingly interdependent world where cultural boundaries are becoming blurred. But the Jain approach transcends pluralism, just as it goes beyond 'tolerance' or 'diversity'. Pluralism, all too often, is about devising mechanisms by which people or groups of irreconcilable views can live together in relative tranquillity. Such mechanisms, necessary and welcome though they might be, do not solve spiritual or even practical human problems, but at best contain them. It is well nigh impossible to legislate tolerance and attempts to do so often result in backlashes, the entrenchment of cultural ghettos and the resurgence of fundamentalisms, religious and secular. Individual needs and desires are not considered, and under the rubric of tolerance individuals tend to find themselves lumped into 'communities' or groups that are convenient for politicians and activists, but nobody else. The Jain concept of intellectual non-violence is different. For it is about the healing of wounds through spiritual progress beyond either/or positioning. It proceeds from the assumption that there are no polarities, merely a continuum, the culture of continuous opposition and sterile debate is based on delusion and obscures the truth.

Thinking in circles rather than straight, narrow lines, seeking overlap and convergence rather than conflict and seeing beyond either/or divisions are all features of Jainism that make it highly relevant to a world where problems are multi-faceted rather than one-dimensional. Jains recognise that truth, reality indeed, can be approached at different levels and from different angles rather than 'confronted' with the crude literal-mindedness of much of today's Western-style debates. They also recognise that intuition, the inner life and rationalism, although essential ingredients of spiritual progress, can also be destructive forces when they are out of alignment with the Three Jewels: Right Faith, Right Knowledge and Right Action. Intuition, when it arises from a distorted consciousness, can give rise to harmful passions, baseless prejudices (including racial or religious bigotry) and irrational attachments that find their logical conclusion in violence and hate. Likewise, the inner life can be a source of spiritual liberation, but its narrow cultivation can be a source of extreme selfishness and delusions of grandeur: mohaniya of the most spiritually poisonous kind. Rationalism, cut adrift from its spiritual moorings, can be abstract to the point of cold-heartedness, the stuff of economists' 'models' that omit all human and ecological considerations, or 'development' experts who ride roughshod over local cultures in the name of illusory progress and growth. Intuition, reason and the inner life become positive forces when they work in harmony with each other in an atmosphere of tranquillity.

The calming of the mind, the stilling of the passions, are the starting points of the Jain quest for knowledge. Although Jainism has many of the characteristics of a 'religion of salvation', personal liberation being its aim, Jains do not divide the world into 'saved' and 'damned', them and us, enlightened and unenlightened. They see patterns in human thought just as the scientist discerns patterns in nature. Thus the search for spiritual truth is, in a literal sense, dispassionate, not in the sense of being morally neutral, but of being free from distorting passion. This means being able to step outside the narrow confines of the self – the material self – and seeing the world and the universe more clearly. Being attuned to the truth is like the sense of inspiration and connectedness experienced when we find ourselves feeling 'at one' with nature. We lose that sense of fragmentation that pervades so much of our daily lives. Instead of fragments, we see kaleido-scopic patterns and in place of separate compartments, we find unity. We see connections that would not usually occur to us and above all, we connect with something far larger than ourselves.

This state of being, beyond mind, beyond conventional thought and the attachments that go with it, is a precondition for under-standing the truth. But to achieve spiritual maturity, far more is needed than an occasional flash of inspiration or understanding. It must become a permanent condition, integrated in our lives rather than confined to special moments of visionary experience. The sense of equanimity and receptiveness to truth is the Jain ideal. At one level, it involves a deep concentration on and identification with the universe. At another, it means stepping outside the self and moving beyond anything previously recognisable as well. This dual state, embedded yet detached, integrated yet set apart, leads ultimately to moksha and so can be achieved only by a minority of ascetics. Yet it is the ideal for all Jains, and something they seek to cultivate in their lives and the way they approach moral or practical problems.

In its search for unity in place of fragmentation, Jainism slots neatly into the demands of a modern world, in which both the old certainties, and the newer ones associated with modernity itself, dissolve before us. Modern men and women, in search of wholeness, display a hunger for an ancient wisdom allied to the emotional life as much as stimulating the intellect. The healing of wounds, ecological and human, requires a combination of creativity and reason, insight as well as systematic thought. The underlying spiritual problem faced by modern humanity lies beyond the alienation of 'man' and 'nature' and the spiral of interconnected human conflicts, expressed through gross inequality, racial and caste divisions, the 'battle of the sexes' and the increasing chasm between (allegedly) developed and underdeveloped worlds. These are symptoms of a much greater malaise, associated with the failure of our assumptions about material progress and economic expansion to produce a society at peace with itself. There is a growing sense that our aspirations, personal or communal, are delusory and dangerous, that there is an inner emptiness in materialistic lives that is reflected in the rise of violent nihilism, the growth of addiction (whether to hard drugs, alcohol or Prozac) and the threat of extremist ideologies and movements. The environmental crisis reflects a human crisis, specifically a crisis of modern, Western humanity whose ideals of development and ever-increasing prosperity have proved insufficient, one-sided and so eventually destructive.

Awareness of this modern crisis of faith helps us understand why, in a technologically driven culture, there is a marked resurgence of interest in folklore, mythology, shamanism and traditional or archaic methods of healing. Such interests, greatly encouraged by the Internet, are most marked amongst those who have undergone the highest levels of modern Western (or Westernised) education. Paradoxically, this very experience which has cut them off from their cultural and spiritual roots has also equipped them with the knowledge that there is something missing and that the search for wholeness and healing requires us to look beyond the progress and growth based ideologies of modernity, or moral systems that divide and polarise. Jainism contains the ancient wisdom of pre-literate cultures and a link, perhaps, to the most ancient settled communities of the Indian subcontinent, such as the 'Indus Valley civilisation' once exalted by Aldous Huxley. In 1935, he wrote at a time of mounting aggression in Europe that:

There are at the present time primitive peoples like the Eskimos, to whom the idea of war seems inconceivable and who make but the smallest use of violence in their personal relations with their fellows. More significant, there now seems to be no doubt that a highly elaborate civilisation – the civilisation of the Indus valley – endured through long centuries without resort to organised violence. In more recent times, members of certain religious organisations in Europe have succeeded, at any rate for a time, in doing almost as well as the Eskimos and the people of Mohendro Dara and Harappa Thus it has actually been demonstrated that men are able to construct a world in which fear and greed are not the mainsprings of action, in which violence plays little or no part .[1]

The language is old-fashioned, but the message is pertinent to a violent, iniquitous world that is searching for equilibrium.

From a Jain standpoint, the answer to the problems associated with modern ideas of progress is more than a mere reaction against progress in itself, or − to use a simplistic slogan of the Beat Generation − 'the return to nature and the revolt against the machine'. Instead, Jainism acknowledges and celebrates human discoveries as contributing to the process of enlightenment. Used properly, inventiveness and creativity are generators of positive karma. They can prevent or alleviate harm, cure disease and extend opportunities to those − such as people with disabilities − whose potential would otherwise remain untapped. Technologies can pollute and poison the Earth, or enslave and exterminate life. But they can also make us understand ecological problems scientifically as well as intuitively, connect areas of the world and promote understanding between cultures, or provide liberation from mindless, repetitive, physically and psychically damaging work. The Jain approach to scientific and technological progress is to regard it as a benevolent force when it is used wisely and in keeping with the Five Vows. That is to say, science and technology are not ends in themselves but means towards the ethical goals of non-violence and living without encumbrance on the Earth. They are integrated with all other human ideas, activities and endeavours, rather than separate from or superior to them. They are not 'beyond good and evil' or 'morally neutral' but powerful moral instruments that can be abused with disastrous consequences, including spiritual regression.

As with Jain ethics in a more general sense, it is the intention behind progressive technological innovation that is important, not the technologies themselves. If the intent – as in the case of weapons of mass destruction – is to exercise power, to frighten or oppress, then the design, maintenance and use of such technologies is as karmically negative as it is socially destructive. Such technologies corrupt the souls of those who depend on them as much as they corrupt societies that depend on violence and force. Thus the Jain path invites individuals to question both their actions and their motives, rather than hiding behind collectivist notions of historical inevitability or the popular cliché that 'you can't stop change'. It invites us to use our creative abilities for the benefit of humanity – indeed all life forms – and the environment. This view of scientific progress as coterminous with all aspects of human life, including the moral order, will be familiar to many Christians, Jews and Muslims, who would wish to restore an ethical dimension to progress. In the same way, it is familiar to many secular rationalists, who seek a humanistic science which gives people control over their own lives, rather than conferring power on corporate and political elites.

Jainism's flexible approach, however, and its refusal to separate or polarise, is in tune with the present trend towards convergence between spirituality and science. As scientific method becomes less linear and more multi-layered, so spiritual inquiry is becoming more rationally based and more rooted in practical experience. Increasingly, in areas such as healing, psychotherapy and ecological awareness, the two branches of human thought converge, overcoming centuries of separation at the behest first of

Judaeo-Christian orthodoxy and then the cold neutrality to which Enlightenment principles were reduced. Jainism provides the ancient wisdom for which there is great hunger in supposedly 'advanced' societies. Yet it balances this sense of eternal continuity with the acceptance of change and the sense of innovation and creativity as moral instruments. Human societies and ultimately the individuals who make them up are charged with the responsibility to use for the common good their ancient wisdom and modern knowledge alike.

Among the Jains, therefore, the quest for knowledge, scientific or spiritual, is based on the interplay of the constant and the impermanent, the shifting patterns and the fixed points. They neither believe that everything is flux nor that all is stable and permanent, but in a process of evolution parallel to the spiritual journey of the soul, which adapts and advances constantly (although it can also regress), but always retains its essence. Jains are equally content with ancient principles and practices, which seem archaic to outsiders, and with modern, indeed sophisticated patterns of living. Continuity and change should not be understood as simple polarities, but as points of reference that continuously overlap and interact. Neither is the truth itself, but both contain areas of the truth. Because Jains have always been deeply aware of the subtle nature of truth and more ready than most to acknowledge the validity of different paths, they are often thought to be relativists.

The Jain doctrine of 'many-sidedness' is sometimes falsely identified with an aspect of post-modernist thinking, prevalent amongst jaded Western intellectuals, which assumes that no absolute truth exists, and that abstract, objective truth is a figment of the human imagination, imposed for reasons of social convenience or authoritarian control. The emphasis shifts, therefore, from a search for objective or 'absolute' truth, which is in itself authoritarian, towards an awareness of the equal validity of all subjective response. From this, it follows that all cultural expressions are 'equally valid' and that different 'truths' can exist for different cultural groups, genders or sexual orientations. The idea of universally applicable values and truths is therefore implicitly (and sometimes explicitly) called into question, even when such questioning impacts negatively on concepts of human rights, equality before the law and the protection of minorities. Critics of this strain of post-modern thought have pointed out that it can justify extreme subjective responses such as Holocaust denial, or be used to defend on 'cultural' grounds practices such as female circumcision. More than this, the result of such extreme relativism is seen at the individual level as a nihilistic and self-centred approach to life, which is spiritually destructive as well as dangerous for the environment and fellow-humans. At the collective level, it finds its logical expression in fanaticism, because it removes all points of reference against which ideas can be tested or modified. In a framework of extreme moral relativism, ideas can be taken to their extreme and totalitarian conclusion and violence in the name of any ideal can be justified. And since there are no objective tests for truth, the ultimate argument must eventually be that of force. Thus as well as giving succour to fundamentalism, the extreme relativist position is a form of fundamentalism itself, because it denies the validity of any reasoned, measured analysis of ideas or any attempt to achieve objectivity. It is therefore quite different from, indeed diametrically opposed to, the Jain concept of 'many-sidedness' or 'multiple viewpoints'.

In Jainism, the concept of anekantvada is intended to illuminate the truth, or assist in the quest for truth, rather than assert that absolute truth does not exist or that all truths are equally 'valid'. Anekantvada means 'many-sidedness', or more precisely 'non one-sidedness'. Viewed superficially, anekantvada resembles the doctrine of liberal pluralism on which Western political life is officially structured – although the West has not always been able to live up to this ideal. The idea of freedom of choice in matters of faith and personal lifestyle, and of competing political and economic philosophies in the secular realm, is certainly a form of 'many-sidedness'. Anekantvada is a powerful philosophical underpinning for modern concepts of democracy and human rights, and this is one reason why Jains have been so comfortable with such ideas and practices. The concepts of religious freedom, social tolerance and the separation of Church and State come naturally to Jains and it is due in large part to anekantvada that Jainism has never been an absolutist sect, and has never used force to promote its ideals. Anekantvada is also highly compatible with the ideal of a multi-cultural society, to which most of the countries of Europe and North America now aspire, as do India and Australia. However it points us less towards the type of 'multi-culturalism' that seems to be favoured by relativists, in which society is fragmented into 'communities' that have little contact with each other and lack a sense of shared values or purpose. Anekantvada directs us instead towards a society in which a variety of cultures respect each others' beliefs but are also able to exchange ideas, interact and, most importantly of all, acknowledge the larger truth of civil society.

Anekantvada is a doctrine of pluralism, certainly, but it goes far beyond the notion of competing 'truths' that characterises Western political or philosophical discussion. It also provides a corrective to the relativising aspect of post-modernism. In anekantvada, truth is acknowledged as the ultimate spiritual goal. For ordinary men and women, it is an elusive goal, but they are still obliged to work towards it, for the sake of their own development and in the interests of later incarnations, future 'selves'. Even the spiritually advanced, including ascetics at the highest level, cannot attain it. In any case, their discipline compels extreme modesty and reticence about their levels of success. Truth, at this level, is relative, but only in the sense that nobody can grasp it fully except for the Jina, the purified soul. This approach makes Jains aware of the supreme spiritual power of truth and induces humility in its pursuit. Dogmatic certainty about the truth is a sign that one is very far from it, as is the attempt to impose that 'truth' by force on others. Dogmatic certainty at the intellectual level leads logically to physical coercion. Intellectual himsa leads directly to physical harm. The fanatic and the dogmatist are further even from the truth than those who content themselves with spiritual apathy. They are in the grip of mohaniya, for both the assumption of privileged access to truth and the assertion that there is no truth are forms of self-deluding karma. Anekantvada is based on the assumption that reality is multi-layered, that it has many sides. Its layers must therefore be examined with caution, precision and the absence of dogma. Science, along with Jainism, has come to accept that absolute truth – or the 'Theory of Everything' – cannot be fully understood by humans but should be pursued nonetheless as an elusive ultimate goal. Both accept that the quest for truth involves clearing the mind of dogma and adopting a position of intellectual flexibility or clear-mindedness.

The idea of many-sidedness is linked intimately to the Jain objective of reducing karma and so at once clearing the mind and purifying the soul. Karmic reduction involves the stilling of the passions, including the passions associated with certainty and dogma. We can therefore interpret at two levels Mahavira's warning to his followers, which resembles a manifesto for spiritual pluralism:

> Those who praise their own faiths and ideologies and blame [those] of their opponents and thus distort the truth will remain confined to the cycle of birth and death.

This can indeed be viewed as indeed a rejection of religious or secular dogma, or an injunction against fundamentalism. It is a call for acceptance of other faiths and paths, not as rival or competing truths as in Western-style pluralism, but as differing paths towards the same truth. Religious or ideological exclusivity is a form of passion, and gives rise to still more destructive passions ranging from righteous anger to the desire to exercise coercive power. Dogmatism is a form of deluding karma, and it is also a form of passion that produces destructive karmic influences and keeps the soul trapped in the cycle of birth, death and rebirth. Anekantvada is a philosophical doctrine, and a practical guide to living and spiritual practice. But it is also a mechanism for reducing karmic influences.

The idea of many-sidedness can be likened to the experience of walking to the summit of a hill or mountain. There is a choice of many paths, from many angles, some winding, some more direct, each offering a different but spectacular view. Yet all lead the walker towards the same summit. Equally, it can be likened to a finely cut jewel whose light is reflected through many facets. A popular Jain story, 'The Elephant and Seven Blind Men' expresses very well the method and purpose of anekantvada:

Once seven blind men, who had never been able to see, were taken near to an elephant. One of the men placed his hands on the elephant's ears, another on his legs, another on the tail of the elephant, and so on. When they were asked to describe the elephant, one man said: 'The elephant is a big flat fan-like animal'. 'No,' said the other, 'I touched the animal, and it is certainly like a thick round post all the way from the ground to as high as I could reach'. The third man shouted: 'You are both wrong. Let me tell you for sure. It is a long rope-like thing with lots of hair on it and it moves up and down all the time. I tried to catch it but it always wriggled away'. Each man in turn claimed that he alone was right.

Finally, the owner of the elephant said: 'All of you are correct in what you have described, but all are also wrong because each of you has touched only one side of the elephant. Had you been able to examine all the sides with all your senses, you would have realised that each of you is right from your individual viewpoint, but the truth is something different altogether'.

This story explains clearly to the lay man and woman the principle of many-sidedness and its potential role in resolving conflicts. It illustrates well the multi-layered nature of reality, which can be experienced from many perspectives and still be equally 'real'. It shows that truth can be arrived at from a variety of angles. However there is a more subtle meaning to the story that is revealed in the final line: 'the truth is something different altogether'. Truth is more than simply the sum of many parts. It exists in its own right, but is manifested through many different aspects. We view the summit from whichever path we take, but the path itself is not the same as the summit. Or rather all paths lead to the summit, but the summit is distinct from the paths and standing astride it is a very different experience from walking up. Truth is not therefore divided into multiple parts, as pluralists on the softer side of post-modernism believe. It *is* manifold, in the literal sense of having 'many folds' or layers, as well as a multiplicity of entry points. It is hidden, it is elusive, but it exists in its own right and is grasped fully at the point of spiritual liberation, in which the true self is realised and becomes all-knowing. Here is one of the paradoxes at the heart of Jainism. The path towards truth (whichever path the seeker takes) is an ethical path. The pursuit of knowledge, the use of reason and even intuitive flashes of insight are subordinated to a much wider moral purpose. This is the living out of the Five Vows, in particular those of non-violence and non-acquisitiveness.

Morality is therefore integral to the search for truth, but truth itself is beyond moral considerations, not neutral, but literally 'beyond good and evil'. That paradox is explained by the Jain perspective on karma. Truth is liberation from karma, whilst the pursuit of truth is part of the karmic journey, still a form of attachment, albeit benign. In this context, anekantvada is the intellectual counterpart to aparigraha. For through the fifth vow of non-acquisitiveness, the practising Jain seeks to minimise his or her attachment to material possessions as ends in themselves, and so steadily reduce acquisitive passions. Through anekantvada, he or she minimises absolutist, dogmatic thinking and the passions, such as fanaticism, to which they lead. In both cases, actions and feelings which cause harm to others, and act as spiritual barriers, are avoided. Aparigraha is a means by which the individual learns to live more lightly and consume less, avoiding ecological damage. Anekantvada is the shedding of intellectual detritus, the clearing of unwanted dogmas, fixations and attachments from the mind so that it can view life more clearly, more objectively. The Jain doctrine of many-sidedness acts as a practical guide to those aspects of life in the secular world that involve forming opinions or responding to the opinions of others. It is also a means of reducing karmic influences and clearing the mind. Aparigraha applies the principle of non-violence or ahimsa to the material realm and so includes – and transcends – the green vision of the modern West, a vision that although nowhere near dominant is gaining ground and making sense. Anekantvada is intellectual ahimsa. It is a non-violent approach to the pursuit of truth, recognising the existence of many paths, many traditions of wisdom or, of equal importance, individual insights. As such, it incorporates the liberal pluralism that is the Western ideal, but also reaches beyond it and offers us something more whole.

In our examination of anekantvada so far, we have presented the quest for truth in terms of an upward movement or a progression forward. This is to be expected, in a sense, because Jains think in terms of spiritual progress, of evolution to higher levels of consciousness. But this is by no means the whole of the Jain vision. Presented on its own, it bears a misleading resemblance to Western linear thinking, in which progress is interpreted in narrow terms. Jainism, however, admits of regression, sideways movements or byways in the spiritual journey. These are inevitable, and in some circumstances may be desirable. Spiritual growth is not necessarily achieved by a slow, steady journey as in the ascent of a mountain by a path on a clear day. That is but one method, one type of spiritual evolution. The walker might pause for lengthy periods, take detours or caves and rock formations. He might finish in a few hours or take the entire day. His path might be occluded by mist, obstructed by rain, hail or snow, or in high summer he might be oppressed by heat as he makes his way. In each case, the experience of the spiritual journey is different, indeed unique. But walking is not the only valid analogy for the spiritual quest. The seeker's journey can just as easily resemble that of the swimmer, moving sideways to evade rocks and currents in the karmic sea that have the power to distract or even overwhelm.

The spiritual quest can involve approaching truth from all sides and angles. Being a radical philosophy, Jainism is not afraid to examine ideological standpoints from the roots upwards. Therefore, it follows that whilst Jains accept that there are many ways of accessing or gaining insights into truth, they also accept a seemingly quite converse viewpoint. This is the proposition, advanced in the *Tattvartha Sutra*, that because each path is incomplete, it is inherently flawed or deficient. Each *naya*, or standpoint, is invalid when considered only on its own terms,

without reference to others, and without being seen as contributing
to something greater than itself:

> All the nayas, therefore, in their exclusively individual stand-
> points are absolutely faulty. If, however, they consider them-
> selves as supplementary to each other, they are right in their
> viewpoints. ... If all the nayas arrange themselves in a proper
> way and supplement each other, then alone they are worthy of
> being termed as 'the whole truth' or the right view in its entirety.

In other words, the many parts of the elephant are not the
elephant itself. On their own, they would be lumps of lifeless
flesh. Likewise the paths, and the summit itself, could not
exist without the totality of the mountain. The doctrine of many-
sidedness leads us back to the idea of connections between all
life forms, underlying the Jain dharma. Being aware of interconnectedness is the beginning of an understanding of truth, and
this applies to ideas and values as much as it does to living
systems. The separation between ideas that forms the basis of most
of modern political and philosophical debate is therefore a fiction,
or a distortion of the truth. The ideas we live by, or use to justify
our lives, have a shared origin in human consciousness – and
human fallibility. No idea can therefore enjoy a monopoly of
truth, but all ideas have ultimately the same roots in the human
experience.

From the Jain perspective, examining the differences between
ideological standpoints is far less interesting than exploring their
shared origins and discovering values that they hold in common.
The truth contained within all spiritual traditions is understood

when we recognise that each of these traditions is a way to the truth rather than the truth itself, that spiritual paths point towards the same goal rather than cancelling each other out. The essence of all spiritual systems, Eastern and Western, ancient or modern, is distilled in the Five Vows of respect for all life, truthfulness, honesty, restraint and non-materialism, and expressed in the Three Jewels of Right Faith, Right Knowledge and Right Livelihood. Rather than claim a monopoly over these insights and virtues, Jains regard them as staging posts in the spiritual quest, and see anyone who shares or, more importantly, attempts to practice them as a fellow traveller, in effect an honorary Jain. For these principles are at the foundations of all the great spiritual systems of humanity. They express universal truths, the validity of which transcend time and place.

This inclusive approach towards the truth is as applicable to secular ideologies, in politics and economics for instance, as it is to spiritual traditions. Their essential truths are rooted in concern for the well-being of humanity and the planet, and the sense that there is something larger than narrow self-interest. Yet on their own, when they refuse to recognise a larger truth, such secular ideologies are mere nayas, propositions that are by themselves incomplete. We have seen, for example, that the Jain view of time, and progress, is cyclical rather than linear, a series of forward and backward motions of a cosmic wheel. This process parallels the natural principle of growth, decline and recrudescence and the karmic principle of birth, death and rebirth through many phases of existence. In similar vein, the principle of life is founded on the balance of continuity and change, rather than one to the exclusion of the other. A many sided universe requires a many sided response from reasoning human beings who are coming to terms with their place within it, and this applies to the social level as well as the disciplines of physics and spirituality. Therefore, those ideologies that reflect tradition alone and exclude the possibility of change produce stagnant societies that stifle individual creativity. Eventually – usually sooner rather than later – they lose touch with their founding principles and decay. Conversely, philosophies of perpetual change and the destruction of any fixed points of reference mutate into harshly authoritarian creeds that trample on individuals and communities and are a travesty of their original ideals.

The doctrine of anekantvada, rooted in the spiritual teachings of non-violence and non-materialism, is given practical expression in Jain culture by the doctrine of *syadvada*, based on awareness of multiple viewpoints. Syadvada derives from the words 'syad' or 'syat', meaning 'in some ways', 'in a certain sense', or 'maybe' and 'vada', meaning a statement or viewpoint. It is therefore the doctrine of accepting multiple viewpoints, or more succinctly 'maybe-ism'. Each naya, or standpoint, is transformed into a question or proposition rather than an assertion or doctrinaire statement of fact. It is accepted that the truths we deal with in our ordinary lives are only partial truths, that reality operates on different levels, which cannot all be accessed by ordinary consciousness. The absolute statement, or *pramana*, eludes the most highly developed spiritual practitioners and the purpose of philosophy is to try to arrive at such statements, the attempt being worth more than the accomplishment itself.

In the context of the pramana, the term absolute does not imply a supreme doctrine, imposed by intellectual or physical force.

Instead, it is the product of all the nayas, a holistic vision that is at once the point of origin and the pinnacle of human thought. Such rounded and full understanding of the truth in all its facets is beyond most human beings, including philosophers and ascetics. However it is, like liberation itself, a goal to work towards in this life, or more auspicious incarnations. And insight comes with the understanding that all our perceptions are relative, our responses subjective, and our beliefs largely the product of conditioning or our limited (and limiting) immediate experience. The element of qualification in Jain thought is far from tentative, as it might at first appear. It is intended to cultivate a frame of mind that is open to alternative perspectives and is capable of absorbing new nayas into a holistic world view. The assumption that there are outstanding questions, that there is more to learn, is a way of opening towards the truth, just as awareness of human limits is a first step to spiritual progress.

Equally, the approach to the truth embodied in anekantvada and syadvada should not be confused with the post-Enlightenment scepticism familiar to Western readers, precursor to the cults of impersonal objectivity and 'moral neutrality'. Enlightened scepticism resembles many-sidedness in that it acknowledges multiple viewpoints and rejects dogmatic or absolutist assertions. Its response to the problem of truth is one of tolerance and constant mediation between competing propositions, which are tested against each other. Sometimes, this is with a view to one proposition 'winning' outright, but often with a view to compromise, a half-full or half-empty solution, by which both parties are only partially satisfied and in most cases return to their dogmas with renewed rigidity. The Jain doctrine of anekantvada includes, but goes well beyond, enlightened scepticism and tolerance. It is interested less in compromise between competing ideas as in finding the hidden elements of shared truth behind these ideas. Anekantvada is quite unconcerned with the 'winning' of arguments or the triumph of one partial truth over another. Since all human belief systems represent journeys to truth, such victories are meaningless. In any case, the pursuit of victory is a worldly rather than a spiritual goal and so a distraction and a source of binding karma.

Most significantly from the Western perspective, the aim of anekantvada is not objectivity or neutrality. It is a training of the mind to arrive at the 'correct attitude' or *samyaktva* that is needed for spiritual liberation. The term 'correct attitude' is free of the negative and authoritarian connotations that it has acquired in many Western circles; it is not in any sense analogous to 'political correctness'. Samyaktva is better understood as an attitude of open-mindedness, in the literal sense of receptiveness to truth, based on the mental practice of many-sidedness and the ethical practice of the Five Vows. Anekantvada is a spiritual exercise that frees the mind from dogma and hunger for power.

Looked at another way, the doctrine of many-sidedness and the accompanying practice of syadvada or 'maybe-ism', enables us to address two seemingly contradictory but parallel processes affecting the modern world. These are the tendency towards fragmentation or dispersal and the movement towards unity and wholeness. Fragmentation is taking place at intellectual level, with the failure of political ideologies to live up to their promises or explain the human predicament, let alone solve it. The collapse of communism – and the generalised crisis of the left – is the most dramatic manifestation of this failure, but the inability of market-based 'solutions' to produce social cohesion is increasingly apparent, as is the widening contradiction between economic growth and integration with nature. At the spiritual level, the certainties and revealed truths associated with the great religions are increasingly called into question or seen as antipathetic and irrelevant. And the phenomenon of globalisation, in which commercial and cultural frontiers are broken down and communication becomes planetary, is fuelling a reaction of retrenchment, in which ethnic or tribal identities are asserted and politics revolves around identity more than ideas. Fragmentation has its profoundly negative aspects: the breakdown of communal ties and the retreat into narrow individualism; the balkanisation of societies by ethnic and religious conflict (or polarisation along other identity-based lines, such as gender or sexual preference); the absence of stability and shared values, and the rise of fundamentalism as an attempt to fill that gap. But fragmentation also has qualities that are both attractive in themselves and potentially positive forces for human development. It includes the rediscovery of local cultures, minority languages and indigenous forms of spiritual or religious practice that have long been suppressed, as witnessed, for instance, by the resurgence of Native American and Australian Aboriginal cultural pride and confidence. Fragmentation involves the questioning of authority and the refusal to accept rigid, oppressive power structures. It is a retreat from uniformity and centralisation, an acceptance, indeed a celebration of diversity and a cultivation of the inner life, the true self and withdrawal from the materialistic demands of mass society. These impulses are part of a spiritual quest, rather than a conventional social or political response. When the fragments are connected together, and then transcended, they amount to the holistic vision of Jainism.

Similarly, the unifying tendency among human beings operates at two levels of consciousness. First, there is a pull towards centralised conformity, impersonal bureaucratic structures and the power of big corporations, towards mass production and consumption in place of craftsmanship, cultural diversity and wise stewardship of resources. Secondly, there is a rising awareness that our interests as human beings are bound up together (bound, a Jain would say, by karma) and that our relationship with the rest of the planet is dynamic, intricate and continuously evolving. That relationship requires subtlety and light living, rather than attempts to dominate and subdue which arise out of false understanding – superficial 'knowledge' - and will harm us rather than assisting our progress. In the movement towards unity, there is also a search for wholeness and healing, for encounter and dialogue between cultures and the convergence of spiritual traditions, because their common origins are recognised. The return to the local and the particular and the quest for unity need not be diametrically opposed to each other, as the proponents of 'globalisation' and 'anti-globalisation' claim. Instead, they can be seen as parts of an emerging consciousness that is new and distinctive, but has profound and powerful ancient roots. Anekantvada is the philosophy and the process best suited to the emerging consciousness, because it moves human relationships – indeed all relationships - beyond the failed culture of opposition and polarisation towards convergence. It moves intellectual discourse, including political, economic and religious, beyond adversarial debate and physical conflict.

Anekantvada is the doctrine of both/and in place of either/or, of unity underlying diversity, of individuality and interconnectedness. As such, it is a potentially powerful ethical force in a world coming to terms with problems, ecological and social, that cannot be solved by traditional approaches to ideology and religion. Applied to the world outside Jainism, the doctrine of many-sidedness and the method of acknowledging multiple viewpoints − 'maybe-ism' - can banish forever the anachronisms of 'left' and 'right', 'progressive' and 'reactionary'. In place of the competition between faiths, they offer the model of co-operation and cross-fertilisation that Jains have lived out for thousands of years. However anekantvada and its corollary syadvada have relevance well beyond the areas of faith and politics. They intersect with new scientific methods and aesthetic sensibilities that are preoccupied with cycles and roundedness rather than simple lines of 'progress', with the continuous rather than the separate, interiors rather than surfaces. The perception of space and time as a continuum matches the Jain view of the loakakasa, the inhabited universe in which the samasaric cycle takes place. So does the concept of the universe as an 'implicate', or enfolded order, in which 'within each object can be found the whole and, in turn, this whole exists within each of its parts'. This many-sided approach was pioneered in the West by David Bohm, a theoretical physicist who engaged in dialogue with Krishnamurti, and Native American elders, and who was guided by the spiritual insights of the East in his pursuit of scientific knowledge.[2]

Bohm called his vision of a manifold universe the *implicate order*. Within that order, components of the many-layered universe which are connected by subtle, underlying patterns instead of adversarial opposites or rigidly separate compartments. This expresses the both/and approach in place of the either/or culture of division that has limited Western consciousness. Ecological awareness, as a scientific discipline and social movement, also asks us to broaden our definition of life to extend to supposedly inanimate objects and include, perhaps, the soul. The sense that natural formations are points of spiritual energy is contained in the Jain dharma, but it has been widely consigned by Western rationalists to the sphere of legend. Today, when we can see that there is more to reason than mere rationalism, the idea of areas of intersection between different levels of being, different 'folds' in the implicate order, seems credible once more. This is reflected in the revival of interest in the healing energies of prana and Reiki, meditation (including the reviving *Preksha* tradition of the Jains) and the therapeutic properties of colours and crystals. Amid the plentiful New Age jargon, there is an understanding of complexity that reasoned modernity and spiritual awareness complement each other, rather than occupying opposite poles. This is the historical insight of Jainism, reflected in anekantvada. The individual spiritual quest, which is identical to the search for objective knowledge, takes precedence over collective ideologies or official dogmas.

In 1921, William Butler Yeats, the Irish poet, wrote in his prophetic poem, 'The Second Coming':

Things fall apart, the centre cannot hold,
Mere Anarchy is loosed upon the world,
The blood-dimmed tide is loosed, and everywhere
The ceremony of innocence is drowned.

The best lack all conviction, while the worst
Are full of passionate intensity.

The imagery of the poem is rooted in Christian and Celtic traditions, but Yeats had a good understanding of Indian spiritual culture, and produced a successful translation of the *Upanishads* with Swami Shree Prohit. The theme of the poem is dissolution and renewal, a cyclical process as familiar to Hindus and Jains as it is to Christians and Jews, and which is represented in Jain teachings through the downward and upward motions of a wheel. The blood-dimmed tide is loosed by adherents of one sided and therefore incomplete world views, which evolve into forms of intellectual violence that resort to physical force. Such one sided ideologies are rooted in the karmic passions that Jainism seeks to still. In this context, we may revisit the idea that 'the best lack all conviction' and interpret it in terms of anekantvada. To one conditioned by Western adversarial culture, lack of conviction implies apathy, nonchalance or selfish indifference. It suggests lack of public spirit and even social backwardness: the term 'idiot' derives from the ancient Greek word for private or peculiar, and was applied to citizens who did not vote or participate in public life. More damagingly still, lack of conviction is a charge levelled against public figures – politicians mainly, but sometimes also spiritual leaders – who are seen as unprincipled, concerned with power for its own sake and influenced by fashionable opinion instead of a solid core of principles.

Conviction, by contrast, is often equated with strength and 'firm leadership', however one sided and doctrinaire those convictions might be. From the Eastern, and especially the Jain standpoint, lack of conviction has a different connotation. It implies the clearing from the mind of dogmatic preconceptions and passionate thoughts that obscure our perception of the truth. In Jain terms, it means casting off the negative karmic influences accumulated by the passions, by partisan thinking, by one sided adversarial positions. Lack of conviction is a state of karmic neutrality, of readiness to become enlightened. It is indifference in the positive sense of the word, achieved by the practice of anekantvada, the doctrine of many-sidedness.

In Jain terms, the best lack all conviction because they have achieved stillness of mind and indifference to material desires, the example of Mahavira and the Tirthankaras. In the words of another Christian poet, T.S. Eliot, they have 'forgot the profit and the loss' and moved beyond worldly certainties.[3] This state of openness prepares the mind for the understanding and practice of ahimsa, which is not one value among many, but an absolute. This remains the eternal paradox of Jainism.

CHAPTER SEVEN

AHIMSA: THE WAY OF HUMILITY

*The sages, who discovered the law of non-violence in
the midst of violence, were greater geniuses than
Newton, greater warriors than Wellington. Non-violence
is the law of our species as violence is the law
of the brute.*

ROMAIN ROLLAND

Jainism is, above all, the philosophy of ahimsa. It is the first, but also the last, of the Three As, the end of the spiritual quest but also its starting point. Ahimsa, in other words, is the essence of Jainism, the crucial ingredient, the yeast. Every other aspect of the doctrine intersects with ahimsa. It is the most complex aspect of the dharma, because it is all-pervasive, but if is also the easiest concept for outsiders to latch onto and believe that they understand. Mahatma Gandhi understood the concept better than anybody and brought it to political life. Recalling the Jain influence on his campaign of non-violent resistance to British rule, he wrote of the ancient doctrine that:

No religion of the world has explained the principle of ahimsa so deeply and systematically with its applicability in life as

Jainism. As and when this benevolent principle of ahimsa is practised by people to achieve their ends of life in this world and beyond, Jainism is sure to have the uppermost status and Bhagwan Mahavira is sure to be respected as the greatest authority on ahimsa. If anybody developed the doctrine of non-violence, it was Lord Mahavira. I request you to understand the teachings of Mahavira, think it over and translate it into action.[1]

Similarly, Dr Rajendra Prasad, India's first President after independence, identified Jainism with the highest principles of Indian civilisation, and saw its doctrine of non-violence as a gift to humanity:

Jainism has contributed to the world the sublime doctrine of ahimsa. No other religion has emphasised the importance of ahimsa and carried its practice to the extent that Jainism has done. Jainism deserves to become the universal religion because of its ahimsa doctrine.[2]

For both men, who were interested in ideas but at the same time profoundly practical, ahimsa was in one sense a simple principle – abstinence from actions that cause harm – but it also required profound and continuous thought. All political ideologies, all forms of economic and social organisation, all cultural practices, should be measured against it. It is a high ideal, and might be the highest possible ideal for humanity, but it also induces humility and dispels the delusions of grandeur that are the worst form of spiritual snare, and which poison our relationships with fellow humans and creatures. It is impossible to achieve in full, except by the Jina at the moment of liberation, and its sheer difficulty is reflected in the discipline of ascetic life. Ahimsa is the foundation of Jainism, and it is also rooted in the ancestral religious doctrines of India, before the philosophies we now call Jain, Hindu or Buddhist were clearly defined. The ideal of ahimsa is diffused throughout Indian thought, and through it the Jain dharma interacts and overlaps with faiths that might otherwise be opponents or rivals. Jains regard their religion as the continuation in a pure form of the most ancient Indian teachings, and this antiquity is reflected in the Vedas, in which several of the Tithankaras are mentioned.

This is one of the many points of contact between the Jain and Hindu dharmas. Jainism and Hinduism are distinctive dharmas, but rather than filing them in separate spiritual compartments, or classifying one as purer or 'superior' to the other, it is more useful to see them as parts of a continuum. As such, they flow into and feed off each other in the search for truth. Many Jains, as noted above, are slow to correct outsiders who assume that they are Hindus. They know their own spiritual identity, but do not see Hinduism as something opposed or 'other'. This reflects the universality of Jainism. As lay men and women, Jains are generally reticent about their faith, living it out rather than talking about it, maintaining their cultural traditions whilst integrating with and contributing to the wider society. At the same time, the most obvious manifestations of Jainism, such as the animal sanctuaries and the rigours of ascetic practice, are ends in themselves, but also challenge the wider human community. These overt manifestations of ahimsa in practice invite us to question our behaviour towards other species, with which we share the journey of life. They encourage us to think about how we can live more lightly, about what material possessions we really need and how much mental and material baggage we can safely cast aside. Such images of Jainism do not reproach us, but they make us think and summon us to question our preoccupations and priorities.

Ahimsa encapsulates the paradox inherent in Jainism. Like the other two 'As', and like the ideal of renunciation, its meaning is minimal and negative, but its implications are enormous and its effects life enhancing and positive. Strictly speaking, anekantvada does not really mean 'many-sidedness' as much as 'non-one-sidedness', the renunciation of dogma. Aparigraha means 'non-possessiveness', the renunciation of materialism. Ahimsa, in turn, means 'non-injury', abstinence from all acts that inflict harm on other creatures, or by extension the environment. From this seemingly sparse doctrine unfolds a guide for living based on austerity for the ascetic but for the lay person a practical guide for daily living. At the heart of ahimsa is the state of equanimity that brings release from karma. The reduction of harm is identical with the reduction of impact on the planet and its resources – hence the appeal of ahimsa to the green movement – but it is also the spiritual goal of withdrawal from the world, which requires an abandonment of worldly concerns, and an acceptance that such desires are transient, karmic and ultimately have nothing to do with liberation. It follows that the ideal of ahimsa is identical with the pursuit of moksha, by which individuals try their best within their own lifetimes but allow for the possibility of many cycles of life. The pursuit of ahimsa means freeing the mind of passions, which harm the spiritual self and lead, almost inevitably, to others being harmed.

In short, ahimsa as concept and practice is the basis of morality and ethics, the great intersecting point, from which all aspects of Jain teachings arise and where they all eventually meet. It is identical with many-sidedness, non-possessiveness and with the training of the mind that leads to samyaktva, the 'correct attitude' of open-mindedness that leads to enlightenment. Ahimsa is also identical with the process of withdrawal from earthly concerns that lead to the reduction of karma. As the *Tattvartha Sutra* demonstrates, all the dangerous acts and thoughts that act as portals for karmic inflow involve the infliction of harm, whether on the self, on others, or the wider community of beings:

The different 'doors' (causes) for the inflow of long-term karma are the five senses, four passions, five indulgences and twenty-five urges.

The five senses are skin (touch), tongue (taste), nose (smell), eye (sight) and ear (hearing). The four passions are anger, pride, deceit and greed. The five indulgences are causing   injury, lying, stealing, incontinence and possessiveness. The twenty-five urges are:

urges that lead to enlightened world view
urges that lead to deluded world view
evil urges of body, speech and mind
the inclination of the ascetic to abstain
urges that produce instantaneous inflow
physical enthusiasm
using instruments of destruction
malicious activity

torturous activity

murderous activity

urges for visual gratification

urges for tactile gratification

inventing and manufacturing lethal weapons

evacuating bowels or vomiting at gatherings of men and women

occupying uninspected and unswept places and leaving things
     there

undertaking others' duties out of anger and conceit

approving of an evil act

divulging the sins of others

arbitrary interpretation of scriptural teachings

disrespect for the scriptural teachings

damage to the environment such as digging earth, tearing
     leaves, etc.

possessive clinging

deceitful actions

promotion of deluded views

harbouring passions and possessiveness

The senses, passions, indulgences and urges collaborate in the production of karmic inflow. Any passionate act, whether good or evil, causes the inflow of long-term karma.

Some of these 'commentaries' might seem archaic in tone, although we could easily apply the injunction on 'evacuating bowels and vomiting' to such modern vices as compulsive eating or binge drinking. Others apply exclusively to the ascetic path. It is ascetic Jains, for instance, who inspect the physical space they occupy and sweep their surroundings with a light brush, to avoid causing harm to small, or even invisible, forms of life. Lay people, by contrast, are asked to respect life and take every possible care, but are not required to engage in extreme or socially controversial behaviour in living out the principle of non-injury. Other 'urges' are of a kind that seem beneficial, and so their listing alongside destructive or compulsive behaviour patterns will puzzle many Western readers. This can be understood in terms of the theory of positive and negative karmic inflow. Passion crosses the frontiers of conventional morality to encompass thoughts, feelings and actions that human societies view as 'good' or 'bad'. There is, however, a more subtle explanation, namely an awareness that the desire to do good to others and the impulse towards enlightened behaviour and thought can very easily become perverted and create harm for others as well as delusions for the self. The enlightened world-view can lead directly to the deluded world-view, when it is not consciously and consistently measured against other ideas, to prevent it from hardening into a rigid dogma or a fanatical ideology, or creating a mood of self-righteousness. We have already noted that in Jainism, as in other Indic traditions, the moral focus is in the motive rather than the action itself. Jains go further than this, however, and argue that even benevolent intentions can be harmful, when they are not grounded in critical thought, or to put it another way, when they become one-sided.

The pursuit of samyaktva, the correct attitude, is an intellectual discipline that involves constant measurement of the self, constant analysis of 'urges' and the restraint of unthinking desire. This attitude of constant care makes Jainism attractive to the outsider, in a society where the consequences of carelessness are becoming ever more apparent, and are reflected in phenomena as varied – yet connected - as climate change, the breakdown of human relationships in families and communities, and the dangers associated with terrorism and war. In Jainism the prohibition of any manufacture of destructive weapons – conventional, nuclear or chemical - is unequivocal and resounding. At the same time, the process of rigorous self-analysis seems to conflict with ideals of spontaneity and the display of emotions that have become popular in the West as a challenge to older traditions of reticence. Jainism is a highly disciplined spiritual path, which is why although its message is universal, it does not set itself up as a mass-based spiritual movement, but remains a repository of wisdom to be found and explored by those who are receptive to it.

Therefore, the Jain path asks for more than spontaneity. It demands a level of precision and rigour in the conduct of one's life, in one's inmost thoughts as well as overt acts that is both difficult and unfashionable. The practice of non-injury, the active avoidance of harm, the reduction of passions that distort and disturb the mind – all these involve the utmost precision, physical and mental, and would seem to make spontaneous actions and the free play of the mind virtually impossible. But as well as making demands of the individual, Jainism allows immense scope for personal judgement and the exercise of rational choice. It takes account of individual circumstances and limitations, and accommodates them flexibly. Its spiritual teachers have a constitutional rather than absolutist role. They advise and warn, rather than command, they offer an education in thinking, rather than imposing an ideology. Each man or woman is, in effect, his or her own guru, engaged in a spiritual search through experiment and experience as well as abstract ideas. And the enlightenment that leads to liberation from karma arises in a moment of inspiration. It is a vision of the whole that arises spontaneously, but can only take place against a background of spiritual cultivation. The strength of Jainism is that it includes the disciplined and the spontaneous.

In Jain philosophy, there is no separation between emotion and intellect, between the spiritual search and the scientific or 'objective' quest for knowledge. Time and history are cyclical, and so in turn is the evolution of human understanding. This is why modern scientific knowledge and sophisticated spiritual systems alike often lead us back to earliest, most basic insights of human communities. The notion that thoughts have inherent power, including power to do good or inflict harm, the awareness of different levels of consciousness – 'parallel worlds' – and a multi-level, unfolding universe are at the cutting edge of scientific research.[3] They are also reflected in the wisdom traditions of preliterate cultures, where journeys to realms outside the known world are commonplace, or in belief systems such as African and Caribbean Vodou which – despite continuing negative stereotypes – use the power of thought for generally benign or defensive ends.[4] According to the doctrine of ahimsa, abstention from harm involves learning to regulate thought so that anger and vengeance do not take the place of reason, and so that reason is balanced by compassionate understanding.

One of the first human insights is a sense of wonder, a feeling for the sacred in the natural world, of the extreme fragility and overwhelming power that natural formations possess, of our own vulnerability despite our capacity to despoil and subdue. Today's renewed interest in the environment, and alarm at the dangerous consequences of pollution and unwise human interference with nature, is forcing us to become aware of human limitations. We are not, after all, the 'measure of all things' and so when we exceed our natural limits, we endanger ourselves as well as the planet. Through the increasing ecological sensibilities of modern times, we are questioning the basic assumptions of the growth and consumption based society we have fashioned over centuries. At the same time, and perhaps more importantly, we are reconnecting with some of the most elementary forms of human understanding.

The primal, intuitive understanding of humanity's place in the universe and our relationship with nature balances the scientific understanding arrived at through reasoned, painstaking research. It gives our renewed ecological awareness the dimensions of poetry, imagination and creative energy. It adds to pure reason an ingredient of emotional commitment, which although 'karmic' in Jain terms, is positive karma, crucial to our understanding and ability to change and grow. The scientific insight, meanwhile, grounds the poetic intuition in the realistic and practical realm. It holds in check the excesses of emotion that can lead to violent passion and oppressive acts. Reason and intuition complement each other, like the forward and reverse cycles of the universe at the point where they intersect. Jainism incorporates both. It is the primal, pre-literate religion of Rishabha, seeing the sacred in all forms of life, as well as inanimate objects or features of landscape, being aware of microscopic and invisible life, including what we now call sub-atomic particles, without being able to prove their existence. But it also the rationalist, scientific philosophy of Mahavira, concerned with detailed study, providing a path to freedom from the constraints of nature and asking us to rise above our limitations as human beings. We do this by overcoming the tendencies in ourselves that make us attempt to conquer and dominate, which give us a false sense of superiority over the rest of nature and other human beings. The goal of ahimsa is therefore the same as the conquest of the material karmic self and the realisation of the true self, the jiva in Jain terms, in Western terms the inner self, the spirit or the soul.

It is here, probably more than anywhere else, that Jainism is relevant to the West. Our civilisation – if such it is – is at a point of transition. We can choose to ignore the consequences of uncontrolled economic growth along with the accompanying pollution, environmental and social instability and gross material inequalities, both nationally and globally. We can choose to ignore the finite nature of the world's resources, which means that we cannot continue indefinitely with unbridled consumption. We can also assuage our social consciences, and our awareness of impending ecological crisis, with the idea that we can have 'sustainable growth', which is as much a contradiction in terms as was 'democratic centralism' in the former Soviet Union. There are many temptations to take this path. In the short term, it is politically expedient, for humans in the mass, including electorates, do not usually appreciate being told they cannot 'have more'. Ignoring the problems associated with growth also means avoiding a rethink of our priorities and goals, whether as a society or as individuals.

The alternative to this strategy of ignoring, thinking in the short-term and hoping to muddle through is to shift our emphasis away from material acquisition and economic expansion. This means focusing on the even distribution of resources and material goods, rather than acquisition and consumption as ends in themselves. It means making time and room for creativity and crafts-manship over uniformity and mass production, using technology for humane ends rather than as a means of control and balancing competitive enterprise with the co-operation that ensures survival. This change - or 'paradigm shift' as it is sometimes called - can be seen as the next stage of social evolution. Yet it also involves breaking free of an addiction to economic activity for its own sake and ending the cycle of perpetual consumption. This in turn requires a realisation that many of our present 'needs' are illusions, foisted on us by the consumer culture and more detrimental than essential to our happiness.

Instead of endless expansion, which is an impossibility anyway, the assumption underlying economic policy would be the need to live within limits, reintegrating with our natural environment and valuing diversity rather than imposing inflexible, uniform solutions. All this requires a profound change of emphasis in economic and social policy, as well as our personal and collective values. Breaking the addiction to growth involves more than mere political change, however. It is a revolution of the spirit, or a return to the spiritual centre, where there is balance rather than conflict, and where materialistic ambitions are transcended. The goal of Jainism is also a return to the centre at the personal level, the reconnection with the soul that leads to self-realisation, the discovery of the true self. And so the social path presented by the challenge of ecological crisis mirrors the individual path presented by the challenge of karma. Karma, as the Jains understand it, can be interpreted as a form of pollution, not the moral pollution of 'sin' as some within the Judaeo-Christian tradition might call it, but a subtle physical and psychic pollution that like the pollution of the environment is caused by over-activity and delusions of dominance. The ecological crisis is the result of an economic and social structure that is based on karmic inflow. Resolving it requires a collective reduction of karma, the pursuit of aparigraha as a social goal as well as part of the individual's spiritual quest.

Jainism is not identical with Western ecological or green consciousness, because although it is about re-attuning to nature it is equally about transcending natural limits and 'urges'. The ideal of non-attachment is at the heart of Jainism and is essential to the practice of ahimsa, because attachment and injury are so intimately linked. Non-attachment corresponds well with the green vision of reducing humanity's ecological footprint, or working with the grain of nature, but is also about withdrawal or escape from nature, which is the opposite of the green ideal. However, if the green movement is to develop a new philosophical and spiritual underpinning, the Jain ethos is as good a starting point as any. In the West especially, it would be a better starting point than the remnants of failed left-wing ideologies and programmes, which despite their pure intentions invariably produce 'urges that lead to a deluded world-view'. The Jain dharma starts with the individual, but provides a rational and compassionate code for the way in which individuals should live in society: 'society' defined as the community of all beings, rather than only human cultures.

Ahimsa is based on such a sense of community, on the sacredness of life because all living things possess individual souls. Its observance rests on the sense that the inhabited universe is everywhere filled with life, and that all life forms, however apparently insignificant, serve a purpose and are part of the same karmic journey. Thus humanity is re-embedded in the natural world and recovers a sense of awe, in its literal meaning of reverential wonder. Humans thereby sense their dependence on nature for survival and the fulfilment of the most elementary needs, and this dependence inspires respect. They see themselves as a part, but a small part, of an eternal universe that persists through endless cycles and is self-generating rather than created by an external force. At the same time, the Jain approach is humanistic, in that it recognises the potential within human beings, not as a 'superior' species, or the most advanced stage of evolution, but as the life form most endowded with awareness of its higher self and the ability to make ethical choices. This consciousness gives the individual the potential to overcome karma, and humanity as a whole to practice 'right living', a just and balanced conduct of its own affairs and its relations with other species and ecosystems. But it also gives humans, individually and collectively, an almost infinite capacity for self-delusion and destructiveness.

As a goal, ahimsa enables humans to realise their best qualities of understanding, healing, co-operation and fellowship, as well as the ability to look beyond immediate concerns. This is realised in the way in which we organise our lives, and in the type of societies we form, which must be based on care for other beings, respect for individual liberty, on retaining the human scale in such as areas as politics, economics, planning and architecture, and on keeping humanity within nature rather than superior to it or seeming to exist on a different plane. Yet there is also the chance to transcend the natural and the mundane, to overcome attachment and connect with something more vital. As such, the path of Jainism, although spiritual instead of mechanistic, is compatible with the best and purest ideals of European rationalism, but it enables us to use that reason to meet new needs. Thus an ancient faith can become the basis for a rational way of living in the twenty-first century. The wheel of human thought can come full circle, so that in ahimsa feeling and reason are as one.

The idea of Jain ethics as a positive cultural influence, and as part of a holistic understanding of environmental and social problems, is quite different from the idea of 'conversion' to Jainism. To suggest that the West become receptive to some of the principal philosophical concepts of Jainism is quite different from the suggestion that Westerners 'become Jains' and throw off their accumulated cultural inheritance. The impulse to convert is incompatible with the principle of many-sidedness. Conversion itself is, for the most part, an act of passion and it is also very often a form of self-delusion, giving rise to self-righteousness and fanaticism. There is therefore a probability that it will lead to harm to others, and the self, as well as attracting karmic inflows of a negative character.

In other words, the approach of 'converting' to Jainism is more likely to do harm than good, socially and spiritually, and also misses the essential point of the Jain dharma. Speaking of Buddhism in the West, the Dalai Lama has noted the problems experienced by converts who come to a new faith without starting with a thorough understanding of their own culture. In the same way, awareness of Jainism introduces non-Jains to new ways of looking at the world. More importantly, however, it enables the Western inquirer to gain deeper insights into his or her own culture, to interpret its sacred and secular aspects in a new light. The enduring principles of Jainism, such as the Three As, the Three Jewels and the Five Vows, are lived out in distinctive ways, but are central to the human quest for enlightenment, finding expression in all cultures and faiths. They reveal the most important underlying questions and challenges for humanity today.

As such, Jainism acts as a subtle influence, rather than as a body of beliefs to be absorbed and copied exactly by outsiders. Mahatma Gandhi was strongly influenced by Jainism, but he remained a Hindu and his commitment to the Vedic path was reinforced and enriched, rather than weakened by that influence, as was his commitment to the politics of non-violence. His contribution to modern Hinduism was a renewed emphasis on the doctrine and practice of ahimsa, a value central to the original *sanatana dharma* (eternal teaching) and emphasised throughout the history of Hindu scholarship, notably in the *Yoga Sutra* of Patanjali. His pursuit of inter-communal harmony has survived as the subcontinent's political goal despite the traumas of partition and continued Hindu-Muslim animosity. It is reflected in a culture of religious tolerance in modern India that has survived against remarkable odds and the greatest challenge to which has come from outside, most recently in the form of evangelising by fundamentalist Christians. Gandhi's devout Hinduism, along with an equal commitment to non-violence and reconciliation between faiths, is an outstanding example of anekantvada in practice. This makes him 'Jain' in spirit, without a literal conversion to Jainism. Likewise Einstein, who expressed the wish to be reincarnated as a Jain, remained a sceptical scientist in the Western tradition. In the Jains, he recognised fellow seekers after truth, who understood that truth could not be confined to calculations and formulae, that knowledge would always be relative but was worth pursuing nonetheless.

One of the essential teachings of Jainism is humility. That

means avoiding intellectual arrogance and false pride, expressed through the conviction that one is 'right' and that others are by definition 'wrong'. Such an approach, quite apart from being deluded, does harm to Jain principles (or any other moral principles for that matter) because it turns ethical codes into stifling and oppressive edicts. This is why Jains, lay and ascetic, are warned against 'arbitrary interpretations of scriptural teachings'. Needless to say, such arbitrariness generates negative karma. At the same time, it obstructs the pursuit of knowledge or renders that knowledge null and void. The critique of formalism, exemplified by the life of Mahavira, acts as a checking mechanism for a philosophy that inclines its followers towards scholasticism and sometimes even pedantry. It is not the same as a revolt against discipline. Indeed it is the reverse, because true spiritual discipline is neither formal nor scholastic, but available to individuals of all educational levels or castes, as much to do with the senses as the intellect.

Formality and dogmatism point logically towards a 'disrespect for the scriptural teachings' because they disregard the original Jain teaching, which is openness and the absence of coercion. In modern times, the Jain's path to enlightenment has at times been compared to the scientist at work in the laboratory. The true scientific researcher pushes back the frontiers of knowledge, but in the process becomes aware of how much he or she does not know, or has yet to understand. In discovery there is also humility, in new insight there is also the revelation of ignorance. It is the same with the spiritual seeker, who must maintain an eternally open mind and be ever conscious of new possibilities for personal growth, new sources of insight. The essence of ahimsa is this sense of humility, of being on a spiritual and intellectual journey, along with all other living things and therefore neither superior nor inferior to them and so unable to judge or coerce.

Jainism's quest for a discipline higher than that of formal scholarship has a unique flavour, associated with non-violence and asceticism and the private pursuit of knowledge. However it also expresses a universal truth about the balance between learning and inspiration in the practice of faith, and the need for continuous renewal to prevent stale hierarchies from stifling or destroying true knowledge. In Mahavira's repudiation of animal sacrifice and warnings against the arbitrary interpretation of scriptures, we can see the same impulses as Christ's repudiation of the money-changers in the temple for their corrupting practices and his critique of the rigidity of the Pharisees, whose excessive legalism and bureaucratic mindset was a travesty of traditional Jewish teachings. The Buddha's critique of the Brahmins and assertion of the universality of spiritual teachings follows a similar pattern, as do the gentle admonitions to Confucius by Lao Tse and Chuang Tzu, who realised that excessive adherence to human-made rules cut us off from the larger discipline of the Dao, or principle by which the universe and nature worked. This latter insight is shared by many environmentalists today, as well as by Jains, for whom ahimsa in its pure form is 'non-interference' with nature. The search for spiritual truth is a journey back to the essence of spirituality, stripping back layers of formalism, dogma and material distractions, just as spiritual practice peels away layers of karma, so that the true self may be realised.

As a non-theistic faith that accepts the universe as both eternal and constantly evolving, Jainism is well placed, perhaps uniquely placed, to challenge intellectual rigidity or intransigent popular fundamentalism. There is no all-powerful Creator in Jainism, whose name religious leaders can invoke as a means of exercising control and on whom followers at all levels can fall back. The Jinas, and living spiritual teachers, are preceptors and guides whose lives are exemplary, who offer a model of how others should try to live, but they are not supreme rulers who determine our destiny. In Jainism, individuals find their own level, their own path towards the spiritual essence, and the assumption of superiority or righteousness sets them apart from that path, as does the attempt to back up spiritual conviction with force. Central to the cultivation of ahimsa is acceptance of the value of each individual life and the repudiation of force, or any interest in the use of force.

The essence of Jainism in practice is therefore individual spiritual growth through a process of disengagement from material concerns such as the exercise of power or control over others and the accumulation of material goods. For the ascetic, this principle is interpreted literally, and so material goods and power relationships are abandoned for a mendicant way of life. For the lay majority, spiritual practice means the wise use of any formal knowledge, power, influence or creativity that the layperson is lucky enough to possess, and the avoidance of activities or occupations that cause harm to others. The arms trade and vivisection are two obvious examples, because they injure and destroy human and animal life.

Spiritual growth involves the use of wealth for socially beneficial ends and the gradual abandonment of material priorities in favour of voluntary simplicity and the cultivation of the spirit rather than the senses. Withdrawal from personal and material ambition is therefore subtly different from the classic 'quietist' position of cultivated indifference and is certainly far removed from indifference. Social engagement is an important part of Jain culture. It has taken the form of charitable works, privately or co-operatively run organisations for human, animal or environmental welfare – or the explanation of spiritual teachings. This latter aim is quite distinct from any attempt to 'convert', but is seen as a form of social commitment as important as any other, for mental processes have the same status as actions, indeed they are seen as actions in themselves. Jains take part in non-violent movements for social change and indeed have had direct and indirect influences on such movements well above their numbers. However Jain social activism must always be modified by humility, the absence of certainty and absolutism, and the refusal to dictate to others, especially those less powerful or articulate. Rather than impose doctrinaire prescriptions for living, which are bound to fail if unwillingly embraced, Jain activists are encouraged to lead by example and practice, by subtle suggestion rather than stridency.

In the West, and societies that follow the Western political path, this philosophy and strategy create the framework for a more effective form of activism than the uncompromising rhetoric, generalisation and moral righteousness that characterises almost every movement for change. This approach is more effective, because in its refusal to endorse coercion its integrity is preserved and its ideals are kept alive. In Western protest movements, all too often, intransigent rhetoric is almost always followed by squalid compromise and ideals dissolve into authoritarian absolutism. The Jain model of subtle activism is, like the highest expressions of

Western thought, founded upon the importance and dignity of each individual. That is not the individual as an isolated, selfish unit who believes that there is 'no such thing as society', but a being with the capacity for positive actions, creativity and spiritual development. Each individual is unique, and yet profoundly connected to all other human – and non-human – lives, as well as bound up with past and future incarnations. Non-violent activism can be seen as the political expression of the private spiritual journey, for it is about reaching beyond illusory divisions such as faith, race and class and finding underlying human truths. It is also about awareness of the artificiality and transience of hierarchical structures and thus transcending human hierarchies and coercive structures. It fosters co-operation rather than competition, consensus rather than adversarialism.

The Jain approach to non-violent social engagement – which is entirely open to non-Jains – offers the possibility of realising the egalitarian goals of Western thinkers and humanitarians, without the imposition of tyranny or bureaucracy. Rooted in the spiritual dimension, it avoids the secular arrogance that has dogged movements as diverse as liberalism, socialism and anarchism in the West. Adherents of these doctrines, however sincere in their beliefs and however ethical their lives, have found their desire for a better world stymied by their assumption that they alone knew how to create it, and that they held the keys to perfection. Rooted in the spiritual dimension, the Jain approach to social change is based on a sense of perspective that distrusts grand designs imposed from on high, but sees social justice as a goal to be continuously pursued and the responsibility of all conscious human beings, not just governments, charities or (to use a fashionable phrase) 'faith communities'.

Thus the social dimension of ahimsa is compatible with the goals of liberty and equality, as enunciated in Western thought. More than that, it offers the possibility of a synthesis of these two principles of a kind that has consistently eluded Western thinkers and lawmakers, so that it is no longer necessary to 'choose' between equality and freedom, individualism and co-operation. Ahimsa as a political concept also presents a more radical critique of Western norms – 'Western Civilisation' in practice – than conventional protest movements. For these become part of, or dramatically accentuate, the 'either/or' aspect of Western political behaviour and the accompanying culture of division and separation. The 'either/or' mentality worsens social problems and produces a culture of intellectual violence that finds ultimate expression in physical force or authoritarian domination. Ahimsa, by contrast, is about the healing of wounds and the resolution of conflict. This applies whether we are speaking of conflict between individuals, between human groups (from families and neighbour-hoods to nations and religions) or within individuals, between their material preoccupations and their higher consciousness. Collective ahimsa is based less on the legislative path and is centred instead on a change of consciousness in human society and within human beings. This does not preclude legislation, which is to be welcomed when it promotes humane values, restrains cruelty and aggression, and points towards priorities other than the material or immediate. But the legislative answer is never enough, and without a change of consciousness can be counter-productive or worse. Ahimsa is individual spiritual development reflected in social practice. It guides us away from the artificial constructions of power, expressed through hierarchy, dominance and competitiveness, towards the true power that lies within the self and which is expressed through co-operation.

One of these artificial constructions of power is human domination over nature. Or, to put it more accurately, ahimsa leads us to question the attempt at human dominance, for it is nature ultimately that is bound to 'win' because of its complexity and inventiveness. The Jain concept of social justice extends beyond humanity to our relationships, personal and collective, with animals and plants, with geographical formations and ecosystems. A rationalist faith whose members are predominantly urban and professional, it retains an ancient regard for natural forces and a sense of the transcendent power of mountains, forests, rivers and rock formations. Such natural formations are points of energy, which influence the way we think and feel, and through which we can access other levels of consciousness. However Jainism eschews the idea of 'conquering' mountains or 'subduing' wilderness. This is because their reverence for nature specifically excludes the notion of wilderness. The whole of nature is filled composed of life and all of these lives have purpose and are linked by karmic destiny. They cannot therefore be conquered, and in the attempt to do so we disrupt our own spiritual journeys as well as doing injury to life on Earth.

At one level, therefore, the Jain dharma takes us above or beyond 'nature in the raw', in that it teaches us that our real self is found in our soul, and not our physical body. Our physical body is associated with material concerns and transient needs, and therefore presents an obstacle to liberation. Moksha involves release from the chains of the physical body and the constraints imposed by nature, as well as the intellectual limitations that act as barriers to ultimate knowledge. The ascetic ideal involves the renunciation of as many physical and sensual stimuli as possible, abstinence from sex and, in the case of some advanced practitioners, the refusal of basic nutrition as the ultimate withdrawal from the world. The lay Jain, who is enjoined to live lightly on the Earth, is constantly reminded of the impermanent nature of attachments, not just material but personal and emotional as well. This negation of the body can be seen to resemble the more extreme or 'hair shirted' aspects of Christian asceticism, associated especially with Medieval Europe, that sees the body as a repository of sin and temptation.

There is, undoubtedly, a puritanical element in the Jain dharma. Often, it is the most immediately visible aspects and so makes Jainism appear unattractive to outsiders, who know little of its finer nuances or its complexity. The puritanical face of Jainism could be said to act as a gatekeeper, repelling the superficial inquirer and challenging us to probe more deeply for the beauty, intricacy and calm behind the austere façade. There is also a more profound and many-sided meaning to the Jain attitude to the body than the one-sided and judgemental concept of 'sin'. For the body is not sinful, but associated with karma and with the entrapment of the soul in the cycle of birth, death and rebirth. In moksha, the soul liberates itself from the physical constraints of the body in the same way that it liberates itself mentally from the restraints of karma. And karma, consisting of accumulated particles of subtle matter, is as much a physical impediment as the organs and limbs of the gross matter body. Release from karma is release from natural constraints, but it is also the release from any desire to exploit or dominate nature, and any delusion that it is possible or desirable to dominate it. This is the point at which the Jain dharma and the growing ecological consciousness of the West overlap, and where they have the potential to enrich each other at both social and spiritual levels.

The Jain ideal is one of escape from nature and worldly constraints. It is freedom from the 'mortal coil' of karma, the cycle of repeated rebirth and the constant round of physical activity and emotional stimulus. The ideal is one of peace in the true sense of stillness, calm and complete emotional balance – or to put it more exactly, the transcendence of conventional human emotions. This has been interpreted as a life-denying philosophy, and certainly there is a sense in which Jainism is not of this world. The goals of immortality and omniscience, identified with liberation, seem to have little practical use to those who are living in the world, dealing daily with its imperfections and their own. Such goals, so far beyond the reach of the overwhelming majority, can give only indirect inspiration or hold out hope for future lifetimes. Yet at the same time as it presents to humanity an other worldly vision, removed from nature as we know it, Jainism also makes human beings conscious of their place in nature, and with that their smallness and vulnerability, despite all their intellectual and creative prowess. When measured against an eternal universe, all of which contains life, human intelligence becomes very relative indeed. However ingenious we might be, we are enmeshed in nature, dependent on it and ultimately impermanent, as individuals and as a species. We are seen as the most spiritually evolved life form, but that very advancement is the most powerful spiritual challenge, because it gives us the possibility of destroying ourselves as well as the capacity for finding enlightenment.

Hence ahimsa is about the wise application of human knowledge. This means being aware of our limitations as much as our possibilities. Rather than being frightened by these limitations, we should use them as an opportunity to live balanced lives, in which we pursue creative interests and useful work rather than wealth for its own sake, in which the quality of life takes precedence over economic growth and development is attuned to the environment rather than perceived as a struggle to overcome it. Far from diminishing us, the Jain conception of eternity presents us with new powers to revise our personal priorities and change the way we structure our society. It is not, after all, anti-life but potentially life-affirming. Jainism's distinguishing feature is its constant reminder to us of the value and fragility of life, our dependence on – and hence equality with – all other beings. As Mahavira proclaimed:

One who neglects or disregards the existence of earth, air, fire, water and vegetation disregards his own existence which is entwined with them.

What better motto could there be for a modern ecological movement, but one that avoided the twin pitfalls of ideological fanaticism and compromise in the interests of personal power? Ironically, the fanatic and the zealot are most likely to betray their principles, because power and vaulting ambition have already become their overriding motives. Jainism provides a balanced philosophy in which ideas, however good, are recognised as human and fallible and so cannot be turned into maniacal obsessions or used to enslave others. This is why even good thoughts and positive actions generate karma, albeit benevolent karma, and so are always regarded as imperfect and fallible. Jain philosophy expresses humanity's place in nature with the aphorism *Parasparopagraho Jivanam*, which means 'all life is bound together by mutual support of interdependence'. This is a recognition of the web of life, in which humanity is entwined. Therefore, rather than seeing austere Jainism as life denying, we should look more critically at the prevailing hedonistic culture of the West. A distortion of the best humanistic principles, it confuses egoism with individual autonomy, instant gratification with the pursuit of happiness and supposed insulation from nature with development and progress. That is the real denial of life, based on delusion and attachment, and reflected in relationships of domination and oppression.

Worse still, the life denying mentality of Western materialism undermines the very concept of community. This is because it sets us up in competition with each other to achieve superficial trappings of success, to 'win' arguments and battles and to control as many of the world's resources as possible. The environment and all non-human life are reduced to the level of resources and nothing more, to be consumed and 'used' to our supposed benefit. Even the concept of human free will, the basis of the Western Enlightenment, is traduced as humans are made the instrument of arbitrary economic forces, secular superstitions such as the 'trickle down effect' and the 'hidden hand' of the market that remove individual and collective autonomy. Seeing through such illusions is a first step towards the awakening of consciousness. At once mechanistic and irrational, they are opposed to the deepest instincts and philosophical underpinnings of Western thought. Jain culture values the intellect, but is concerned with the way in which it is used and the reasons for its use. But it is also aware that human inventiveness confers extra challenges and responsibilities. Like Western humanists, Jains emphasise the role of men and women as independent moral agents, capable of choosing between creativity and destruction, compassion and cruelty, and morally obliged to make that choice. The incentive to choose the creative and compassionate route is couched in terms of altruism, but also the rational self-interest that accompanies the realisation that all life is bound together in a common project. In Mahavira's words:

You are that which you intend to hit, injure, insult, torment, persecute, torture, enslave or kill.

Exploitation and cruelty - towards fellow-humans, animals and the Earth itself – is not only ethically wrong and a generator of negative karma. It is also against our interests as human beings. The goal of spiritual development thereby overlaps with practical considerations of human survival as a whole, and the survival of each individual human being. By acts of violence against others, we are inflicting violence on ourselves. This violence might be physical or psychic, but the effects are ultimately the same, and always result in more violence and an increase in negative energy that can pervade whole human cultures. The practice of ahimsa is the process of turning away from negative emotions, destructive impulses, fears and the desire for domination or revenge. It is the projection outwards of compassion without sentimentality, justice without dogmatism, but it is also the cultivation of the inner self and the realisation of our true self-interest. Thus an other-worldly ideal translates into practical guidance for our daily lives, a rational goal to work towards in our thoughts and our actions.

For Jains, the word *daya* means not only compassion and the exercise of charitable works, but empathy, in the sense of identifying ourselves and our interests with the lives and interests of other beings. Ahimsa is at once an aspect of daya and the origin of daya. *Jiva Daya* is the process of identifying with, and sharing with, all beings, all those that have jiva, instead of competing with or destroying them. As the former Indian High Commissioner in London, Dr L.M. Singhvi, himself a Jain, expressed it:

Jiva Daya entails universal friendliness (maitri), universal forgiveness (kshama) and universal fearlessness (abhaya). Jains, whether monks, nuns or householders, therefore affirm, prayerfully and sincerely, that their hearts are filled with forgiveness for all living beings, that they crave the friendship of all beings, that all beings give them their friendship and that there is not the slightest feeling of alienation or enmity in their hearts for anyone or anything. They also pray that forgiveness and friendliness may reign throughout the world and that all living beings may cherish each other.[5]

And so ahimsa is far from a dogmatic programme of abstinence and self-punishment. On the contrary, it is an ethos of balance, between individual and society, humanity and nature, creativity and restraint. Within Western society, there is a rising awareness that the material path, despite its superficial advantages, has failed to satisfy our deepest needs or tune in to our most positive instincts and desires. Because of this, it threatens the stability of our civilisation, mocks the values of liberty and equality that we uphold and even endangers our survival as a species. The doctrine of abstaining from harmful acts, and the principle of Jiva Daya, identification with all life, can steer us in a positive direction when we decide to turn away from sterile materialism. It can broaden our spiritual vision but at the same time keep us anchored in reason, inspire us to change our lives but inoculate us against intolerance and extremism. For ahimsa is the way of humility. It gives us a sense of perspective about our own lives and our place in the cosmos, so that as we admit to our vulnerability, we access our true power. Once again, it is Mahavira who expresses with elegant simplicity the moral and intellectual basis of non-injury:

There is nothing so small and subtle as the atom, nor any element so vast as space. Similarly, there is no quality of soul more subtle than non-violence and no virtue of spirit greater than reverence for life.

CHAPTER EIGHT

ANCIENT WISDOM FOR AN AGE OF ANXIETY

They say that the Jaina religion is practised only
by the few.
I say that the Jaina code of life is destined to be
practised by the many.

They say that Jainism is confined to the shores of our
Mother India.
I say that the heart and soul of Jainism will eventually
be embraced by humanity as a whole. Indeed, that
blessed day is fast approaching.

SRI CHINMOY

The radical aspect of Jainism is found in its silence, subtlety and restraint. For the West, this seems a strange kind of radicalism. We associate radicalism with clarity of thought and clear lines between ideas or philosophical systems, with collectivism and the promise of far-reaching change, or with an attitude of 'definiteness'. The Jain dharma, by contrast, celebrates complexity and seeks common ground between systems of thought. It is more concerned with the inner light of freedom and spiritual awareness within the individual than it is with collective trappings or the assertion of social agendas. Jainism is an inward path, about individuals searching for an elusive truth, rather than submitting to authority, whether that authority is intellectual or coercive. This is why Jain ascetics do not have the status of priests, whilst gurus and teachers, the acharyas – even the Tirthankaras themselves – cannot compel obedience. In Jainism, every man or woman is a 'community leader' or 'spokesperson'. There is no monopoly of truth, no eternal hierarchy, no ultimate goal except the ultimate individual goal of escaping the karmic cycle.

There is a sense in which Jainism is anything but radical, at least as far as human society is concerned. Life in the material world is temporary, transient and unsatisfactory. It can never be more than second best, because it is inherently karmic. Life on earth, indeed, is the imprisonment of the soul in the physical body and the imprisonment of the intellect in *avidya* or ignorance, because worldly knowledge can only be limited. Worldly life is not really 'life' at all, but a second-rate substitute for living. At most, it is a preparation for the true life conferred by moksha, whereby the jiva – the life monad – ceases to be an entrapped soul but becomes a unit of pure existence and consciousness, immortal because it is all-knowing. This view of earthly existence conjures up for Western readers of today some vague and uncomfortable reminders of the Medieval Christian world-view. In those pre-Renaissance, pre-Enlightenment times, the worldly existence was interpreted literally as a 'vale of tears' from which escape was a form of release. Human life was at most only barely satisfactory, but could never be ideal and was primarily to be endured in preparation for eternity. This is indeed very similar to the Jain approach and helps to explain why Jainism is so often treated as a curiosity, or as an alien cult of austerity to be admired or vaguely feared.

To those schooled in the unquestioned certainties of enlightened progress, faith in technology and belief in only that which can be measured in material terms, such other-worldly doctrines seem pessimistic and conservative. They appear to be obstructions to change because they imply that the good life, like the early Christian Kingdom of God, is a state that is not of this world. Such critics, when they think about the issue at all, regard the Jains as fatalists who have turned their back on the world and equate karma with faith. The idea that a philosophy such as Jainism can offer a radical promise to the world is for them a new – and radical - proposition that turns their intellectual map upside down and gently challenges them to rethink their entire 'progressive' world view.

From the Western standpoint, the potential strength of Jainism is its ability to expose our radical traditions as not radical enough, our progressive impulses as representing something far less than progress. This is because they approach the human predicament from a restricted angle and so imprison us in narrow certainties that have become both dangerous and redundant. For a society that is increasingly frustrated by its inability to match material and technological development with well-being or peace of mind, the Jain approach offers a model of integration and balance. It seeks out points of connection rather than emphasising differences, because it is interested in underlying unity rather than overt disunities. It is concerned with content rather than form, with depth of meaning rather than superficial expression. This is why Jains have been able to bring the resource of ancient, unassuming wisdom to the societies in which they live, so that they become a force for good with their quiet example of non-violent tolerance and restraint. More than merely survive, they have created wealth and expanded the frontiers of knowledge. A perpetual minority, the Jains have maintained their culture and values without stridency and aggression, influencing rather than confronting others, integrating without being absorbed. Jains effectively invented the concept of 'inter-faith' work and engaged in dialogues with other faiths many millennia before this approach became a Western liberal fashion. Such dialogue does not imply the dilution of faith, but its widening and deepening.

Although – or rather because - the Jain path rejects formal authority, it is a path of discipline, requiring depths of inner strength and restraint. To live in accordance with Jain principles, the individual must weigh up each of his or her actions, from the apparently superficial gesture to a decision with global ramifications. The Svetambara ascetic who sweeps a brush in front of him and covers his mouth to protect tiny life forms is living out the principle of ahimsa in a literal and uncompromising way. But in his preventative actions he also provides a visual explanation of Jain principles. This is because Jainism draws no distinction between grand gestures, usually the luxury of the few, and the small or everyday actions that are integral to our lives. Both can be creative or destructive, compassionate or ruthless, measured or impulsive. Both affect other lives as well as shaping our own. If anything, it is the seemingly small actions that have the most crucial impact on those around us, and our karmic destinies, whilst the most trivial decisions have more relevance than exalted thoughts. The decision to swat or spare an insect, to give coins to a beggar or to ignore or insult him, to compliment a friend or make a sarcastic remark are at least as central to our moral status as human beings as our spiritual practice or our vision of how the good society should be organised. Acts of trivial oppression, meanness or spite undermine and destroy our higher ethical principles because they turn them into abstract concepts, without meaning or value.

By refusing to distinguish between small and large actions, lofty ideas and trivial or transient thoughts, Jainism seems to demand much of the individual. One might argue that it demands too much for the stressed, overstretched man or woman of today. Yet viewed from another angle, the Jain path can be seen to promote a balanced approach to life, in which compassionate acts are valued for their practical benefits as well as their moral worth. The avoidance of harm to others takes precedence over short-term gains, which are seen as fleeting, giving only the superficial impression of contentment when they are the result of indifference or contempt for others. Material advances – in society as well as for individuals – are viewed by Jains with unflinching critical realism. When they are 'won' by exploitation, conquest or other bad ethical choices, they are tarnished, transient and a source of anxiety and discord, rather than peace and right conduct. When they are acquired virtuously, they confer obligations of further virtue, indeed sacrifice. Both types of material gain, the vicious and the virtuous, are generators of karmic inflow and so they keep enlightenment as a distant goal.

The Jain world view therefore asks us to examine every action, every decision we take to determine whether it is likely to do harm. At one level, this creates a mentality of constant caution, eternal questioning of motives as much as outcomes and, some would say, aversion to risk. From another standpoint, the ethos of avoiding or at the very least reducing harm has moral clarity and practical efficacy. Furthermore, it provides a sense of perspective that is conducive to calm, the avoidance of stress and at the same time a creative and rewarding life. This enables us to avoid delusions about our own importance and power, fanaticism, imposing our ideas or assumptions on others, blind obedience to leaders or acceptance of doctrinaire theories, and being in thrall to material possessions. We see real power in the compassionate act, real wealth in the quality of life (of others as much as ourselves) and real faith manifested in the restraint we exercise in avoiding actions that inflict harm or exploit.

Jains advocate detachment from the world, in the sense of understanding that earthly concerns are relative rather than absolute, transient rather than eternal. This arises from an understanding that spiritual liberation is 'not of this world', but it is also an enlightened objectivity that enables us to decide our priorities whether as individuals concerned with our inner lives, or members of a human community, or inhabitants of the planet and 'lived-in' universe. In other words, the Jain path of detachment and restraint enables us to step back from one-sidedness and material goals as ends in themselves. In the heightened consciousness that arises, we understand intellectually and experience emotionally the interconnectedness of all life: Parasparopagraho Jivanam. By transcending narrowly selfish interests, we become aware of the interests we share with all living beings, all beings that have souls and so can attain freedom from karma. By focusing on our inner spiritual development, instead of outward forms and structures, we appreciate our need to co-operate with each other to survive in the short term and over time grow in knowledge and compassion. As well as co-operation between humans, that means humans co-operating with all creatures, and the planet itself, to ensure the continuity of life. Such understanding, inherent in the Jain way of life, is the product of meditation, detachment and continual restraint from acts of harm. In detachment from selfish interests, we arrive at rational self-interest. Mahavira made it clear to his followers that 'He who hurts [other] creatures or, gets them hurt by others, augments the world's hostility to himself'.

In cultivating the self, we become aware of our connections with others, in seeking release from worldly bonds, we find our place in a constantly evolving, yet eternal universe. Far from cutting us off, Jainism allows us to experience life with greater colour and intensity than before, to view it with tranquillity as something benign and from which we can learn, rather than with passion as something we must conquer or subdue. This inner richness is apparent to Sri Chinmoy, himself a Hindu spiritual teacher, who writes of the contrast in Jainism between austere appearance and life-affirming reality:

They say that Jainism is stark austerity-life.

I say that Jainism expects austerity from those who have the capacity to renounce the world for the world-illumination, and self-control from those who are still enjoying the pleasure-life.

They say that Jainism is too difficult.

I say that Jainism is easier than the easiest of you have but one feeling deep inside your heart: love and sacrifice to each and every living thing in the universe.[1]

Jainism is a philosophy of universal love and friendship (*maitri*), but also of objective reason, of detachment and integration, of intense individualism and at the same time a sense that the destinies of all forms of life are interlocked. To Jains, these positions are anything but paradoxical. They are not even opposites, but can be seen as principles that continuously overlap and flow into each other, or as facets of the same jewel, paths to the same summit. To be Jain is to reconcile principles that we in the West have come to regard as opposed or incompatible: faith and reason, intellect and intuition, equality and freedom, conservatism and radicalism, tradition and modernity. It does not merely mediate between these principles, but fuses them together into the holistic understanding known as *jnana*, or pure knowledge, which incorporates all ways of knowing – intellectual or instinctive, physical or tactile, religious or spiritual – and turns them into something at once richer and simpler.

As a result, the Jain does not even have to make a choice between religious belief and atheism, for his is a non-theistic faith, without a supreme deity, and in which the energy of life cannot be created or destroyed: this is why the jiva, as a unit of pure energy, achieves eternal life. Jains take the long view of existence, thinking well beyond their present, temporary, material lives and rejecting short-term gratification in favour of rational self-interest, which is the same as the common good. While it demands hard decisions in one's personal life and practice, Jainism abolishes the adversarial 'choices' on which much of Western political, economic and even religious debate are founded. But in replacing either/or with both/and, it does not do away with the need for questioning. In fact, it does the opposite. The practice of ahimsa and the organisation of the mind according to anekantvada both require a continual process of questioning our own motives and the impact of our actions on others, including the smallest and (in Western terms) least elevated life forms. More than that, and in common with many faith traditions, the Jain path stresses the limits of human knowledge.

Jnana, as inclusive knowledge, is a broad canvas, which also includes the awareness of how much we do not know. For it is understood that those who claim overall knowledge, or who believe that they know 'the answer' for all of humanity, merely reveal the extent of their ignorance and limitations. However like the scientist, the Jain is obliged to continue to ask questions and to retain his scepticism. Permanent self-criticism joins with permanent social criticism. These do not take the forms of self-punishment, carping criticism of others, or malign pessimism about society and human potential. Instead, they involve the search for knowledge and the attempt to achieve balance and reconciliation. Without inner reconciliation, it is impossible to project benevolent impulses outwards and exert a positive influence on our surroundings.

We have already noted the way in which so many activists for good causes become embittered and intolerant, and why revolutionaries become dictators. This is because such people are not reconciled with themselves and do not understand their own imperfections. Therefore, they are unable to exert a positive influence on the societies around them. The causes of peace and freedom cannot be successfully advanced by those who are eaten up with anger and motivated by the will to power. Anger, even righteous anger, consumes the highest human ideals, just as on the spiritual plane it acts as a magnet for the negative inflow of karma. Power, in this context, loses its moral force and with that loss rests only on brutality and coercion. The lesson of Jainism for Western radicals is that even the most humanitarian cause can be destroyed by passion, which is the ultimate weakness although it confers superficial strength.

From a Jain standpoint, human perfection cannot be achieved, because it is a contradiction in terms. Yet as spiritually aware beings, humans still have a duty to come as near to perfection as they can, to strive for greater knowledge and insight, to practice compassion and voluntary simplicity. The sense that human life is imperfect is far from an expression of pessimism and gloom, which are in themselves negative passions. Instead, it provides a sense of perspective that wards off fanaticism. One who is always questioning cannot become a fundamentalist, because the fundamentalist perspective closes down the questioning process. Those who realise that humanity is imperfect will not seek to impose the perfect society by force, because they sense that this leads inevitably to disaster. The path to enlightenment is built on critical questioning and with it the struggle to improve both self and society. Therefore, the seeker of enlightenment is still involved with humanity and nature, more keenly so than those who remain attached to selfish conflict and cannot see beyond immediate needs or material desires. Detachment and involvement are two more artificial 'opposites': the spiritual seeker is more deeply involved precisely because he or she has chosen the path of detachment. In the same way, the awareness that perfection is impossible, that we can always 'do better', makes for more effective reformers and gives social criticism a stronger, more creative edge.

In the early twentieth century, the German ethical anarchist Gustav Landauer defined the state, and resistance to the state, in terms that strike a remarkable chord with Jain consciousness:

> The state is not something which can be destroyed by a revolution, but is a condition, a certain relationship between human beings, a mode of human behaviour; we destroy it by contracting other relationships, by behaving differently.[2]

Translated into Jain terms, the state is samsara, the karmic cycle which entraps us, limiting our ability to act and think, standing between us and knowledge of who we are. The institutions of the state are karma, because they create division and promote false values. The dissolution of the state is the elimination of karma, the achievement of inner freedom and the release of the true self. Landauer, along with many of his contemporary radicals of the left, rejected organised religion, but he was strongly influenced by Jewish and Christian teachings. He was a spiritual revolutionary, in that he recognised that without a change in the consciousness of the individual, there could be no worthwhile external social change. Without our 'behaving differently' in our personal lives, including the most trivial actions, we would not achieve the frame of mind needed to create a more civilised community – or to reduce the karmic power of the state, which restricts our consciousness and our potential to do good.

Landauer was writing at a time when humanism in the West was tightly defined, in terms only of 'a certain relationship between human beings'. For thousands of years, the Jains have realised that true humanism involves humanity's relationship with other creatures and awareness of its place in a universe of life. This insight means more to the West today, when the flaws in mechanistic thinking are more obvious and the results of our separation from nature more menacing. Landauer's is a revolution from within, based on the practice of compassion in our everyday lives rather than grand designs imposed by well-intentioned but rigid idealists. He realises that political revolution is not enough, when individual sensibilities have not been transformed, and so he takes a long-term view of revolution, with the anarchist as social critic and questioner, rather than angry advocate or violent agitator.

This vision of society is anarchic only in the sense that external authority structures have become redundant. However it has an underlying order that is more stable and profound than is found in more rigidly controlled societies. The new forms of social relationship that we 'contract' are founded on inner discipline, instead of the threat of external force. We 'behave differently' because we have learned to 'think differently', and this in turn is because we have evolved, and not because we are afraid to do otherwise. Two of the central motifs of Jain doctrine are evolution and freedom from fear. Evolution is interpreted in spiritual terms. This means that no distinction is made between the development of more advanced life forms and the spiritual progress of the individual.

Within the inhabited universe, humans represent the pinnacle of spiritual evolution, and this is reflected in their capacity for conscious ethical thought, and their ability, to reason, invent and plan ahead. From these abilities, we derive inherent power over other species, and the planet – the power to create or to destroy, oppress or liberate, heal or pollute. To evolve, as an individual human being and as a species, this power must be used sparingly and wisely, and then eventually overcome. The ethical choices conferred (whether we wish it or not) by our intelligence are reflected in the lives of each individual human being who, rather than being merely a passive element in a larger evolutionary process, is the agent of his or her own moral development. Jainism is compatible with the broadly Darwinian concept of evolution, which is accepted in the West by all except Biblical literalists. It comes to terms easily with such ideas as adaptability, natural selection and a hierarchy of species based on intelligence, inventiveness and level of consciousness. Unlike the conventionally held Western view, humanity in its present form is not necessarily the final evolutionary stage. The Jina, after all, is not human, but represents a more evolved state of consciousness. As a species, and as individuals, humans are reminded that they can always do better. Human intelligence, moreover, does not confer the 'right' to exercise power, dominion or ultimately even stewardship. The successful evolution of consciousness is measured by abstinence from power, the exercise of which is associated with lower forms of life and states of mind. Human spiritual evolution is therefore expressed first through good works and benevolent actions, then eventually through withdrawal and a cultivated state of equanimity.

Jain concepts of evolution therefore include the individual spiritual progression as much as the collective development of species. Unlike the Western view, they encompass the social, cultural as well as the physical and intellectual aspects. They are all viewed as parts of the same process, essential to each other, much in the same way as Jains do not distinguish between thought and action, intention and outcome. Evolution can also work backwards through the samsaric cycle. Humans are reborn at lower states of intellectual aptitude, or as members of other species, 'hell-beings' or static devas, before they rise again to relative spiritual maturity. Civilisations regress to barbarism and are then eventually reborn, and even species or worlds are destroyed and reconstituted. As might be expected, evolution is viewed as cyclical instead of linear. But it is an aspect of the karmic journey, and as such it offers the possibility of redemption for the individual soul. The most highly evolved being is that which has overcome negative karmic influences, and moksha is escape from karma as well as the highest achievable point of evolution: from the karmic body to pure consciousness.

Spiritual evolution ultimately involves abandoning social concerns to reach the true self, beyond the ego and the physical body. Yet sociable impulses, which attract beneficent karma, are also the most important stage in human spiritual evolution. In the spiritual journey, they connect the human with the super-human, which we in the West would call the divine, because the positive karma they generate points towards freedom from attachment. The Jain path starts with the human person, but each individual transformation has an impact on the wider society and social change is the sum total of individual transformations. Real change involves a shift of emphasis that is subtle, often imperceptible and comes from within, rather than being imposed from without by force or by fear. The truly enlightened human being pursues an ethical way of life *because* of freedom from fear, and the test of a successful community is the absence of force, which means people making ethical choices because they wish to do so, and not because they are compelled to do so. As the American political philosopher David Wieck puts it:

> An ethical society composed of persons not voluntarily ethical is not only a severely limited ideal, perhaps even a contradiction in terms, but it is also a first step in justification for governments which know what is 'good for' people.[3]

The Jain tradition provides an ethical code that enables human beings to learn to 'behave differently'. It guides us towards avoiding coercive behaviour and recognising that material goals are neither the most important nor the most valuable, but are likely to be the most corrupting and destructive. Jainism offers a blueprint for a quiet revolution, in which human society is reformed from its roots upwards. But unlike the movements to which politically conscious Westerners dedicate themselves, Jain consciousness is based on unity rather than division, reconciliation rather than conflict. Rooted in the individual conscience, it is innately anti-authoritarian. No lawgiver, no priesthood, no political system however democratic can be an adequate substitute for that conscience, and nor can they compel the 'correct' ethical choices. Yet that conscience itself acts as an inner authority more compelling than any external law or custom. In the Jain view of society, we can find the idea propagated by many Western campaigners, feminists for example, that the distinction between the social and the intimate is arbitrary and artificial. Jains go along with this, to an extent, but they go further than this, because their definition of 'personal' is beyond selfish interests or the assertions of one human group at the expense of another. Personal development means striving to achieve inner calm, peace of mind, the transcendence of passion. In the social sphere, this means learning to co-operate with others, both for moral reasons and as a guarantee of survival.

Co-operation is a powerful source of wisdom and spiritual growth, attracting benign karma and pointing in the direction of moksha. Its role in the evolution of species, as well as human development, is now increasingly acknowledged. The absence of co-operation produces social breakdown and insecurity for all, including those who seemingly benefit from such divisions. Lack of co-operation is also a barrier to personal growth, because it creates atomised units rather than rounded, clear-minded individuals. The Jain path is not a race, and we do not compete with each other for spiritual progress. Competitive urges are negative passions, which are gradually discarded. Co-operative impulses are benevolent feelings, and therefore they are steps towards enlightenment.

Thus Jainism, a philosophy of ultimate withdrawal, can also become a spur to social engagement. Always an unobtrusive movement, and powerful precisely for so being, its influence is indirect or underlying, and so often barely acknowledged. Dr L.M. Singhvi paid tribute to the impact of Jain thought on Gandhi's non-violent campaign against British rule and the philosophy to emerge from it:

In the twentieth century, the most vibrant and illustrious example of Jain influence was that of Mahatma Gandhi, acclaimed as the Father of the Nation. Gandhi's friend, Shrimad Rajchandra, was a Jain. The two great men corresponded, until

Rajchandra's death, on issues of faith and ethics. The central Jain teaching of ahimsa was the guiding principle of Gandhi's civil disobedience in the cause of freedom and social equality. His ecological philosophy found apt expression in his observation that the greatest work of humanity could not match the smallest wonder of nature.[4]

To walk the Jain path does not require initiation into Jain doctrines or even adopting distinctively Jain customs. The strength of this ancient faith is that its insights can help us to understand our own culture more fully. Or, put another way, we advance further towards an underlying truth expressed in different ways, at different times, and crossing the boundaries of faith (or non-belief), political ideology, nation, language, caste or class. Thus there is no such thing as 'Jain politics', 'Jain economics' or a model 'Jain society'. It is more helpful to think of Jainism as an attitude of mind, a way of looking at the world, from which people of all faiths and none can draw and which can help to clarify the visions of conservatives and radicals, ascetics and entrepreneurs.

The Jain dharma frees us from the superficial choices between 'pairs of opposites' that now impede so much of Western thought, so that we can make the choices that are crucial to the survival of all life – the choice between continuous growth and the conserving of finite resources, between pollution and healing, spiralling inequality and social justice, creativity and destruction. How we make these choices is our decision, for there is no blueprint. The Three As, which give Jainism its universal aspect, appear restrictive but are in fact infinitely flexible, far more so than the competing ideologies of economic expansion and religious literalism, which promise freedom but offer homogeneity, conformity and intolerance.

Unlike those doctrines, religious and political, that emphasise human weakness and the ideal of submission, Jainism reminds us constantly of our power. This can be an uncomfortable reminder, because it demands that we take responsibility for our lives, rather than allowing ourselves the luxury of submission to 'the party', 'the state' or even to God. Jainism is a conscious awakening from karma, which divides human beings from each other, and from nature, and fragments human thought into conflicting beliefs, all of which are illusions when isolated from each other, but are also pieces of a universal truth. In choosing to recognise this universality, we begin to move beyond enslaving passions and acquire a new clarity of perception. We become aware of our power, and the sacredness of each of our lives. Yet we also see ourselves as belonging to a great network of life, on which we depend for our survival and our spiritual growth. We become dispassionate observers, and at the same time we learn infinite compassion.

The Jain path frees our minds from karmic ideological constraints. It does not give us 'the answer', but equips us to ask the right questions.

NOTES

Preface

1. There are, according to varied estimates, between four and ten million Jains today. This includes India and the Diaspora, chiefly East Africa, Europe (including the United Kingdom) and North America.

Chapter One

1. Vine Deloria, Jr, *Red Earth, White Lies: Native Americans and the Myth of Scientific Fact* (Golden, Colorado: Fulcrum Publishing, 1997).

Chapter Two

1. Padmanabh S. Jaini, *The Jaina Path of Purification* (Delhi: Motilal Banarsidass, 2001), p.53. The term 'Jaina' is synonymous with Jain.

2. For a more detailed discussion of Jain scriptures, see Jaini, op.cit., pp.42-88. The quotations from Mahavira in my book are drawn from Hermann Jacobi's translation of the *Acaranga Sutra*, English versions of which were published in 1882 and 1895. Quotations from the *Tattvartha Sutra* are taken from a recent translation, *That Which Is*, edited by Nathmal Tatia and published by the Institute of Jainology and International Harper Collins, London, 1993.

Chapter Three

1. The Jain pursuit of ahimsa has earned the respect of

successive Indian elites, both religious and secular. One of the
most notable examples of this phenomenon was the influence
exerted by a Svetambara monk, Hiravijaya-Suri, on the
Islamic Mughal ruler Akbar (1556-1605). Akbar personally
renounced hunting and fishing, ordered the release of caged
birds and imposed restrictions on the killing of animals.

2. Bede Griffiths, *The Marriage of East and West* (Tuscon,
Arizona: Medio Media, 2003), p.134.

3. See Christopher Isherwood, *My Guru and His Disciple*
(Minneapolis: University of Minnesota Press, 2001).

Chapter Four

1. Jean Herbert, *Shinto: the Fountainhead of Japan* (London:
George Allen & Unwin Ltd, 1967), p21.

2. ibid.

3. Quoted in Swami Prabhavananda, *The Spiritual Heritage of
India* (Hollywood: Vedanta Press, 1979), p.157

4. K.V. Mardia, *The Scientific Foundations of Jainism* (Delhi:
Motilal Banarsidass, 2002), p.7.

5. Mardia, op.cit., p.13.

6. Bernard Levin, *In These Times* (London: Jonathan Cape Ltd.,
1986), p.121

Chapter Five

1. Swami Vivekananda, *The Yoga of Action: Karma Yoga*
(Kolkata: Advaita Ashrama, 2003), p.131.

Chapter Six

1. Aldous Huxley, *Pacifism and Philosophy: An Aldous Huxley*

Reader (London: Peace Pledge Union, 1994), p.13. The leading essay in this volume, 'Pacifism and Philosophy', is a slightly abridged version of a talk given by Huxley to the Society of Friends (Quakers) in London on 3rd December 1935.

2. David Bohm, *Wholeness and the Implicate Order* (London: Routledge, 2002).

3. Eliot used this phrase in *The Waste Land*, which he wrote in 1922, several years before he was received into the Anglican Church. At this stage in his life, he was exploring Eastern as much as Western spiritual traditions, and the poem makes frequent reference to the *Upanishads* and early Buddhist texts such as *The Fire Sermon*.

Chapter Seven

1. Quoted in Sri Chinmoy, *Jainism: Give Life, Take Not* (1998). www.srichinmoylibrary.com/jainism

2. ibid.

3. See Michio Kaku, Parallel Worlds: *The Science of Alternative Universes and Our Future in the Cosmos* (London: Allen Lane, 2005).

4. See Reginald Crosley, M.D., *The Vodou Quantum Leap: Alternate Realities, Power and Mysticism* (St Paul, Minnesota: Llewellyn, 2000).

5. Sri Chinmoy, op. cit.

Chapter Eight

1. www.srichinmoylibrary.com/jainism

2. Quoted in Colin Ward, *Anarchism: A Very Short Introduction*

(Oxford: Oxford University Press, 2004), p.8.

3. See David Wieck, 'The Negativity of Anarchism', in Howard J.Erlich et al (eds), *Reinventing Anarchy* (London: Routledge, 1979).

FURTHER READING

The Western seeker will find far fewer detailed studies of the Jain path than the Hindu and Buddhist dharmas. However, as I hope this book has shown, the principal themes of Jain philosophy have increasing relevance and resonance. They are also beginning to attract serious academic study and more popular contemplation.

Sri Chinmoy's *Jainism: Give Life, Take Not* provides a good-humoured introduction to the Jain tradition, conveying powerful ideas with a refreshingly light touch. Published originally in booklet form in 1998, it is now available on-line at www.srichinmoylibrary.com/jainism. Swami Prabhavananda's book *The Spiritual Heritage of India* (Hollywood: Vedanta Press, 1979) has a detailed and helpful chapter on Jainism, which is described from a sympathetic Hindu viewpoint.

For a 'pure' academic approach, Paul Dundas's *The Jains* (London: Routledge, 2002) provides an excellent read and a wealth of information on all aspects of Jainism. Dr Dundas is Reader in Sanskrit at Edinburgh University and applies to Jain history and philosophy a scholarly analysis that is at once rigorous and humane.

K.V. Mardia's *The Scientific Foundations of Jainism* (Delhi: Motilal Banarsidass, 2002) unites the ancient teachings of the dharma and the conclusions of modern science. Dr Mardia is a Jain and a physicist, and these two aspects of his thought both complement and reinforce each other. His book is exhilarating and thought-provoking in equal measure.

In *The Jaina Path of Purification* (Delhi: Motilal Banarsidass, 2001), Professor Padmanabh S. Jaini of the University of California at Berkeley gives an account of Jainism that is at once scholarly and inspirational, invaluable to academic researcher and spiritual seeker alike.

GLOSSARY

Abhaya, universal fearlessness, 221

Acharya, spiritual leader or teacher, 150

Aghatiya karma, non-destructive karma, 107, 112

Ahimsa, non-violence, principle of non-injury to life, xvii, 31, 32, 37, 40, 44, 83, 94, 122, 129, 131, 134-7, 161, 165-6, 180, 193-222, 226, 231, 239, 241

Ajiva, non-sentient, everything that is not spiritually alive, 81, 90, 92, 97-102

Ananda, bliss, state of benign understanding, 102

Anekantvada, many-sidedness, acceptance of different paths to the same truth, 122, 158, 159-92, 208, 231

Angas, 'limbs' or aspects of the Jain canon; texts that provide post-Mahavira Jainism with a 'body' of written knowledge, 39-40

Antaraya, energy obstructing karma, 108

Anu, minute or sub-atomic particles, 86

Anuvratas, Lesser Vows, undertaken by lay men and women, 129, 158

Aparigraha, non-possessiveness, non-materialism, 31, 37, 121-2, 123-58, 161, 180, 196, 205

Ardha-Magadhi, dialect of Prakrit (q.v.) in which many post-Mahavira Jain teachings were spoken and written, 25

Asata-vedaniya, karma of displeasure or sorrow, 112

Asrava, inflow of karmic particles, 99, 101, 103

Asteya, avoidance of theft; concept of theft extends to unjust prof it, exploitation or gain at the expense of others, 31, 135

INDEX

O

is a symbol of the world,
of oneness and unity. O Books
explores the many paths of wholeness
and spiritual understanding which
different traditions have developed down
the ages. It aims to bring this knowledge
in accessible form, to a general readership,
providing practical spirituality to today's seekers.

For the full list of over 200 titles covering:

- CHILDREN'S PRAYER, NOVELTY AND GIFT BOOKS
- CHILDREN'S CHRISTIAN AND SPIRITUALITY
- CHRISTMAS AND EASTER
- RELIGION/PHILOSOPHY
- SCHOOL TITLES
- ANGELS/CHANNELLING
- HEALING/MEDITATION
- SELF-HELP/RELATIONSHIPS
- ASTROLOGY/NUMEROLOGY
- SPIRITUAL ENQUIRY
- CHRISTIANITY, EVANGELICAL
  AND LIBERAL/RADICAL
- CURRENT AFFAIRS
- HISTORY/BIOGRAPHY
- INSPIRATIONAL/DEVOTIONAL
- WORLD RELIGIONS/INTERFAITH
- BIOGRAPHY AND FICTION
- BIBLE AND REFERENCE
- SCIENCE/PSYCHOLOGY

Please visit our website,
www.O-books.net

A Heart for the World

The interfaith alternative

Marcus Braybrooke

This book is really needed. This is the blueprint. It has to be cherished. Faith in Jesus is not about creeds or homilies. It is a willingness to imitate Christ-as the Hindu guru Gandhi did so well. A must book to buy. Peacelinks, IFOR

1905047436 168pp £12.99 $24.95

A World Religions Bible

Robert van de Weyer

An admirable book to own personally for reflection and meditation, with the possibility of contemplating a different extract a day over an entire year. It is our hope that the use of this splendid anthology will grow. We recommend it to all for their personal enrichment.

The Friend

1903816157 432pp full colour throughout 180/120mm £19.99 $28.95

Created in the Image of God

A foundational course in the Kabbalah

Esther Ben-Toviya

(new, May '07)

This book provides a foundational course in the Kabbalah which

speaks to the universal truths of the human experience, and is relevant to people of all backgrounds.
1846940079 272pp £11.99 $21.95

Everyday Buddha

A contemporary rendering of the Buddhist classic, the Dhammapada
Karma Yonten Senge (Lawrence Ellyard)
Foreword by His Holiness the 14th Dalai Lama
Excellent. Whether you already have a copy of the Dhammapada or not, I recommend you get this. I congratulate all involved in this project and have put the book on my recommended list.
Jeremy Ball Nova Magazine
1905047304 144pp £9.99 $19.95

Good As New

A radical retelling of the scriptures
John Henson
Fully lives up to the sub title description. At the heart of his inter-pretation is his understanding that Jesus' genius lay in putting into language understood by ordinary people things obscured by the scribes' sophistication or pedantry and he has applied this philoso-phy to powerful effect. A 450 page immensely valuable addition to scriptural understanding and appreciation.
Methodist Recorder

Popol Vuh II

A literal, line by line translation

Allen J. Christenson

A definitive document of rhetorical brilliance.

Stephen Houston, Jesse Knight University Professor, Brigham Young Univ.

1903816572 280pp 230/153mm £25.00 $37.50

Popol Vuh: The Sacred Book of the Maya

The Mayan creation story

Allen J. Christenson

The most accurate and comprehensive translation ever produced. His work is an extraordinary masterpiece of scholarly analysis.

Karen Bassie-Sweet, University of Calgary.

190381653X 320pp 230/153mm £19.99 $29.95

Son of Karbala

The spiritual journey of an Iraqi Muslim

Shaykh Haeri

A new dawn has appeared in spiritual travelogue with the publication of Son of Karbala. It deserves a place among the great spiritual odysseys of our time, right next to Gurdjieff's Meetings with Remarkable Men, which it at once resembles and exceeds in its honesty and clarity.

Professor Bruce B. Lawrence, Duke University, Durham NC

1905047517 240pp £14.99 $29.95

The Bhagavad Gita

Alan Jacobs

Alan Jacobs has succeeded in revitalising the ancient text of the Bhagavad Gita into a form which reveals the full majesty of this magnificent Hindu scripture, as well as its practical message for today's seekers. His incisive philosophic commentary dusts off all the archaism of 1500 years and restores the text as a transforming instrument pointing the way to Self Realization.

Cygnus Review

1903816513 320pp £12.99 $19.95

A short review cannot begin to persuade readers of the value of this book. Buy it and read it. But only if you are brave enough. Renew 2nd printing in hardback

1903816734 608pp £19.99 $24.95 cl

1905047118 608pp £11.99 $19.95 pb

The Ocean of Wisdom

The most comprehensive compendium of worldly and spiritual wisdom this century

Alan Jacobs

This anthology of 5,000 passages of spiritual wisdom is an awesome collection of prose and poetry, offering profound truths to everyday guidance. It would be a valuable reference for any writer or historian, but it also makes for a good fireside or bedside book, offering bits and pieces of wisdom at whatever pace the reader wishes.

Academy of Religion and Psychical Research

190504707X 744pp 230/153mm £17.99 $29.95

The Principal Upanishads

Alan Jacobs

Alan Jacobs has produced yet another literary masterpiece in his transcreation of the 'Principal Upanishads', which together with his 'Bhagavad Gita', aim to convey the nondualist teaching (Advaita Vedanta) of the ancient Indian scriptures as well as explore the author's own poetic expression.

Paula Marvelly

1903816505 384pp £12.99 $19.95

The Spiritual Wisdom of Marcus Aurelius

Practical philosophy from an ancient master

Alan Jacobs

Most translations are literal and arid but Jacobs has paraphrased a selection of the best of Aurelius' meditations so as to give more force to the essential truths of his philosophy. The following meditation summarises Aurelius' beliefs: "Everything is interconnected, the bond is holy. All has been coordinated to combine for universal order, balance and harmony...." Modern quantum physics could hardly explain it better.

The Light

1903816742 260pp £9.99 $14.95

The Thinker's Guide to Ethics

Peter Vardy and Julie Arliss

September '07

The Thinker's Guide to Evil

Peter Vardy and Julie Arliss

2nd printing

As a philosopher of religion Peter Vardy is unsurpassed.

Dialogue magazine

1903816335 196pp full colour throughout £9.99 $15.95

The Thinker's Guide to God

Peter Vardy and Julie Arliss

2nd printing

What a magnum opus! From Pluto's feet to Dawkin's Selfish Gene, this provides a magisterial survey of Western thought about God.

Rev Henry Kirk, Principal Examiner

190381622X 276pp full colour throughout £9.99 $15.95

The Thoughtful Guide to the Bible

Roy Robinson

A liberating experience. There is a great deal of factual information. The difficult questions are not avoided. Roy Robinson does not pretend that the Bible is always historically accurate or morally admirable. He has no time for a simplistic fundamentalism that trivialises the concept of inspiration. But from a critical position he offers a strong defence of the Bible as the church's main source of authority.

Reform

1903816750 360pp £14.99 $19.95

The Thoughtful Guide to Christianity

Graham Hellier

A rough guide to the Christian faith for anyone within or without the Church, and a resource for teachers, preachers and discussion groups. Designed to give material for reflection, the guide is drawn from over 700 sources, including some of which are deeply critical of Christianity and the Christian Church. Reform

1903816343 360pp £11.99 $17.95

The Thoughtful Guide to Faith

Trevor Windross

2nd printing

This is a splendid book! Its author is ambitious for Christianity and his aim is the development of a voice coming from the Church that is truly radical and can be heard alongside those of traditionalists and fundamentalists, without trying to un-Church people from those backgrounds. Hasten to your bookshop. SoF

1903816688 224pp £9.99 $14.95

The Thoughtful Guide to God

Making sense of the world's biggest idea

Howard Jones

The wide scope of this fusion of theology, philosophy and science makes this an important contribution to a study of the divine that is easily readable by the non-specialist.

Dr Verena Tschudin, author of Seeing the Invisible

1905047703 400pp £19.99 $39.95

The Thoughtful Guide to Islam

Shaykh Haeri

About as timely as any book can be, should be read, and re-read, not only by so-called Christians but by many Muslims too.

The Guardian

1903816629 176pp £7.99 $12.95

The Thoughtful Guide to Religion

Why it began, how it works, and where it's going

Ivor Morrish

(new, November '06)

This is a comprehensive and sympathetic approach to all religions of the world, including the lesser-known ones, sects, cults and ideologies. Broader than "comparative religion", it uses philosophy, psychology, anthropology and other disciplines to answer the key questions, and provides a holistic approach for anyone interested in religious or philosophical ideas.

190504769X 400pp £24.99 $24.95

The Thoughtful Guide to Sufism

Shaykh Haeri

A Sufi is a whole human being, primarily concerned with the "heart" that reflects the truth that exists within it beyojnd time and in time. The aim is to reach the pinnacle of "his" self by achieving physical silence. The Sufi path is one of self denial. I found this book an absorbing and heartfelt source of information. Sangha

1903816637 128pp £9.99 $14.95

You Called My Name

The hidden treasures of your Hebrew heritage

Esther Ben-Toviya

We are entering a new era of Jewish-Christian dialogue. This offers the reader a guided tour of Judaism, the religion of Jesus, that will enhance the spiritual lives of all who follow the religion about Jesus, Christianity. This is more than a book. It is a cherished resource. Rabbi Rami Shapiro, author of The Divine Feminine.

1905047797 272pp £11.99 $19.95

1000 World Prayers

Marcus Braybrooke

This book is the most comprehensive selection of prayers from different traditions currently available. It is divided into five major sections: God (including silence, love, forgiveness), times and seasons, the changing scenes of life, the world and society, and the natural world. There is a contemporary as well as traditional flavour. Scientific and Medical Network Review

1903816173 360pp 230/153mm £12.99 $19.95

Bringing God Back to Earth

John Hunt

Knowledgeable in theology, philosophy, science and history. Time and again it is remarkable how he brings the important issues into relation with one another... thought provoking in almost every sentence, difficult to put down. Faith and Freedom

1903816815 320pp £9.99 $14.95

Guide to Interfaith

Reflections from around the world

Sandy and Jael Bharat

For those who are new to interfaith this amazing book will give a wonderful picture of the variety and excitement of this journey of discovery. It tells us something about the world religions, about interfaith history and organizations, how to plan an interfaith meeting and much more - mostly through the words of practitioners.

Marcus Braybrooke

1905047975 320pp 230/153mm £19.99 $34.95